THE INNER TEACHINGS OF

THE PHILOSOPHY AND RELIGION OF INDIA

THE INNER TEACHINGS OF

THE PHILOSOPHY AND RELIGION OF INDIA

Yogi Ramacharaka

BHARATIYA KALA PRAKASHAN

Delhi :: (India)

First Edition : 1918
Revised Edition : 2009

Published by **C.P. Gautam**
BHARATIYA KALA PRAKASHAN
3421-A, IInd Floor, Narang Colony Tri Nagar,
Delhi-110035. Phone : 27393083, 32967505
E-mail : bkp3421@yahoo.co.in

ISBN : 978-81-8090-220-8

Printed by :
D.K. Fine Art Press (P) Ltd.
Delhi

Contents

Introduction

This book is composed of the inner teachings of the Philosophy and Religion of India.

Chapter-I talks about the contribution of India to the world in terms of language, philosophy through Vedas and Upanishads, spirituality, the theory of the One Supreme Soul, etc. How western philosophies got influenced by the Hindu Philosophy, what is *Atma* (soul) are discussed in this chapter in detail.

Chapter-II is about the inner teachings by the great sages. How the sages gathered around them the most intelligent young men to forumulate and expound philosophy of pure reason. Aspect of ultimate reality, attributes of Reality Laws of Nature are talked about in a very lucid manner. Theory of Reincarnation, Rebirth of Soul and Meempsychosis is also explained in the chapter.

Chapter-III deals with the great system of Hindu philosophy knows as. The *Sankhya* system. The meaning of the term 'Sankhya', the basic proposition of the *Sankhya* System, which is known as *Prakriti* and *Purusha* have been discussed in detail. The charge of atheism against the Sankhyas also discussed. Similarity of the Buddhist teachings with those of the *Sankhyas.* Doctrine of love and hate of atoms which explained the mutual attraction and repulsion of the particles which are evident through the universe, and which action and reaction account for the greater part of the physical phenomena. Three *Gunas—Satva, Rajas, Tamas*—with their effects have been thrown sufficient light upon. Besides, twenty-four *Tattvas* or principles, five Tanamatras, the Manas or Mental Substance have also been discussed.

Chapter-IV talks about the leading school of Hindu philosophy in India, the *Vedanta* System, which also bears the name of *Uttara Mimamsa*. It is discussed how the *Vedanta* prostulates the existence of THAT or *Brahman*, as the only Reality and only Existence. *Advaita* school of *Vedanta*, founded by *Sankaracharya*, *Vishishtadvaita* school of *Ramanuja*, *Maya*, *Brahman*, *Avidya* or ignorance, the *Rupa*, *Prana*, *Linga Sharira*, *Buddhi*, *Atman* and the theory of Reincarnation and *Karma* have been discussed in detail.

Chapter-V throws light upon the *Patanjali's Yoga* System, commonly known as *Yoga* system. It discusses the existence of a world Purusha, Universal Soul, Personal God or *Ishwara*. It also discusses the subject of Chitta or Mind-Stuff, Mind of Thought *(Manas)*, the determinative faculty *(buddhi)*, the Self-consciousness *(ahamkara)*, etc. In addition are discussed Eight Steps leading to Attainment—Self-control *(yama)*, Religious Duty *(niyama)*, Postures *(asana)*, Control of the *Prana (pranayama)*, Control of the Mind *(dharana)*, Meditation *(dhyana)*, Transcendental Contemplation *(samadhi)*, etc. *Ida*, *Pingala*, *Kumdalini*, *Raja Yoga*, and *Hatha Yoga* have also been discussed.

Chapter-VI talks about other miner systems such as the Vaisheshika System, the Purva Mimansa System, the Nyaya System and Agnostic and Materialistic Systems, Charvakas. *Drava* or Substance, *Guna* or Qualities, *Karma* or action, *Samanya* or Generality, *Vishesha* or Atomic Individuality, etc. are discussed under *Vaisheshika* System. The Freedom of the Soul by means of the Observance of the orthodox rites, ceremonies, worship, prayer, etc. are discussed under the '*Purva Mimansa* System. And, Materialism is discussed under the Charvakas.

Chapter-VII Source of Pain and way of Escape, Renunciation of Life by the killing out of Desire, Karmic Cause and Effect etc. It also talks about the four truths of Salvation such as the truth of suffering, the truth of the cause of Suffering, the truth of the Cessation of Suffering and the Truth of the path that leads to the cessation of suffering.

Chapter-VIII thorws light upon Sufuism, which the philosophical and religious system of a large body of Mystics sheltered beneath the wing of the Mahomenedan religion. This chapter contains the teachings of Suficism, union with God, Consciousness Ecstasy, or Illumination, absorbtion in the Divine (Fanah Fillah), Mystic Teachings (shariat), the following of the Mystic Path (tariqat) etc. Besides, some incidents of the famous *sufis* have also been spoken about.

Chapter-IX is composed of the philosophical idiology of the Religions of India. What is Sanatana, Avatar, Law of Karma, Rebirth, Maya, Samsara have been touched. And Shiva, Vishnu, Lingum, Shakta worship Vaishnavas, Shaivas are the discussed ones as well.

Chapter-X spekas about the Religiouns in India with their branches such as the Shaivas, the Vaishnavas, the Shaktas, the Sikhs, the Jains, the Theistic Sect, ramakrishna, Hindu Religions images and the Ram Avatar and the Krishna Avatar with short stories of their life. Brahma Samaj, Arya Samaj and Prarthana Samaj have been touched under the Theistic Sects.

Chapter-XI talks about the wonder-working exploits of the ascended masters or *yogis* or *fakins.* How they are possessed of high spiritued powers, the telepathic powers etc. Their ability to defy the gravitation power and the way of chantings can change the movement of some thing. Also discussed are Prana, Rythemic Breathing and Concentrated will.

Chapter XII discusses the Vedas such as Rig-Veda, Yajurveda, Sama-Veda, and Atharva-Veda, the Brahmanas, the Upanishads such as Brihadaranyaka, Chandogya, Aitareya, Kaushitaki, Taittiriya, Katha and Mandukya, etc. This chapter also talks about the pronunciation of Sanskrit.

Chapter XIII explains the glossary of Sanskrit terms.

Chapter I

The Land of the Ganges

India—the Land of the Ganges—the home of Sanskrit, the Root-Language of the world—the Mother of Religious and Philosophies—the Twentieth Century and the Western World greet thee! From thy sources have come the languages of the world, in which men have expressed the thoughts arising in their minds—thy word-symbols have made possible advanced thinking and expression of thought. From thy thinkers and teachers have come the root-ideas which have since grown into many a religious and philosophical tree, with bud, leaf, flower, and fruit. To thee may be traced the great philosophical conceptions and religious truths that have animated and inspired man's thought for centuries. Thy hundred centuries of deep thought and meditation upon the Mysteries of Existence—the Secret of the Absolute—have proved as the leaven which has lightened the bread of life, and has raised the sodden mass of materiality and changed its character so that it may be partaken of without harm by reason of the transforming power of thy leaven.

The history of India runs back for many centuries, the Hindus themselves claiming that their records and traditions carry them back over a period of a hundred centuries—10,000 years—and that back of even this great period of time their people existed and had their successive civilization and periods of race test. Centuries before our present civilization had dawned—centuries before the Christian religion was established—centuries before even the time of Abraham, and still longer before the time of Moses and the practical beginning of the Jewish religion—the Hindu teachers of philosophy had formed great schools of thought, which in turn had been subdivided by their followers, the teachings of which have come down along the line of the centuries even unto to-day. The Vedas and the Upanishads were written centuries ago—beyond the time of recorded history—and have been handed down from teacher to pupil ever since. Before the days of the Sphinx and the Pyramids of Ancient Egypt, India's great religious and philosophical teachers had formulated their doctrines and founded their schools of thought. Surely such antiquity of teaching, and the corresponding vitality of the doctrines which has kept them alive and vigorous through the passage of these great periods of time, must arrest our attention and command our respect.

The leading scholars of the Western world have long since recognized and appreciated the great value and importance of the work of the Hindu thinkers along the line of philosophy, and have freely give credit to them for their fundamental work upon which a great body of the Western thought has been built. In fact, it is difficult to find any form of Western philosophy that has not used the Hindu philosophies as a basis—or, at least, which has not, perhaps unconsciously, restated the fundamental truths uttered centuries before by some Hindu thinker. Every possible form of human philosophical speculation, conception, or theory, has been advanced by some Hindu philosopher during the centuries. It would seem that the Hindu philosophical mind has acted like the finest sieve, through which strained the volume of human philosophical thought, every idea of importance being gathered and applied, by someone, at some time, in India. Professors Max Müller and Paul Deussen have testified to the fact that India has been the fountain-head of philosophical thought, and that in the Vedas and the Upanishads may be found references to every philosophical conception that the Western mind has since evolved. This is no mere boast of the Hindu—an examination of the authorities will satisfy the most rigid proof on this point, as the best authorities freely admit.

Victor Cousin, the French writer upon philosophical history, has said: "When we read the poetical and philosophical monuments of the East—above all; those of India, which are beginning to spread in Europe—we discover there many a truth and truths so profound, and which make such a contrast with the meanness of the results at which European genius has sometimes stopped, that we are constrained to bend the knee before the philosophy of the East, and to see in this cradle of the human race the native land of the highest philosophy. *India contains the whole history of Philosophy in a nutshell.*" Sir Monier Williams, in his great work on the Hindu Religions, said : "Indeed, if I may be allowed the anachronism, the Hindus were Spinozites more than two thousand years before the existence of Spinoza; and Darwinians many centuries before Darwin; and Evolutionists many centuries before the doctrine of Evolution had been accepted by the scientists of our time, and before any word like 'Evolution' existed in any language of the world." Many writers have held that the great Grecian thinker and philosopher, Pythagoras, received his instruction from Hindu teachers upon his sojourn in India, and some of the legends hold that upon his return to his native land he brought a company of Hindu philosophers with him, in order that the Greeks might receive the benefit of their instruction. Whether or not this latter statement may be true, it is undoubtedly true that the vitality of Grecian philosophical thought was due to Hindu influences. Prof. E. W. Hopkins has said: "Plato was full of Sankhyan thought, worked out by him, but taken from Pythagoras. *Before the sixth century B.C. all the religious philosophical ideas of Pythagoras were current in India.* If there were but one or two of these cases, they might be set aside as accidental coincidences, but such coincidences are too numerous to be the result of chance . . . *Neo-Platonism and Christian, Gnosticism owe much to India.* The

Gnostic ideas in regard to a plurality of heavens and spiritual worlds go back directly to Hindu sources. Soul and light were one in the Sankhya System, before they became so in Greece, and when they appeared united in Greece, it was by means of *the thought which was borrowed from India.* The famous Three Gunas of the Sankhya reappeared as the Gnostic 'three classes.' Davies says : "*Kapila's System is the first formulated system of philosophy of which the world has a record.* It is the earliest attempt on record to give an answer, from reason alone, to the mysterious questions which arise in every thoughtful mind about the origin of the world, the nàture, and relations of man and his future destiny." The same authority says that : "The philosophy of Schopenhauer and Hartmann is a reproduction of the philosophical system of *Kapila* in its materialistic part, presented in a more elaborate form, but on the same fundamental lines. In this respect *the human intellect has gone over the same ground that it occupied more than two thousand years ago*; but on a more important question it has taken a step in retreat. Kapila recognized fully the existence of a soul in man, forming indeed his proper nature—the absolute of Fichte—distinct from matter and immortal; but our latest philosophy, both here and in Germany, can see in man only a highly developed organization." Hopkins says : "Both Thales and Parmenides were indeed anticipated by Hindu sages, and The Eleatic school seems to be but a reflection of the Upanishads. The doctrines of Anaxamander and Heraclitus were perhaps not known first in Greece." Schlegel has said :"The divine origin of man, as taught in the Vedanta, is continually inculcated, to stimulate his efforts to return, to animate him in the struggle, and incite him to consider a reunion and reincorporation with Divinity as the one primary object of every action and reaction. Even the loftiest philosohy of the Europeans, the idealism of reason as it is set forth by the Greek philosophers, appears in comparison with the abundant light and vigour of Oriental idealism like a feeble

Promethean spark in the full food of heavenly glory of the noonday sun, faltering and feeble and ever ready to be extinguished."

Of the Vedanta System of Hindu Philosophy, Max Müller says : "This constitutes the unique character of Vedanta, unique compared with every other philosophy of the world which has not been influenced by it, directly or indirectly." Speaking of the daring philosophical conceptions of the Vedanta in its denial of the reality of the phenomenal, and the assertion of the reality only of the Absolute One, Max Müller says : "None of our philosophers, not excepting Heraclitus, Plato, Kant, or Hegel, has ventured to erect such a spire, never frightened by storms or lightnings. Stone follows on stone in regular succession after once the first step has been made, after once it has been clearly seen that in the beginning there can have been but One, as there will be but One in the end, whether we call it Atman or Brahman." Sir William Jones has said: "It is impossible to read the Vedanta, or the many fine compositions in illustration of it, without believing that Pythagoras and Plato derived their sublime theories from the same fountain with the Indian sages." Schopenhauer, the great German philosopher, said : "There is no study more beneficial and elevating to mankind than the study of the Upanishads. It has been the solace of my life, and it will be the solace of my death." Paul Deussen says : "God, the sole author of all good in us, is not, as in the Old Testament, a Being contrasted with and distinct from us, but rather our divine self. This and much more we may learn from the Upanishads : we shall learn this lesson if we are willing to put the finishing touch to the Christian consciousness, and to make it on all sides consistent and complete."

× × ×

The Western student who wishes to become acquainted with the Philosophies and Religions of India is placed at a great disadvantage by reason of his remoteness from the authoritative teachers, and also by reason of his inability to distinguish between the true and the untrue—the genuine and the spurious—the truth and the half-truth—among the voluminous writings on the subject. He finds a mass of literature relating to India and her religions and philosophies, written in English by various persons who often have made but a superficial study of the subject, and he is unable to reconcile the many conflicting statements that he finds in these books. He finds the various authorities flatly contradicting each other, and, in his ignorance; he is unable to decide upon the question of the relative and comparative reliability of these sources of information. This is not to be wondered at, when it is remembered that the majority of the English writers on the subject have had their own information not from authoritative sources, but gleaned from various disconnected sources, the writers not being possessed of the power of intelligent discrimination, so foreign is the subject to their previous lines of thought and so opposed to their mental, religious, and philosophical training. It is true that there are a number of very good English works on the subject, but they are greatly outnumbered by the mass of incompetent, erroneous, and sometimes prejudiced and biased treatises on the same lines.

For anyone to write intelligently upon the subject of Hindu Philosophy or Religion, it is necessary that he must be in sympathy with the Hindu mind and *soul*—not necessarily a believer in their religions, or a follower of their philosophy, but most certainly possessed of a mind in sympathy with the fundamental conceptions and *spiritual basic principles* of the Hindu people. This is true regarding the teachings and beliefs of any people—imagine a Chinaman who lacked a Western training attempting to write a correct statement of the Western beliefs, philosophies, etc., from disjointed and contradictory sources of information, and you will have an idea of the difficulties in the way of the average Western person who would write of the Hindu Philosophies. In fact, our Chinaman would have an easier task, for the greater part of the Western thought has been expressed in books, whereas much of the Hindu thought exists only in the shape of verbal teaching, tradition, and "reading between the lines" of printed books. For one to write intelligently of Hindu thought, he must possess not only the best sources of information, but also the "instinct" whereby he is able to discriminate between the authoritative teachings, and those which contain but half-truths—and above all, he must be possessed of the Hindu Spirit, whereby he may see things as the Hindu sees them—that subtle spiritual sense which enables one to go at once to the heart of the Inner Teachings—that Key which unlocks the Door of the Temple.

When it is remembered that many of these English attempts to interpret the Hindu Philosophies have made by men who have lived in India as Christian missionaries, and whose duty it has been to discredit the native beliefs in the minds of the Hindu people in hope of winning them over to the creed and belief of the missionaries, it will be seen how prone to error such attempt must be. For no matter how sincere, honest and conscientious such a writer may be, his account must necessarily be coloured by his point of view and the duties of his life—he is in the position of a paid attorney for one side trying to describe the case of the party whom he is opposing—an almost impossible task to fulfil with bias and prejudice. The paid attorney, zealous for his client's interest, and impregnated with the one-sided view of the case, is not very likely to manifest a purely judicial mind and point of view, no matter how honest he may be.

And then again, the fundamental opposition between the basic philosophical conceptions of the Hindu philosopher and the Christian theologian can scarcely be imagined by one not familiar with both. As a slight instance, we may say that while "creation" is one of the basic propositions at the Christian theologian, the Hindu philosopher will not admit the existence of such a thing—he regards "creation" in the doctrine of *the making of something from nothing*, a conception which is filled with error for him, and which is absolutely unthinkable and insane from his point of view. To the Hindu mind *nothing comes from nothing*—everything that *is* either an eternal thing, or else a form or manifestation, or appearance, emanation or phase of some eternal thing. The "miracle" of creating something from nothing is absolutely incomprehensible and unthinkable to the Hindu's mind—no matter how hard and honestly he may try to form a mental image of the thing, he confesses himself baffled—it is like asking him to think that twice two is something else but four—and that the shortest distance between two points is other than a straight line. To him, "naught" is always "naught," and never can become "aught" by any process, human or divine.

Then again, to the Hindu mind, a mortal thing can never become immortal by any means. *An immortal thing must always have been immortal, or else it never can become so.* And therefore everything that is born must die sometime—and everything that dies has been born sometime. To him Eternity must exist on both sides of the Now; in fact the Now is but a point in Eternity. Thus the Hindu is unable to accept the teachings of immortality for the soul, unless previous immortality be conceded to it. He cannot conceive of any power "creating" a soul from nothing, and then bestowing immortality upon it for eternity. And while the Western philosopher, likewise, is unable to think of "aught coming from naught," the subject presents no difficulty whatever to the Western theologian who readily conceives the thing being done by Divine fiat.

And, so you see how little the missionary writer is apt to grasp the fundamental Hindu conceptions or point of view—his training and life-work prevents it. And what is true of the missionary is also true of the average Western investigator of the Eastern philosophies and religions. As the Hindus say, he who would grasp the Inner Teaching of the Hindu Philosophy *must have a "Hindu Soul,"* no matter what may be his race, or country. There are many Western people who have these "Hindu Souls," as the increasing number of Western people who are interested in, and who intelligently and sympathetically understand the Hindu Teachings, may testify to. The Hindus, when they find such, explain it upon the theory of Reincarnation, saying *"Once a Hindu, always a Hindu,"* no matter in what race the Hindu Soul may incarnate—the concentrated force of the ancient teachings are indelibly impressed upon the soul, and give it a tendency toward the Hindu thought in future lives. In fact, the Hindus hold that the souls of the ancient Hindu teachers, or rather of certain of them, are now incarnating in the West to lead the newer races toward a conception of the Truth, and their first disciples are the reincarnated Hindu souls abiding in the Western lands.

There is another difficulty attending the attempts of the Western writer who wishes to grasp the true meaning of the Hindu Philosophies, but who has failed to catch the *spirit* of the Hindu thought. We allude to the Inner Teachings which are to be found in all of the Oriental thought. The Oriental mind works upon entirely different psychological lines from the mind of the Western man. In the Western lands the impulse is to publish and proclaim every detail of the thought on any subject, sometimes in advance of its actual acceptance by the leading minds working along the lines of the particular subject. But in the Orient the tendency is precisely the opposite, and the sage is apt to reserve for him- self and his close circle of personal students and followers the cream of the idea, deeming it too important to be spread broadcast to the unthinking and unappreciative public. Moreover, in the West the philosophy of a man is regarded as a purely intellectual matter, and he is not expected to live up to the philosophy that he has enunciated—while in the East the philosopher takes his teachings very much in earnest, and so does his public, and he is expected to live out his teachings in his everyday life or else be considered a hypocrite. This being the case, the Oriental holds back his Inner Teachings for himself, until he is able to live out and manifest them in his life. And what is true of the individual is true of the great body of thinkers, who instinctively reserve for the few the Inner Teachings of their philosophies, deeming it almost a sacrilege to divulge the inner truths to anyone who has not proven his worthiness and right motives.

Moreover, there is always the great body of the Inner Teachings of the Hindu Philosophies which are tacitly accepted and recognized by the students of the philosophies, but which are not openly taught. These basic truths are deeply impressed upon the Hindu consciousness, and are absorbed almost with their mother's milk. Consequently, the English investigator, finding no clear and detailed statement of these fundamental truths mentioned in the books, is apt to ignore them, and consequently is unable to understand the true meaning of certain secondary truths and ideas based upon the fundamental conceptions. This is apparent to anyone who has grasped the inner meaning of the Hindu philosophies, and who is able to see the common basis for the apparently contradictory theories and opposing schools, when he reads the essays and books written by Westerners who treat the different schools as diametrically opposed to each other and having no common basis of agreement. The truth is that *all the various Hindu philosophies and religions are but various offshoots from a common trunk and root*. If one discovers this root-thought, he is then able to follow out the subtle differences of interpretation and doctrine, and to reconcile their differences, whereas to the Western man who fails to perceive the common trunk and root the whole system of Hindu Philosophy is a tangled mass of contradictions, lacking relationship and harmony. In these lessons we hope to be able to so present the subject that the student may be able to see the common trunk and root, and then to follow out the diverging branches to the end, from the point of apparent separation ; or on the other hand, to follow a line of thought back from its extreme point to the point where it diverges from the common trunk.

If the above statements regarding the difficulty of a correct understanding and interpretation of the Hindu Philosophies be true, what must be said of an attempt of the Western mind to understand and interpret the Hindu Religious systems, in all of their branches, denominations and division down to the finest hair-splitting degree. To the average Western mind the subject of the Hindu Religions is one of extreme perplexity and confusion, seemingly based upon an unstable foundation, and lacking coherence or any reasonable common basis or foundation. The Western mind sees and hears on one hand the highest, spiritual teachings, and the most refined and subtle philosophy coming from the master minds of Ancient India, and on the other hand sees and hears the grossest superstition and credulity accompanied by the most absurd forms of ritualistic nonsense and exhibitions of greedy and tyrannical priestcraft. On one hand he sees the most elevated spiritual conceptions, accompanied by the most austere and ascetic lives of their followers, while on the other hand he sees the exhibition of what appears to him to be the grossest forms of the old Phallic Worship accompanied by the most shocking exhibitions of immorality and obscenity. Can such things have a common origin—can there be any connection between the highest forms and the lowest? The inquirer forgets that in the history of all religions there have been witnessed these extremes and contradictions, but usually they are separated by periods of time and eras of thought, while in India they exist contemporaneously and almost side by side.

Then again, the Western mind sees the highest form of religious philosophy taught and practised under some of the more elevated forms of the Vedanta, beyond which no human mind has ever dared to venture, so ethereal and tenuous are its conceptions, the Truth being followed until it faded into a transcendental vagueness impossible of being grasped except by the mind trained in the highest philosophic methods. And, opposing this, the Western observer sees what appears to him to be the crudest form of idol worship, and debasing credulity and superstition—almost a form of devil worship and fetishism. He is justified in asking whether there can be any common root and origin for these opposing conceptions and practices. It is no wonder that the Western world, hearing some of the reports of the missionaries and travellers, and then reading the high doctrines of the Vedas and Upanishads, fails to understand, and gives up the matter with a shake of the head and the thought that India must be a very nightmare of theological, religious and philosophical vagaries and conceptions. And, when to this he adds the reports of the "Wonder-Workings" or "Magic" of some of the Hindu fakirs or magicians, it is still more perplexed; the difficulty not growing less when he hears the Hindu teachers declaring that these "miracles" and "wonder-workings" are not performed by high spiritual people, or by spiritual methods, but that on the contrary they are the result of methods along the lines of the "psychic," understandable by every-one who cares to investigate the subject, and often performed by men most unspiritual and lacking morality or religious merit and often ignorant of even the rudiments of the higher philosophies. All this is most confusing to the Western mind, and we hope to be able to throw some light on the dark corners of this subject, also.

× × ×

One of the explanations, of the prevalence of the lowest forms of fetishism, superstition and religious debasement in India, alongside of the highest forms of religious and philosophical knowledge and teaching, is the mental atmosphere of India itself, and a study of the history of thought in that land. It must be remembered that for countless centuries the Hindu mind has confined itself closely to an investigation of "the other side of Life" to a degree not to be imagined by the Western mind. While the newer lands of the West, with their active pioneers in activity, have been pushing forward toward material advancement and progress, India has been resting quietly, dreaming of that which lies back of the material world, and under and above physical existence. To the Hindu mind the physical and material world is more or less of an illusion, inasmuch as it passes away almost while it is being formed, and is a thing of the moment merely—while the spiritual world is the real one and the one to which the mind of man may most properly be turned. Mind you, we are merely stating the fact and existing conditions that you may understand them, not as urging that the above method is the better. For, to be frank with you, we consider the general tendency of the Hindu mind to be as much "one-sided" as that of the Western world—the one leans to the "I Am" side, ignoring the "I Do" side ; while the other places entire dependence upon the "I Do" phase, almost entirely ignoring the "I Am" phase. The one regards the side of Being, and ignores the side of Action; while the other regards Action as the essential thing; ignoring the vital importance of Being. To the Western world the Physical is the dominant phase—to the East the Metaphysical holds the lead. The thinking minds of both East and West clearly see that the greatest progress in the future must come from a combining of the methods of the two lands, the Activity of the West being added to the Thought of the East, thus inspiring the old lands into new activities and energy; while to the Western activity must be added the spirituality and "soul-knowledge" of the East, in order that the rampant materiality may be neutralized and a proper balance maintained. And close observers see in the eagerness of the East to take on Western activity; and in the hunger and thirst of the West for knowledge of the soul and "that which is back of all life and the universe"; the indication of a wonderful future for the whole world, East and West together.

The people of India are separated by but a very thin veil from "the other side of life," and anyone who lives in India and who allows himself to "feel" the current of thought and life manifesting there, soon becomes aware that there is a vast psychological difference between the ancient land of the Ganges and the Western world. It is "in the air" of India and none can live there without feeling its subtle effect and influence. No Western man who was lived in India for a half-dozen years is ever the same man afterward, even if he returns to his own land. He never loses the feeling of the vague and nebulous Something Alive that is in the very air around him and about him. Scoff as he may, and materialist of materialists though he may be, he still feels that Something around him—he has caught the psychic atmosphere of India.

And this fact of the mental and psychic atmosphere of the land of the Hindus has a bad effect as well as good one. Just as does the rich ground of the tropical countries, under the blazing sun and other influences of Nature, bring forth a luxuriance of fruits, flowers and vegetation of a kind desired by Man, so does the same soil, under the same impulses, bring forth a rank growth of noxious weeds and vegetation—the fertile fields on the one side bearing marked contrast to the wild, fierce jungles on the other. And yet both conditions arise from the same soil, under the same sun, and rain, and atmospheric conditions. And, again, just as the wonderful sun of the tropics and the semi-tropical lands tends to bring forth the wonderful harvests and vegetable growths, so does it, at times; and under certain conditions, burn up, parch and destroy the grain, fruit and nutritious growths of the land, in a fierce and deadly drought, the result being that grim famine reigns where bountiful harvests formerly held court, and thousands perish from hunger instead of being nourished by Nature. And, as on the physical plane, so on the mental and spiritual in India. The mental soil so rich and so filled with materials for spiritual growth under the Sun of Spiritual Knowledge, also becomes a field ripe for the noxious growths of superstition and credulity, devil worship and frightful debasement of thought and practice. And, again, just as the sun produces the bountiful harvest in one section, and the deadly drought in another, so does the rich spiritual development of India have its dark side in the degenerated teachings and "shadow" among the same people.

India is a land of marked spiritual contrasts—the highest and the lowest are to be found there side by side. But, to those who are able to get behind the scenes and probe to the heart of the matter, it always is evident that the debasing forms of religion in India, are always found to be but *the degenerated and debased sides* of the true religious teachings of the Hindus. Just as men may and do degenerate morally, mentally and physically, so may and do men degenerate spiritually. Just as in the Western centres of civilization are to be found human monsters performing deeds more savage than those of the most ignorant savages—just as men of intellect are found guilty of acts and practices below the level of the beasts—so do we find in India the lower and ignorant classes of people so far fallen away from the magnificent spiritual teachings of their race that they are lower in the scale of true spirituality than the ignorant savage who has no spirituality at all. The greater the height, the greater the fall therefrom—the further the pendulum swings the one way, the further the swing in the other direction. The universal laws which manifest on the physical plane, are likewise in operation on the mental and spiritual planes as well. Perhaps, when you have studied these lessons, you will be able to understand the true and the false about India's religions—and to see that while her philosophies reach the summits of the highest mountains of human knowledge, at the same time certain forms of her religions dwell in the darkest, lower crevasses and canyons devoid of sunshine and the vivifying influences of the more favoured sections.

India has a population of nearly or quite, *three hundred million people,* spread over an immense territory closely populated. Its population is made up of numberless peoples and races, of all shades of religious opinions and practices, among which are, the millions of Orthodox Hindus (with their many forms of creeds and beliefs); Christians ; Mahommedans ; Jews; Parsees; Buddhists ; Jains ; Sikhs; and others, including about a half-million of aboriginal people, not Aryans or true Hindus, who adhere to their old form of ancestral worship. It is not to be wondered at that all shades and degrees of religions thought are to be found among these peoples, just as in Europe there is to be found every form, grade and degree of religious belief, from the highest to the lowest—and just as in America there is to be found the most advanced religious thought, side by side with some of the most superstitious and degrading forms among the ignorant—from the religious conception of an Emerson to the degrading beliefs of some of the southern negroes, little above the level of the Voodoo beliefs of their ancestors.

How few of the American people, of all classes just as one meets them on the streets, are capable of comprehending the sublime teachings of their country-man, Emerson! As in the East—so in the West—the law is universal. To those who ask: "Why is it that with the high conceptions of the Hindu Philosophy the masses of the Hindu people are not able to rise to a higher level?" we would answer : For the same reasons that the high teachings of the Western Philosophers have not reached the understanding of the masses of the people of the Western world—the cause is the same, and lies far behind the distinctions between peoples and countries. In all lands there are advanced souls, and those less advanced—and still those which are far down in the scale. The man of the world-wide view of life does not make narrow provincial comparisons between peoples, for he sees everywhere in operation the same universal laws of human nature, manifesting under the guise of local features and traits, but ever the same laws.

The peculiar local feature and traits among the Hindus—the features in which they differ the greatest from the Western peoples—is the fact that we have mentioned a moment ago, that *in India the veil between the Visible and the Invisible is much thinner than in the Western lands.* In India the crust between the surface of phenomenal life, and the great underlying noumenal life, is very thin indeed, and the sensitive soul may sense the throbbings of the underlying life, with its heart-beats and tumultuous currents of being. This being so, while the advanced soul is thus brought into close touch with the Inner Life of the Universe, and is able to mount to a higher plane, the soul far back on The Path of Spiritual Attainment not having the intelligence or powers of discernment to apply the Hidden Forces of the Soul, is still conscious of the existence of the Underlying Life, and is apt to develop along the lower psychic lines, instead of along the higher spiritual ones, and accordingly tends toward superstition and credulity, and low spiritual ideals, instead of mounting upward. *The weed grows in the tropical climate as well as the fruits and flowers.* Perhaps with even this slight explanation you may be able to understand this subject just a little better than you did before reading it. Let us trust so.

And now let us proceed to the consideration of the Basic Principles underlying the entire system of the Hindu Thought. And then let us pass on to an examination of the interpretation and teachings of each system, school cult and sect of that land so fertile and prolific of thought of Things Behind the Veil.

SPECIAL MESSAGE I

By Yogi Ramacharaka

This month we begin the study of "The Philosophies and Religions of India." It is a subject of the greatest interest to all who have studied with us the previous lessons on our conception of the Yogi philosophy. You will be able to trace step by step the progress of the great Hindu Philosophical Thought from the beginning down to the present time, in all of its branches and variations. You will be made acquainted with the Inner Teachings and the Fundamental Doctrines of the Hindu Philosophers, which will enable you to perceive the exact points of divergence and difference in interpretation, and the various points of reconciliation and agreement between the various schools and sects. With the key of the Fundamental Teachings you will be able to swing wide open the heavy outer doors of the Temples of Thought. And, moreover, as these Fundamental Teachings are basic and universal in their application, you will be able to unravel the tangles of Western Philosophy, as well as the Oriental Philosophy, by the means of your acquaintance with these Basic Principles, tracing each conception back to its origin, and placing it in its proper class. Moreover, you will see wherein *our own System of Philosophy* agrees with, and differs from, the various differing schools of the Hindu Philosophy. You will see that while we do not "wear the label" of any of the various schools, yet there are many points of agreement with the various ones in some of their divisions and subdivisions. We belong to what is known as the Eclectic School of Hindu Philosophy, which is really no crystallized school at all, but which founds itself firmly upon the solid rock of the Fundamental Teachings, and then "takes its own wherever it finds it" from the teachings of India's thinkers for the past five thousand years. "Eclectic," you know, means Selective; Chosen from various sources and systems, etc. ; and is the very reverse of "Dogmatic" and "Sectarian." We have many points of agreement with the Monistic school of the Vedanta; and likewise many points of agreement with the Sankhya school; and some points of common thought with Patanjali's Yoga school; and also some points of agreement with

Buddhism ; but at the same time we take exception to many points put forth by each school. Besides, we have availed ourselves of that very great, and to us very important, body of independent thought outside of the regular Hindu systems, and which is held by the independent thinkers, teachers and philosophers of India and other parts of the East; besides drawing liberally upon other sources of Oriental Occult Teaching. To those who, not acquainted with the history of the Hindu Philosophy, might object that an "Eclectic" System of Hindu Philosophy was a "new thing," and a product of modern tendencies, and therefore lacking the weight of ancient authority and precedent; we would quote the following from Prof. Richard Garbe, the well known German authority on Hindu Philosophical History. Prof. Garbe says : "In the first century of the Christian Era, there was started in India an Eclectic movement which was chiefly occupied with the combination of the Sankhya, Yoga and Vedanta theories." Such a "movement" (not a school or system, remember) which has been in existence for two thousand years, and which occasioned the production of some of the most virile philosophical thought during that time, may be pardoned for declining to be called "new" ; and for claiming its rightful place in the Hindu Philosophy.

And now, in approaching this study, let us lay aside all prejudice and preconceived conceptions and misapprehensions—and with open mind examine, consider and weigh the claims and teachings of these various systems—testing each with the touchstone of the Fundamental Principles which shall be given you, and above all perceiving the Unity in Diversity apparent to the student who has caught a glimpse of Truth. Let us Meditate on the idea that Truth is Universal, and that no one person, or body of persons, ever has; has now : or ever will-have ; a monopoly of Truth. That there is Truth in all teachings—but that none have All the Truth. And so, seeing the Truth in All, and ALL in the Truth, let us lay aside prejudice and bigotry, and with clear eyes perceive the reflection of the Sun of Truth in the waters contained in the many earthen jars of Dogma, Doctrine, Creed, Sect, School and System—but always remember that the TRUTH itelf is something far above these earthen receptacles, with their stores of water, each reflecting the Light of the Truth which proceeds from Above. And in so Meditating let us carry in our minds the words of the thousands-of-years-old *Rig-Veda*, which says :

"The Truth Is One—Men Call It By Many Names."

And in this thought is to be found the Secret of Tolerance, Broadness and Brotherhood, as in its absence appear Intolerance Narrowness, Bigotry, Sectarianism, Dogmatic Assumption, Persecution, Hostility, Hatred and Separateness. There is but ONE TRUTH—to know that Truth in its entirety is to BE that Truth—the bits and glimpses of Truth that we see in human Dogma, Creeds, and Closed Systems, but the reflections of the Sun of Truth, far above in the heavens, as seen on the surface of the muddy water of the Earthen Jars standing in the Courtyard. Remember this and seek ever the Sun. But the Jars must be examined in turn that we may know to distinguish the Truth from its reflection. Such is the Teaching of the Wise. Peace to Thee.

Chapter II

The Inner Teachings

It is difficult to trace back to the beginning of the great Aryan Philosophies, so far removed from the present are those beginnings in point of time. It is estimated that the Aryan Race is at least one hundred centuries—10,000 years—old, at the present time, and some have thought that its teachings were based on those of some still older civilization. The Aryan civilization is certainly the mother of modern thought — yes, even of the languages of the civilized world, and Professor Max Müller has said that nearly all the word-concepts now in use by the civilized may be traced back to a few Sanskrit roots. Not only has the Aryan mind given us our subjects for thought, but also the very words by which these thoughts may be conceived and expressed.

Centuries upon centuries ago, the Aryan Race descended upon the plains of India, conquering and driving out the dark-skinned aboriginal inhabitants of that land. From whence the Aryans came, historians are undecided, but the legends indicate that they came from some unknown land at the North. Some have supposed that they came from the region of the North Pole, the former conditions of which region were quite different from present conditions, while others have supposed that they were the survivors of some great nation whose home had been destroyed by some convulsion of nature. Some of the old legends hold that the Aryans were the survivors of the lost continent of Lemuria, which is said to have been situated in what is now known as the Pacific Ocean, and parts of the Indian Ocean, and which included what we now know as Australia, Australasia, and other portions of the Pacific Islands, which islands are really the surviving portions of the lost continent—its highest points—the lower portions being sunk beneath the waves. The legends hold that prior to the great cataclysm which destroyed the land and the people of Lemuria there was an emigration of a large number of Lemurians, led by certain religious leaders who had foretold the coming destruction of the land. The people and their descendants took refuge on some of the higher points of the distant northern parts of the land, which were turned into islands at the time of the cataclysm. Dwelling on these islands for centuries, they afterwards emigrated to the mainland of the new country, which had risen from the sea toward the south, and which is now known as India. They found the land occupied by dark-skinned aborigines who had been driven there from other lands by the convulsions of nature, the descendants of the Aryans overcoming them by reason of the superior Aryan mental development. It is interesting to note, however, that that there are nearly a million of the descendants of these non-Aryan aborigines still living in parts of India, the Aryans having allowed them to dwell in peace and who still adhere to the primitive religions of their forefathers of centuries back, their conquerors having respected their beliefs, and having refrained from forcing their own religions upon them.

The Aryans prospered in the new lands, and from them descended the present Aryan races of India. A portion of them, however, passed on to what is now known as Europe, and their descendants to-day are known as the Germanic, Italian, Celtic, Greek races, etc. Few people in the West realize that the Aryan Hindus and the dominant races of the Western world are descendants of the same stock, and are not separate people, as are the Chinese, Japanese, etc. The fact of the common origin of these peoples accounts for many of the underlying beliefs common to the several races in their earlier history, namely, that of Rebirth, etc., which the ancestors of the Western races held.

During the period of their emigration, wanderings, re-establishing fixed conditions, etc., which extended over many centuries, the ancient Aryans lost much of their culture and veneer of the old civilization, as has always been the case among pioneers from an older land entering into a new land in which they must "begin from the bottom" and build up a new civilization. Confronted with new, and trying conditions and environments, they gradually relapsed into a condition of primitive simplicity, the old truths and knowledge passing away and being replaced by traditions, legends, and vague memories of the past teachings transmitted by the old men of the people to their grandchildren and great-grandchildren, and thus being kept alive. But although the greater part of their philosophy was lost, and their religion passed from a condition of subtle metaphysical doctrine back into a condition of primitive, simple religion, still there were some fundamental truths that never were lost to them. The old teachings had been of a great, universal One Absolute Being from whom all else emanated— and from whom the individual souls proceeded "as the rising sparks from the blazing fire"; and of the Immortality of the Soul, which never was born and never could die, and which was subject to rebirth, under a universal law of cause and effect. And, although the ancient Aryans lost the full understanding of that One Absolute Being, they never wandered away from the idea of a great Nature-Spirit of which in some mysterious way they were a part—nor did they lose their hold on the doctrine of Reincarnation. These fundamental doctrines clung to the race throughout the centuries, and still continue with it.

These simple, primitive people naturally fell into the ways of all people of their degree of civilization, and they proceeded to create gods and demi-gods without number, according to their conceptions and the demands of their imaginations, the number increasing, and the differences began to manifest more clearly, as the race rapidly increased and divided into tribes, peoples and nations. But the Aryan mind in India never lost sight of the fact that above and over all of their gods there existed the One from which even the gods proceeded. Even in the most backward of the tribes, who had relapsed into a state of idolatrous practices and whose collection of gods included many crude conceptions, some of which were practically forms of devil-worship, still above all they had their tradition of their "God of Gods." And so the race began its upward climb again, passing through all the stages that all races, have manifested in the evolution of their religious beliefs—but always having their inherited ideas of The One manifesting its subtle influence, and striving to unfold itself once more into the religious consciousness of the race.

At a period estimated at about five thousand years before the Christian era, many of the Hindu people, particularly in certain favoured sections in which the struggle for life was not so severe, and in which the people had risen to a comparatively high state of culture and knowledge, began to manifest a great interest in Philosophy. The Hindus claim that this was caused by the Reincarnation of many of the old teachers of the root-race, who, returning to the earth and incarnating in the bodies of their descendants, began to revive the old knowledge which had been lost during the centuries of emigration, wandering, and building up of the new civilization. About this time, whatever may have been the cause, there began a wonderful revival of philosophical speculation and thought, the effects of which are manifest in India even unto this day. At that time appeared those great thinkers whom we now call the "Ancient Hindu Sages," the memory of whom is kept alive in India of to-day by tradition. These men antedated the writing of the Vedas and the Upanishads, the ancient and sacred works of the Hindus. These Sages started the Hindu School of Philosophy which has since exerted so marked an influence upon the race.

So far as we are able to gather from written and verbal tradition—particularly the latter, for the Hindus always have passed along the bulk of their teachings in this way—the Sages gathered around them the most intelligent young men of their race and began to formulate and expound a philosophy of Pure Reason. The students were instructed to lay aside all of their preconceived ideas, and religious teachings, so far as philosophical conceptions were concerned, and as we would now say in the West, "to begin from the ground up," laying a firm foundation, and then carefully erecting the structure of thought thereupon. In fact, so concerned were the Sages in establishing a firm foundation for the new philosophy, that it may be said that their entire work was in the direction of laying the Great Foundation of the Hindu Philosophy, leaving for their followers through the centuries the work of erecting the superstructure thereupon. And so well was their work done, that although many philosophies have come, and many have gone, in India during the past fifty centuries, the Foundations of the Sages still remain, as sound and as firm as when first laid, unchanged, unhurt, and unaffected by the binding up and tearing down work that has gone on over them in the many years since they were laid. Surely such Foundation Work must be sound, and well worthy of the attention and consideration of all thinkers, no matter what their belief, or race, or country. Let us now consider the work of the Sages, and the Foundation they laid.

In the first place, the Sages bade their students observe that there was nothing Constant, Abiding, Fixed, and Imperishable in the phenomenal aspect of Nature and the Universe. At this place it may be well to give their idea of the meaning of "Phenomenal." To them the Sanskrit word conveying the idea that we now express by the word 'phenomenal' meant "that which appears to the senses—that which is seen, felt, heard, smelled, tasted, or sensed in any way." The Greek word 'phenomenal' is defined by Webster as: "An appearance; anything visible; whatever is apprehended by observation"— the two words being almost identical in meaning. The Sages then bade their students observe that the phenomenal world was but a series of changing, shifting forms and events, nothing being abiding or permanent. To the mind of the Sages none of these phenomenal things—nor all of them combined—was or were 'Real,' the term being used in the sense of "existing; fixed, permanent, constant"—just as we use the term in connection with "Real Property—Real Estate—Realty," etc., in law today. And, accordingly, the Sages bade their students recognize that the Phenomenal Universe not 'Real' in the philosophical sense of the word.

The next step was to bid the students recognize that underneath all the changing and shifting manifestations of the Phenomenal Universe there must be something that was Real and Substantial upon the face or surface of which occurred the constant play of matter, force, and life, as the ripple and waves played upon the surface of the ocean, or as the clouds passed before the blue of the sky. They held that Pure Reason must convince any Philosophical mind that there must be Something Real and Substantial under and behind the Phenomenal Universe, else the latter could not exist even in appearance—that there must be a Background of Reality, or a Foundation of Substance. Their term, from which the concept of 'Substance' arose, may be understood by the definition of 'Substance,' which is given by Webster as follows : "That which underlies all outward manifestations; substratum; that in which all properties inhere, that constituting anything what it is; nature; real or existing essence; etc." (Kindly remember that the word is not used in the sense of "Matter, or Material Things.") And that, consequently, this Universal Substance must be Real—and that in its totality it was necessarily the only Reality. The next step was the recognition that this Substantiality must be but One in its essential being, otherwise there could not exist that continuity and orderly trend of manifestation observable in the Phenomenal Universe.

The next step in the logical reasoning was that this Ultimate Reality must be above all phenomenal attributes and qualities, including those of man, and consequently that its Inner Nature, or Essential Being, was beyond the cognition, knowledge or even the imagination of man, and was Unknowable in that sense, and therefore beyond definition or name —therefore the Sages styled this Ultimate Reality by the Sanskrit word 'TAT,' from which the English word 'THAT' is derived—a pronoun referring to something supposed to be understood—in this case implying no qualities, attributes or name. And the Sanskrit word, *Tat*, and its English equivalent, "THAT," is still used even unto to-day to designate or point out (but not to describe) the Hindu idea of the Ultimate Reality behind the Phenomenal Universe—and in these lessons we shall so use the term, or its more popular Hindu equivalent 'Brahman,' or 'The Absolute,' our own favourite term.

The next step in the chain of reasoning was that, applying the fundamental Hindu axiom : " Something never can be caused by, or proceed from, Nothing," and as there was nothing other than THAT in Real Existence, or which could have caused it, and as Reality even could hot have been Self-created from nothing, it must follow that THAT must always have existed, and must be Eternal. And, also, applying the Hindu axiom that "Something cannot be dissolved into Nothing," THAT cannot cease to be, and must be Everlasting. Therefore, THAT is to be considered as Eternal.

The next step was that, inasmuch as there was nothing outside of THAT with which, or by which, it could be defined, bounded, determined, affected, caused, or influenced, it must be held that THAT is Infinite. It was also held that as there was nothing else that could act as a Cause of the Phenomenal Universe, THAT must be its only efficient and sufficient Cause. But in this connection the subtle mind of the Hindu Sages escaped the placing of THAT in the category of other Causes, as some of philosophers have done when they call it "the first Cause." Instead, they held that it is the Causeless Cause—the Only Real Cause—and that other than THAT there can be no Real Cause. Following this line of reasoning they discovered that all that we call Cause and Effect in the Phenomenal World is but a series or sequence of Consecutive Effects, that is, a series or sequence of objects or events following in an orderly train; successive; uninterrupted; continuous and constant, and all proceeding from the One Cause—THAT. In the Phenomenal World each object or event is both a Cause and an Effect (relatively speaking)—that is, an Effect of the preceding object or event, and the Cause (relative) of the succeeding object or event—the Effect being the Cause (relative) reproduced—each Effect thus being in the Cause (relative). This being so, it follows that the Laws of the Phenomenal Universe are continuous, regular and uniform, and to be depended upon. Therefore THAT may be considered as The Only Real Cause.

The next step was to recognize that THAT was necessarily Unchangeable, there being nothing to change It; nothing into which It could be changed; and, moreover, as there was nothing but Itself that it could be, It, being All that Is, there is nothing else. It could change itself into, as there cannot be anything created from nothing, and even THAT could not create Itself into any Reality other than that which It is, any more than It could change Itself into Nothingness or Non-Reality. And, moreover, it was held that THAT could not divide Itself into parts, for there was nothing else to divide it, or by which it could be divided, or with which to separate the parts—moreover, if it were divided there would be two or more THATS or Realities, instead of but one; and its Infinite nature would be destroyed, something which the Sages deemed impossible. Therefore it was held that THAT was Unchangeable and Invisible.

The next step was to declare the truth that as all that truly IS must be Real (in the sense of the term that we have explained) and as THAT being all that is Real must be ALL that IS—then it followed that other than THAT there could be nothing that IS. And, accordingly, all that seemed or appeared to be, must lack true reality and existence, and must be either nothing, or else an emanation of some kind, or manisfestation of some kind of THAT. And upon this Basic Proposition the Hindu Philosophers that all Truth regarding the Universe must be based. They would not admit the "creation" (real) of anything phenomenal, for they claimed that axiom, "Something cannot be created from Nothing," when applied, demonstrated that even THAT could not have "created" the Phenomenal Universe of the Individual Souls from nothing, nor could THAT have 'created' anything from its own substance or essence; nor was there anything outside of Itself that THAT could have used with which to 'create' anything—therefore it followed that nothing had been, or could have been really created" and that therefore the Phenomenal Universe, and all it contained, including the Individual Souls, must have "emanated from," or been 'manifested by' THAT in some manner and by means of processes beyond the power of the mind of man to determine, although not beyond his power to imagine. And upon that Basic Proposition the Sages rested their speculation and reasoning regarding the Phenomenal Universe. And upon that firm basis have been erected the many structures of subsequent Hindu Philosophy. And, now, let us give you a little summing up of the conclusions that were arrived at by these Ancient Hindu Sages, and their earlier followers, before we pass to the subsequent developments of the philosophical thought of India.

× × ×

To begin with, the Hindu Sages assumed Three Axioms, or Self-Evident Truths, upon which they based their Thought regarding the Phenomenal Universe, and the reality which they held was to be found behind it. These Three Axioms were as follows :

I. From Nothing, Nothing can come; Something cannot be caused by, or proceed from Nothing; Nothing Real can be Created, for if it Is Not Now, it never Can Be—if it Ever Was Not, it Is Not Now—if it Is Now, it Ever Has Been.

II. Something Real cannot be dissolved into Nothing; if it Is Now, it A ways Will Be; Nothing That Is can ever Be Destroyed; Dissolution is merely the Changing of Form—the resolving of an Effect into its Preceding Cause (real or relative).

III. What is Evolved must have been Involved; the Cause (real or relative) must contain the Effect; the Effect must be the reproduction of the Cause (real or relative).

As we have seen, from the beginnings of the Hindu Philosophical thought, there was manifested an almost intuitive desire to go back and through the phenomenal aspect of things—back through the things which bore names, even though these things were conceived of as universal principles—back still further, and further, until at last was to be found THAT which was not capable of further analysis or refinement—and which could not even be called a Something—and which the Hindu mind has always called THAT, because no other term could be applied to it without ascribing attributes or qualities—THAT which would be left even after all the universe had been thought away in the refinement of metaphysical speculation. The early thinkers asked the questions: "When the universe distintegrates, what is it that absorbs it? What is the Reality behind, and under the world of change and destruction? Upon what permanent foundation does the universe of impermanency rest?"

The old legends tell of the Hindu philosophers thousandse of years before the Roman Empire, asking ultimate questions, such as: "What is there that we still exist though there be no universe; no heavens; no gods; no anything?" The answer agreed upon by the sages being

"Infinite Essential Space."And so space was considered as a Reality that could not be thought away even by the use of the most powerful imagination. But their conception of space was not that of an immense, infinite Nothing—for the Hindu mind abhors ideas of Nothing, and will not admit that Anything can proceed from Nothing—instead, their idea of Essential Space was that of an Actual Reality—an Absolute Substantial Reality from which all Things were manifestations, emanations, expressions or thoughts. They thought of Infinite Essential Space as a No Thing, but not as Nothing. To them Space was not only "an infinite capacity for exteneding objects," which is the physical aspect of it—but something more—an Infinite Bare Abstract Subjectivity, which the human mind was compelled to admit in all of its conceptions, and yet was unable to think of as 'in-itself.'

In the second place, the early Hindu thinkers were compelled to admit the reality of Motion, as an aspect of the Ultimate Reality. They reasoned that there was manifested an Activity which proceeded from THAT, and which evidently was not merely a phenomenal manifestation but rather an inherent and essential aspect of Itself. They held that as all Activity arises from Motion, therefore the Essence of Motion must inhere in THAT. And so they formulated the idea that Absolute Essential Motion was a second aspect of THAT—but in their conception of that Absolute Essential Motion they regarded it as of such infinite degree of power and rate of vibration that to all human thought it must be regarded as Absolute Rest—Motionless Motion consisting of vibration of such a high rate and degree that to the highest human consciousness it would appear as absolutely at rest, just as a rapidly whirling wheel seems to stand still. Therefore the Hindu's second aspect of THAT may be stated as Absolute Essential Abstract Motion-at-Rest, if the term is permissible—something that is unthinkable 'in-itself.'

In the third place, the early Hindu thinkers were compelled to recognize the Real Existence of a Law which was manifested in all the phenomena of the Universe, and which was constant, fixed, unchangeable and possessing all the attributes of Reality. They could not reason, think, or imagine this Law out of existence, nor could they conceive that it had ever Not-Been, else they would be committing the absurdity of assuming that the fundamental facts recognized by the reason could ever, at any time in the past, not have been—for instance, that the principles of Geometry of Space ever could have been not-true; that mathematical principles and the laws of logic ever could have been untrue and non-existent; in short, that things which were perceived to be superior to change and time, and which manifested all the elements of reality, ever could not have been, or ever could have been otherwise than they are. Therefore, the philosophers were forced to recognize Absolute Abstract Law as a third aspect of THAT—their conception being of an Abstract Absolute LAW which was impossible of being understood "in-itself," but which existed as an aspect of THAT, and which governed all of the phenomenal manifestations of Motion, or Matter, or even of Its own expressions in the shape of the Laws of Nature, in which shape it manifests in the phenomenal world. The Law was sometimes regarded as the WILL of THAT.

It was held that just as all phenomenal manifestations of Matter must be an appearance, reflection, expression, or emanation of the first aspect of THAT—Absolute Essential Space; so all phenomenal manifestations of Physical Energy or Force, or Power must be an appearance, reflection, expression, or emanation of the second aspect of THAT—Absolute Essential Motion ; and all phenomenal manifestation of Universal Laws must be an appearance, reflection, expression, or emanation of the third aspect of THAT—Absolute Abstract Law. But these three aspects were recognized as but different views of the One Reality, and not as three "parts" or "principles," or "persons." It was not a Trinity, but a One viewed from three viewpoints. As to the abstract conceptions of these three aspects—so far removed from phenomenal manifestation, it is scarcely a matter of wonder that Western thinkers have thought that the Hindu metaphysicians taught that "All is Nothing," so high did their Conceptions soar up into the thin and rarefied air of transcendental philosophy. But the 'No-Thingness' of the Hindu is very far removed from the "Nothingness" of the Western Mind.

The Western thinker often expresses surprise that Life and Mind are not included in the list of aspects of THAT, by the Hindu thinkers. But the latter considered the Mind and Life of the phenomenal world as merely reflections of appearance of the BEING of THAT, and not as any of the aspects of it—that is, as phenomenal counterparts or reflections of the WHOLE Being of THAT, rather than of any of its aspects. They could not conceive of the BEING OF THAT as possible without an Infinite Existence and Knowing, but they made a subtle distinction, and would not say THAT 'lived' or 'thought' (these being phenomenal manifestations and attributes), but simply said THAT 'IS,' the statement of Real Being carrying with it the conception of Infinite and Absolute Life Existence and Knowing, of which Life and Mind are the phenomenal reflections.

From this Hindu Root-Thought of the One Reality—THAT—proceed all of the various conceptions regarding the Universal Substance—the Universal Energy—even the Universal Soul—the highest conception being that they all proceed from THAT, and that THAT is thinkable when all these secondary conceptions are thought away. THAT is the one thing behind which and beyond which the human mind is unable to think—which the human mind cannot think out of subjective existence, for it is the very foundation, or the background, of Thought itself. And it will be found that THAT is back of all conceptions of Deity, personal or impersonal—all god conceptions emanate from this fundamental conception. The best Hindu teachers have always held that THAT was incapable of being expressed in words—was unthinkable and unspeakable in terms of description—that to "define It was to limit It, and thus consequently to deny It"—It transcends the power of the human understanding and imagination, and is beyond the range and reach of human thought. But yet, the human mind, if it thinks of the subject at all, is inevitably compelled to conceive of the existence of THAT. It cannot be thought out of subjective existence in the consideration of the Nature of Things, any more than can the "I" be though out of existence by the individual when thinking of personal things. It defies the power of description, and yet must be postulated as existing. When we reach the consideration of the various philosophies and religions of India we shall see the structures that men have attempted to erect upon this basic foundation, and under all of them we shall discover the same elementary conception of the Ancient Hindu Teachers, although often almost covered up and hidden by the temporary structures built thereon. And these structures will pass away as have all of man's theories and creeds—but so long as human thought exists these Fundamental Truths must be accepted as basic and necessary. And if you will examine the philosophies and religions of the Western world, you will find the same basic foundation under them all—if this were not so they could not stand.

The above mentioned Fundamental Truths of the Hindu Philosophy regarding THAT are regarded by their best thinkers to be axiomic and beyond doubt or question. In order that you may understand the reasoning manifested through the subsequent lessons, when the various conceptions are considered, it would be well for you to acquaint yourselves thoroughly with the above lines of reasoning of the early Hindu sages. You will find that once well grounded in them you will be able to consider any metaphysical or philosophical question with a new clearness of thought and discrimination. They are the Axiom of the Hindu Thought, which were formulated many centuries ago by the keenest philosophical intellects of which we have any record. And they are well worth the careful consideration of everyone who wishes to think along philosophical lines.

× × ×

It will be noticed that in the formulation of the above mentioned Fundamental Principles of the Hindu Philosophies, the early teachers considered the problem exclusively from the standpoint of Pure Reason, and independent of any religious teachings or the voice of religious authority. This occurred not because the early teachers wished to express their disbelief in the prevailing religions of their day, but because they felt that Truth must be above the exercise of mere Faith, or acceptance of doctrines and dogmas issued upon the bidding of real or assumed authority. They felt that man had been given Reason wherewith to examine for himself into the great problems of life, being and the universe—Reason which was not required for the needs of the struggle for material existence, but which was evidently evolved for the purpose of purely intellectual work and function—and, this being so, it became the duty of advanced men to exercise this Reason to the utmost—to inquire of its highest reports and conclusions, and then to abide by the results of the inquiry.

And there were other reasons inspiring these early thinkers to formulate schools of philosophy, which should run along side by side with the religious teachings of the race. These wise men foresaw the rise of dogmatic religious teachings, or theology, fostered and nurtured by a priesthood which would profit thereby, the end being that the populace would have borne upon them a mass of dogma and so-called "authoritative " teaching, ceremonies, ritual and creeds utterly foreign to the essence of the true faith, and which would end by something true religious philosophy by the cover of ecclesiasticism. This fear has been found to be well grounded, by the experience of men in all times and lands—the growth of organized churches and priesthoods having invariably been accompanied by a decrease in the philosophical freedom and clearness of thought, and a perversion of the original teachings of the religion in question. Such seems to be the laws of church organization and the crystallization of creeds. And, so, these ancient sages wished to establish a co-ordinate branch of thought—one founded on Pure Reason rather than on Faith and Authority—and which would tend to keep pure the teachings and bright the flame of Truth, even when the pall of ecclesiasticism would descend upon the Hindu Teachings, from time to time.

And this precaution has tended to keep true philosophical thought alive in India for over five thousand years—fifty centuries. From time to time the religious teachers and leaders would become more and more orthodox, and ritual, form, ceremonies and creeds would cause the people to forget the Ancient Wisdom. Gods, demi-gods and supernatural creatures and beings of all kinds would take the place of the thought of THAT in the minds of the people, and THAT would appear only as a shadowy and nebulous background to the personifications of Deity, and the numerous *Avatars*, or Incarnations of the Divine And so religious forms would flourish and the religious spirit would wither and fade away. Then here would be sure to arise some Heretic or Dissenter—Protestant or Reformer—Who would return to the ancient teachings and philosophies of the Fathers, sounding again the old note of THAT, and the employment of Pure Reason as a basis for Faith rather than the ecclesiastical formalism and dogmatic theology upon which so much so-called 'religion' is based. These reformers would attract many of the thinking people to them, who would be followed by a number of the less intelligent ones, and a new school, or form of religion would be adopted, and if based upon sound reasoning and practical precepts would grow and flourish and prosper as did the old denominations. But sooner or later the apathy and numbness of old age in church life would come to the new school also, and then would rise another schism or reform. And so, on through the centuries, school after school has arisen—schism after schism has sprung into existence—each having its birth, rise, decline, death and decay—and each having as its source of inspiration the Philosophy of the Fathers, which had been handed down principally by tradition and legend, the Oriental memory being remarkable in this respect, the teachings of many centuries ago having been handed down intact from teacher to pupil, by pure memory, even unto this day.

After the lapse of several centuries, there began to be numerous bits of writing on the part of the Hindu poets and others, into which naturally crept mention of the early teachings and philosophy, much of it being related in a style coloured and tinged with the poetic fancy of the writer. Then, after a time, learned teachers would form schools of teachings and thought from which would arise philosophical writings on the part of their followers. In this way arose the Upanishads, that wonderful collection of ancient Sanskrit writings, in which is contained scraps of the highest philosohical thought and wisdom that ever emanated from the mind of man. If one has the Master-Key of the fundamental teachings, such as we have mentioned in this lesson, he may read from the Upanishads an elaboration and exemplification of these doctrines that will prove a source of the greatest delight to him, and which will result in the opening up of his mind to the highest and most elevating thoughts. The boldness and daring whereby some of these old thinkers pursue an idea to its logical conclusion is a revelation to the mind trained in the cautious and time-serving methods of many of the Western philsophers of the past. Surrounded on all sides by orthodox religions and peoples, the writers of the Upanishads did not hesitate to reason out a line of thought, even if thereby the entire dogmas of the prevailing religion would be swept away. And, stranger still, India has ever been almost entirely free from religious persecution and tyranny, and even a powerful priesthood has never been able to overcome the inherent Hindu prejudice in favour of allowing all comers a free use of the philosophical arena in which to display their mental and spiritual might and muscle.

As we shall see, the differences in the schools of philosophy arise chiefly by reason of the attempt to interpret the process and methods where "the One becomes Many"—that is, upon the questions of the Origin, Nature and Destiny of the Soul, and its relation to the One. With the Fundamental Principles in mind, we will find it interesting to follow up the Hindu thought on this subject, in its many wonderful turns and windings, its by-paths and side-journeys, in all of which many bits of valuable truth may be picked up.

But, before closing the lesson, let us call your attention to the fact that none of these leading divisions of philosophical thought have ever thought it necessary to 'prove' the existence of the soul—this question was considered answered by the consciousness of every individual, and all attempt to 'prove' it was considered folly—the Hindu mind never has had any Doubt on this subject. The Buddhists attempted to prove that the soul was not a true entity, but this was merely a metaphysical hair-splitting.

And again, the question of Reincarnation, or Rebirth of the Soul, always has been accepted as an almost self-evident fact on the part of the Hindu thinkers, and it has been held that the glimpses of recollection that every person experiences, and the fragments of "memory of past lives" that nearly all if not every one of the Hindus are conscious of, takes the matter out of the ordinary realm of philosophical speculation. To the Hindu mind Reincarnation, Rebirth or Metempsychosis is as much an accepted fact of life and nature as is Birth and Death—it is never Doubted, and the Hindu mind passes on to a consideration of the 'Why' and 'How' of the problem. For one hundred centuries the Hindu religions have accepted Reincarnation—for fifty centuries Hindu philosophy has included it among the proven facts of life. It is regarded as a part of the universal phenomena, and as forming a part of the natural law, and to be studied in that branch of human thought and education, rather than in connection with the Fundamental Principles. To the Western mind this seems odd—but the Hindu consciousness sees it in a different light. No Hindu Philosophy or Religion ignores or denies Reincarnation any more than it denies Thought.

The essence of the Inner Teachings has always been the Reality and Being of ONE UNIVERSAL SPIRIT PRINCIPLE, from which all other life, being, principles were manifested by emanation, reflection or otherwise, and which manifestations had their ONLY REAL BEING in the ONE SOURCE. We ask you to remember, always, this one fundamental principle of the Inner Teaching, for without it you will lose your way in the labyrinth of Hindu Philosophy, while with it you always will have the Light which will illumine The Path of Knowledge.

While, from the first, there was ever the dispute about the 'Why' or 'Reason' of the Emanation, Reflection or Manifestation—there never was any dispute about the fact of the manifestation, or nature of the universe of phenomena. And, arising from this axiomic doctrine, there arose that feature of the Hindu thought which regarded the phenomenal universe as an illusory world, producing the pain and dissatisfaction that comes from the fact of separateness from the Source. Hence arises that which the West has called "the Pessimism of the Hindu thought," but which even the Western religious philosophies reproduce in their conception of "this life below being one of sorrow, sin and unhappiness," of the "better world" awaiting these who escape the present one with a record of good deeds and the proper faith and belief. The Western conception of "the world of Sin and Sorrow" is no less pessimistic than the Hindu conception of the "world of Ignorance, Illusion and Separateness from the

One." The thought that the phenomenal world is one of sorrow and unhappiness, and lacking the bliss of some other plane of being beyond it, is a universal conception of the human mind—common to the race.

And the religions of India, like those of the West, teach that escape and 'salvation' from this 'world of sorrow' is possible to those who accept the doctrines of their church, and who live 'good' lives. But the Hindu philosophies go further than the religions of either East or West, and point out that Emancipation, Freedom, Release from *Samsara*, or the Chain of Existences—or 'Salvation,' to use the Western term—may be obtained by an Understanding of the Truth; a Realization of the Real Self; a Perception of the identity of the Individual Spirit with the Universal Spirit ("Tat tvam asi," "That art thou !"); and the killing out of Desire for Material Life and Objects, and a concentration of the whole mind upon The One.

And this ONENESS of Reality—this doctrine of the manifestation of The Many, and of the Universe, as an emanation, reflection or phenomenal appearance of the One, is the Inner Teaching underlying all of the many forms of the Hindu Philosophy and Religions. And you will find this Inner Teaching running like a silken thread through all the beads of the systems of philosophies and religions of India, from high to low, as we proceed. Plainly asserted and insisted upon in the Monistic forms of the *Vedanta*; apparently contradicted in the outer form of the *Sankhya*; apparently ignored and supplanted by Nihilism in Buddhism; disguised by personifications in the Orthodox Religions of India—still ever we shall see this Inner Teaching of THE ONE running through each and all, in spite of appearances. THE ONE is the background; the Foundation and Support; and the Roof, of all Hindu Philosophical and Religious Thought, and will be seen always by those whose vision is sufficiently clear, and *who know where to look*.

And so, now passing on to the consideration of these

various systems, we must ask you to be ever keen to perceive the Inner Teaching under its manifold disguises, names and veils. Be not deceived by the outward appearance, but look ever BEHIND THE VEIL—for there ever abideth The TRUTH.

SPECIAL MESSAGE II

By Yogi Ramacharaka

There is but one Truth. All so-called 'truths' are but some of the many aspects of the one Truth. Truth is "that which is." That which 'is' must exist in reality, verity, and certainty—must exist as a fixed established principle, law and state of being. Truth is present everywhere; is infinite power; is infinite intelligence; is the foundation and background of the universe. Truth is but one, though men call it by many names. Truth is God divested of the idea of personality. Truth is not material; neither is it mere energy, as the physical scientists conceive it; neither is it mind, as men understand the term. Truth is Spirit and nothing else. Spirit is Truth and nothing else, Truth and Spirit are identical. All else is Untruth.

Just what Spirit is, is impossible of expression in words, for words are designed to express relative things, and the Absolute cannot be expressed or defined by relative terms. As Spinoza has said, "To define God, is to deny Him." Enough to know that Spirit Is.' You will remember the words of Jesus, who said: "God is Spirit." There is no qualification in the sense of asserting that God is *a* Spirit, that is, one of a number of Spirits. The statement is plain, positive and unmistakable in its assertion. God is SPIRIT, itself. That is, that God and Spirit are identical. There cannot be two Spirits any more than there can be two Gods. And there cannot be two Truths, any more than there can be two Spirits, or two Gods. For God, and Spirit, and Truth are identical—merely words to represent and symbolize the one Reality. Other than Truth, there can be only Untruth.

Spirit—God—Truth ! These are the three terms expressing the one idea. The words Spirit of Truth are preferred by many metaphysicians to the term God, for the reason that the latter has become confused in the minds of many who have used it, and who imply the existence of the attributes, qualities and natures of personality to God. Truth is the conception of God in His highest aspect—His aspect of Being, divested of the attributes and qualities of personality, which have been added to Him by many people who dwell upon the plane of personality, and who fail to perceive Him in His transcendental Being.

Truth is that which Is, and Spirit is *that which* Truth *is*. Truth is Spirit; and Spirit is Truth. There is no Spirit but Truth; and no Truth but Spirit. These are axioms which must be learned and realized by you before you may enter into an understanding of the operations attendant upon the understanding of Truth.

Our meditation for the coming month is as follows :

"TRUTH IS ALL THERE IS—ALL ELSE IS UNTRUTH !"

In order to grasp the spirit of the words of the meditation, we must remember the above statements concerning the identity of Truth with Spirit; and of Spirit with God, divested of the attributes of personality.

Truth is all there is—all else is Untruth. And Untruth is that which is not—the essence of Nothingness, Illusion, Error, and *Maya*. Peace to Thee.

Chapter III

The Sankhya System

In the great system of Hindu philosophy known as The *Sankhya* System, we have one of the oldest forms of philosophical conceptions known in that land of old systems of thought. While it is customary to ascribe to *Kapila*, who lived about 700 B.C., the honour of having originated this great system old thought, still Sanskrit scholars have discovered the fundamental portions of *Kapila*'s teachings in the older writings of the race, and the probability is that the teaching itself is many centuries older than *Kapila*, and that he merely arranged the fragment of older systems into a clearly defined school of philosophy, discarding the outside accumulations that had gathered around the older teachings; and emphasizing certain fundamental principles that had been overlooked. At any rate, traces of the teachings now known as the *"Sankhya"* System may be found as far back as 2000 B.C., and the fundamental conceptions probably run back still further. The term *'Sankhya'* means 'correct enumeration' or 'perfect classification.'

The basic proposition of the *Sankhya* system is that there exists in the universe *two active principles*, the interaction of which produces the activities of the universe, including those of life—the play and interplay of the two manifesting in countless forms, combinations, and infinite variety. These two principles are known as (1) *Prakriti*, or the primordial substance or energy, from which all material forms and energies evolve; and (2) *Purusha*, or the Spirit Principle, which "ensouls" or seeks embodiment in *Prakriti*, and thus gives rise to all the various forms of differentiation, from atoms to man; and which is not conceived of by the *Sankhyas* as forming one Universal Soul (as do the Yoga scholars), but which is held to be composed of countless 'spirit atoms,' monads, or individual spirits—which Units as a whole compose a Unity of Units, which may be considered in the light of a Principle.

There are many points of difference between the various conceptions of the real nature of *Purusha* and *Prakriti*, particularly on the part of Western writers on the subject, some of which are totally at variance with the beliefs and conceptions of the advanced Hindu adherents of this philosophy. We shall consider each of the three leading conceptions in turn, pointing out the errors where they exist.

I. The first conception of the nature of *Purusha* and *Prakriti,* and the one which is favoured by the majority of Western writers on the subject, is that which holds that *Kapila's* theories are artheistic and practically materialistic, inasmuch as he ignores the existence of a Supreme Power, *Brahman*, or THAT and postulates a dual Eternal Thing, one half of the duad being Matter. This view interprets the teachings of *Kapila* to mean that there are Two Eternal Things, the first of which is Matter, and the second of which is Spirit, divided into countless atoms—both *Purusha* and *Prakriti* being held as eternal, infinite and immortal, and both of which are self-existent and sustaining, requiring no Supreme Power as a basis or background. This conception is decidedly in error, and the spirit of the philosophy has been lost to those who so hold. The error regarding the discarding of the belief in THAT or *Brahman*, however, is easily explained. In the first place there is nothing in the teachings of *Kapila* or of his early followers, in which the existence of THAT is denied ors condemned—there is simply a silence regarding it, just as is the case in Buddhism, and the cause is the same in both cases. Both *Kapila* and *Buddha* accepted the centuries old doctrine of THAT, which no Hindu philosophy had questioned, and both then proceeded to account for the phenomenal universe. Had *Kapila* attempted to discard the universal conception of THAT he would have certainly attacked the doctrine, and have set up arguments against it, accompanied by illustration parables, and analogous proofs, with which the Hindu philosophers always have been so well supplied and which they have used so freely. But *Kapila* does not mention the matter, but calmly proceeds to elaborate his system explaining the phenomena of the universe. To those who have penetrated beneath the surface of the *Sankhya* System, and who are familiar with the Hindu methods of thought and teachings, it readily will be seen that there is nothing atheistic or materialistic in the conceptions of the *Sankhya* System. Among the Hindus, the charge of atheism made against the *Sankhyas* comes principally from the followers of *Patanjali*, the Yogi, who hold to the existence of a Supreme *Purusha* or Universal Over-Soul, and who, consequently, resent the *Sankhyas'* failure to recognize their conceptions. And the charge of materialism comes from the *Vedantists*, who deny the existence of matter, considering it as *Maya* or Delusion. In fact, *Prakriti* is rather the Source of Matter, rather than Matter itself, as we shall see a little later on.

II. The second conception of the nature of *Purusha* and *Prakriti* is in the nature of a half-truth which is also a half-error. It holds that *Purusha* and *Prakriti* must be regarded as 'aspects' of THAT or *Brahman*, and which aspects are eternal and constant, and which cannot be withdrawn into THAT or *Brahman* as emanations may be, but which are fixed aspects or "natures" of THAT, which always have been, and always will be, in periods of activity and periods of non-activity between the cycles of activity. The error of this conception consists in ascribing eternal and real existence to these two principles, thus ascribing a duality to THAT instead of a Oneness. This conception, while much nearer the truth than the first mentioned, still contains the fatal error just noted which condemns it in the minds of the most logical of the

Hindu thinkers, who see the Truth of *Kapila's* idea in the third conception, which we shall now consider.

III. The third conception of the nature of *Purusha* and *Prakriti,* and which the best thinkers accept as correctly expressing *Kapila's* meaning, is that both *Purusha* and *Prakriti* are "emanations" from or "appearances" of THAT or *Brahman*—both having equal substance and degree of reality, but both being finite and being destined to pass away in time; that is, to be withdrawn into their common source—THAT—at the end of great period of activity, when the great period of 'cosmic rest' begins, which in turn is followed by a subsequent period of activity, and so on. In this conception the fundamental principle of the Hindu philosophy—the existence of THAT as the Only Reality—is recognized as a necessary basis for the teaching, and as a necessary background for the doctrines concerning the phenomenal universe. And *Purusha* and *Prakriti* are seen to be but the primal forms the two great principles of phenomenal activity, Spirit and Body, which are apparent in all phenomenal things, from atom to man, and beyond man. And both of these principles are emanated from, or cast into apparent being by THAT or *Brahman,* in the process of world-making. Instead of their being 'aspects' of THAT, they are merely manifestations, appearances, or emanations, or even 'thought-forms' in the Mind of the One, as we have described in our previous series of lessons.

So you see that *Kapila's* teachings fit into the general framework of the Great Hindu Thought instead of being an exception to, and in opposition to it. In this connection, we would call your attention to a frequent use of the word 'eternity' in some of the Hindu writings. In many cases the term is used as in the Western sense, that is to say in the sense of "duration without beginning or end; a condition of infinity and time," but inasmuch as the true Hindu philosopher ascribes and attribute this quality only to THAT, and denies it all else, it may be seen that outside of THAT the word is meaningless to him, and cannot be employed. But finding the need of the word in a secondary sense, he applies it to things having a continuous existence during the entire period of cosmic activity, which extends over great spaces of time, but which ceases to be when all is finally withdrawn into THAT, and the cycle of activity ceases and is succeeded by the cycle of non-activity—when all manifestations, appearances, emanations and phenomena or ideas are withdrawn into THAT, which then dwells alone until another period of cosmic activity begins. As. H.P. Blavatsky says in a, foot-note to her "The Voice of the Silence": "Eternity with the Orientals has quite another signification than it has with us. It stands generally for the one hundred years or age of *Brahma*, the duration of a *Maha-Kalpa*, or a period of 311,040,000,000,000 years." So you see that the reference to *Purusha* and *Prakriti* as 'eternal' does not conflict with this conception of their nature, and their impermanence as compared with THAT. And this third conception of the Inner Teachings of The *Sankhya* System agrees with our understanding of them, and we can see no reason for withholding our approval of the schools of the *Sankhya* thought which so holds. Any other conception would be in direct opposition to the general trend of the Hindu thought, and contrary to reasonable belief on the part of those who are familiar with the thought of *Kapila's* time, and the methods of Hindu philosophy in general. Let us consider the details of the teaching concerning *Purusha* and *Prakriti* in view of this conception.

Purusha, according to *Kapila*, is to be thought of not as one great World Spirit, or World Principle of Spirit, in the sense of an undivided Unity, but rather in the sense of a countless number of individual spirits, or spirit atoms, bound together with filaments of attraction and harmony arising from them common nature, but nevertheless free, independent, and individual. *Kapila* pointed out that if *Purusha* were but One, separated into countless tiny parts, they would be alike in nature, equal in every respect, and manifesting no variety, whereas all nature shows a constant and infinite variety. There is no Universal *Purusha*—no *Ishwara*—no Personal God—in *Kapila's* philosophy. As one writer says: "He found no need for one—his conception of *Purushas* was deemed sufficient to explain the ensouling of matter, under Natural Law !"

Kapila holds that *Purusha* is Pure Spirit, or Substantial Transcendental Intelligence (independent of *Manas*, or Mind-Stuff), but that it is above attributes, or qualities (possessing neither), and in its natural condition is unaffected by joy, pain, or other emotions or sensations (which the soul experiences by reason of its embodiment in *Prakriti*, which has evolved mind, sense-organs, etc.); and is in nature and pure condition, until, entangled in *Prakriti*, it dwells in a state of pure bliss, peace, and rest, engaged in absolute meditation which is "the knowing of nothing." When the soul becomes involved in material existence, through its connection with *Prakriti*, it illuminates the mental and physical organism and faculties with its 'spiritual light,' and the soul is enabled to enter into its existence of experience, or personal life, in the physical world. It acts upon the *Prakriti* as a Magnet upon bits of steel, magnetizing them and giving to them power which they did not before possess, and which they could not possess without being in its 'field of influence' or induction. But it is held to possess no actual volition of its own, and is therefore unable to express itself except through, and by means of, the various forms and phases of *Prakriti*. The involvement of the *Purusha* in the body of the *Prakriti* produces what is called a 'soul,' that is a *Purusha* surrounded with its mental environment and instruments and organization. And the soul becomes subject to the laws of '*Samsara*' (which is the Sanskrit term implying "The Cycle of Existence"), with its chain of Cause and Effect; *Karmic* Results, and Rebirths. And *Samsara* brings pain to the soul, and the effort of the imprisoned *Purusha* is to free itself and return once more to its state of bliss. And, therefore, the effort of the teaching is to bring to the imprisoned and suffering *Purusha* the means of Liberation, so that it may pass beyond *Samsara*, Rebirth, *Karma*, and Experience, and regain its normal and natural state of unconscious freedom and bliss, beyond change and pain, of which 'dreamless sleep' is the physical symbol.

The *Sankhya* System holds that the *Purushas* were originally in a state of pure spiritual existence, freed from the attraction of *Prakriti*, and from the desire of material life. But that being attracted and seduced by the glamour of *Prakriti* they plunged into the latter, and once there became entangled in the manifold webs of material life. Bewildered by their strange surroundings, the *Purushas* lose their original state of freedom and clearness of perception, and become deluded by the *Maya* or Illusion of Matter, and are led a merry dance in working their way out of the material plane in which they have become immersed. Like a fly that has taken a dip into the honey-pot filled with 'Poppy-made Honey,' the *Purushas* flounder around and are unable to use their legs and wings, and the more they struggle the worse is their condition—the more the narcotic of the poppy-honey intoxicates them. Finally awakening to a realization of their former state of existence, and the real situation, the *Purushas* begin a process of extrication, and through long series of reincarnations work themselves from lower to higher states, slowly but surely, toward their former condition of Bliss. This idea has been expressed by an English poet, Edward Carpenter, who says: "Slowly and resolutely—as a fly cleans its legs of the honey in which it has been caught—so remove thou, if it only be for a time, every particle which sullies the brightness of thy mind."

The *Sankhyas* hold that from the combined action and reaction of the *Purushas* in *Prakriti*, all forms and varieties of life are created, and all varieties matter are produced, it being held that every atom matter is *Prakriti* ensouled by an individual *Purusha* manifesting activity and life. In this way the entire phenomena of the universe is accounted for, from the movement and activities of atoms, to the revolution of suns, and the manifestation of life, vegetable, animal, human, and super-human. The *Purushas* combine in activities; forming all sorts of varieties of combinations (in the wrappings of bodies of *Prakriti*, of course) which account for the variety of material elements, and life. The entire phenomena of the material world, including matter and energy, as known to modern Western science fits into the *Sankhya* idea, as the corpuscles of which matter is now known to be composed, as well as the aggregations of atoms, molecules, etc., and the various forms of force, may be considered as occasioned by the imprisoned *Purushas*, in their bodies of *Prakriti*, ever changing and moving, and evolving—provided the fundamental theories of the *Sankhyas* be accepted. *Kapila* taught inorganic and organic evolution over 2,500 years before the days of Darwin and Herbert Spencer, and several centuries before Heraclitus, the great Grecian evolutionist.

Kapila's conception of *Prakriti* was not that of gross Matter, as so many of the Western writers on the subject are wont to assume. Instead, his conception may be expressed by the word 'Nature,' as used by Bruno and other thinkers—that is, as a subtle, ethereal substance, partaking rather of the nature of an Energy, rather than of Matter—a substance far more subtle and ethereal than the Universal Ether of modern Western science.

Prakriti is the Cosmic Primordial Energy, or Substance from which the universe is evolved, and into which it again resolves itself, in endless cycles of change. *Prakriti* he held, was not composed of ultimate atoms, as some other Hindu philosophers had claimed, but was atomless and continuous, the atoms being but centres of influence and activity caused by the embodiment of the *Purushas*, which gave activity to them, and which afterward formed the atoms into combinations. Mind was composed of *Chitta,* or Mind-Stuff, which arose from the action of *Purusha* upon *Prakriti. Prakriti* is described as active according to energies of its own, along almost automatic lines, but it is insentient and mindless in itself, the sentient qualities being possible only when instigated and inspired by the *Purushas.*

Some of the illustrations used bring out the above mentioned point clearly, as for instead the ancient one in which *Purusha* is pictured as a "lame man possessed of eyesight and the other senses," and *Prakriti* as "a man in whom the senses of seeing and hearing, etc., had been omitted, but who possessed a good pair of legs." According to the fable, a combination is made and the lame man (*Purusha*) mounts up on the shoulders of the blind man (*Prakriti*) and together they move along briskly and intelligently, whereas separately they could make no progress. In the *Sankhya* conception of *Manas* or Mind as being of a semi-material nature, the conceptions of modern science of the materialistc school are approached. But still, the *Sankhya* are far from being materialists, for they postively deny to *Prakriti,* the essence Matter, any intelligence, mind, or sentiency, ascribing the latter to the action of *Purusha,* or Spirit, which is above mind just as *Prakriti* is below it.

One may read Ernest Haeckel, the German scientist, with new understanding, if he will interpret it by the light of the *Sankhya* teaching—Haeckel's 'soul of the atom' being understandable in the light of *Kapila's* theory, as in no other way, *Kapila* undoubtedly inspired the German philosopher, Schopenhauer, and his successors, who took from the Hindu philosopher at least a portion of his fundamental conception. *Kapila's* thought renders Materialism thinkable, as it adds a new element which explains the activities and evidences of sentiency in low material forms, and the evolution therefrom—whereas the gross Materialism of the last century is unthinkable in its denial of mind, or soul qualities. And to think that all this was thought out by *Kapila* some 2,500 years ago, and that his teaching was based on still older teaching! And yet, the West speaks of the poor, ignorant, heathen Hindu, crying for the knowledge of the West! And not only this philosophy, but many others of India, anticipated by over two thousand years many of the latest conceptions of modern Western science and philosophy! Verily, History repeats itself.

Kapila teaches that the *Prakriti*, since its junction with, or impregnation by, *Purusha*, has been in a state of constant change and evolution, from succeeding form, and combination, the original condition of *Prakriti* having been altered so that it is difficult for the mind to conceive of its original and primitive or virgin condition. From a state far more ethereal than any form of ether known to science, it has assumed atomic combinations, and molecular arrangements, until in response to the never-ceasing demands of the *Purushas* to manifest in action and life, the *Prakriti* has been compelled to assume many gross and unethereal forms. In response to the developing senses of the mind occasioned by the evolving manifestations of the embodied *Purushas*, *Prakriti* has assumed forms and appearances recognizable by the senses of sight, hearing, smell, taste, etc., so as to be sensed by the sense-organs. And the *Purushas* have lost their original and primitive state of pure being, losing their original freedom as they became enmeshed in the web of *Prakriti*—becoming slaves to the senses, as they yielded to the caressing seduction of material manifestation. *Prakriti* in its original state was subtle, ethereal, diffused, tenuous, and without the qualities that are registered by sense—it could not respond to sense, nor could it arouse sense. *Purusha* in its original state was free from desire or attachment, and devoid of qualities, attributes, action, or attachment, as we understand these words in their material sense.

The *Sankhyas* hold that because of these changes it is almost impossible for the individual mind to now grasp the nature of the original *Prakriti*, or to even imagine the state of excellence of *Purusha* before it yielded to the seduction of material existence. But they hold, by means of true knowledge and scientific reasoning, in addition to right living and detachment from passion, the mind can be brought to a state of understanding whereby it may grasp the nature of the *Purusha* original state, and the true nature of *Prakriti*. And this knowledge is one of the ways of Liberation and Freedom sought by the *Sankhyas*—the road whereby the 'short cut' may be taken to Freedom, instead of the road of repeated rebirth and material life.

In all of the Hindu Philosophies, it will be noticed, there is this constant repetition of the fact that material life is but an illusion and a snare—the result of ignorance and mistaken desire—and that the part of true wisdom is to escape from it as soon as possible. Death does not release the soul from material embodiment—for rebirth is always there to claim it. As the *Sankhyas* say, the *Purusha* never escapes the embrace of *Prakriti* by the road of Death, for Death only weaves a more subtle covering for it, in which it dwells until rebirth draws it once more into the vortex. There is no escape by the road of Death—the road of Life is the only possible avenue of escape. The method of escape is by Right Living in combination with the Development of Wisdom, whereby the Spirit is enabled to perceive its true nature and original conditions, and also the true nature and meaning of the enfolding *Prakriti*.

Akin to the teachings of the Buddhists is that of the *Sankhyas*—both hold that Material Existence is foreign to the Spirit, and consequently the latter is never permanently satisfied or happy in material life, but, instead, is always wanting something other than that which it possesses, and is always seeking to be at some other place than its place of abode at that moment. It is always crying "More, more—change, more change—something else—somewhere else—someone else." And the more it gains the more it wants—possession destroys the desire, and gives birth to desire for other things. He who seeks happiness in material things pursues the will-o'-the-wisp, which he never overtakes. The only true happiness comes from renunciation of material things, and the resolute setting of the face toward the Far-off Land of the Soul's Desire—the Land of the Lost Home of the Spirit. Such is the teaching of *Kapila*, the great *Sankhya*. The fly is told to disentangle itself from the honey which entangles its feet and holds it a prisoner—the poppy-honey which seems sweet, but yet which holds the tang of bitterness and intoxication.

The *Sankhya* System is far more of the nature of a scientific-philosophy, however, rather a religious-philosophy. It concerns itself principally with an analysis and explanation of the process whereby *Prakriti*, played upon by *Purusha*, evolves itself into the phenomenal or material universe, including into the manifestation of life. *Kapila* recognized the existence of material atoms as postulated by *Kanada* in his *Vaisheshika* System (see subsequent lesson), but he opposed the latter's theory that these material atoms are "things-in-themselves" or eternal, indivisible, and indestructible, and he taught, instead, that the atoms are simply centres of force in the great principle of *Prakriti*, the centres being established by the presence of the *Purushas*. *Kapila's* teaching regarding the combinations of the atom closely resembled the teachings of modern Western Science, with its theories of Ions, Corpuscles, or Electrons, which combining into atoms form certain material elements, which in turn combining into molecules form other grades and styles of matter. *Kapila* also taught another doctrine which is now favoured by the modern science of the West—that doctrine of the love and hate of atoms which explained the mutual attraction and repulsion of the particles which are evident through the physical universe, and which action and reaction account for the greater part of the physical phenomena.

Kapila taught the doctrine of Evolution, beginning with

the atoms or ultimate ensouled particles, which, combining by reason of love or hate, formed more complex forms, from which in turn evolved more complex combinations, and so on, and on, until at last organic matter was produced, and then the lifeforms began to appear, rising higher and higher in the scale until man, and super-man is reached, and still the urge of evolution continues on toward higher and still higher forms. But *Kapila* rejected any idea of purely material evolution—he held that unless the *Purushas* were ensouled in the *Prakriti* and thus gave to it intelligent activity, there would be no material evolution. He made this distinction because of the Spirit being the active cause of Evolution, rather than because of any inherent quality in *Prakriti* itself. *Kapila's* philosophy exerted a marked effect upon the thought of the Grecian philosophers, and the doctrine may be traced directly back to the *Sankhya* teachings. In turn the Greek philosophers have largely influenced the modern scientific thought, as may be seen by referring to any recent work on physical science, in which credit is freely given to the Greeks. The idea of evolution, material and spiritual, which shows throughout the Greek and Neo-Platonic philosophies, and which is incorporated in all of the occult teachings, was arranged into a systematic form by *Kapila*, even though he obtained its germ ideas from his Hindu predecessors. As Prof. Hopkins has said: "Plato is full of *Sankhyan* thought, worked out by him, but taken from Pythagoras. Before the sixth century B.C. all the religious-philosophical ideas of Pythagoras were current in India. If there were but one or two of these cases, it might be set aside as accidental coincidences, but such coincidences are too numerous to be the result of chance . . . Neo-Platonism and Christian Gnosticism owe much to India . . . Soul and light are one in the *Sankhya* system before they become so in Greece, and when they appear united in Greece it is by means of the thought which it borrowed from India. The famous Three Qualities (*Gunas*) of the *Sankhya* reappear as the Gnostic 'three classes.'" John Davies, in his well known work "Hindu Philosophy," speaks of *Kapila's Sankhya* System as "the first recorded system of philosophy in the world—the earliest attempt on record to give an answer, from reason, alone, to the mysterious questions which arise in every thoughtful mind about the origin of the world, the nature and relations of man, and his future destiny." The same writer gives to *Kapila* the credit for having influenced the German thought as expressed by Schopenhauer and Hartmann, their work being spoken of as "a reproduction of the philosophic system of *Kapila* in its materialistic part, presented in a more elaborate form, but on the same fundamental lines. In this respect the human intellect has gone over the same ground that it occupied more than two thousand years ago; but on a more important question it has taken a step in retreat. *Kapila* recognized fully the existence of a soul in man, forming indeed his proper nature—the absolute of Fichte—distinct from matter and immortal; but our latest philosophy, both here and in Germany, can see in man only a highly developed organization."

In India, likewise, the influence of *Kapila* and the *Sankhya* has been great. Not only has it tinctured the other philosophies, and made for itself a place in the metaphysical thought of the majority of the Hindu religious systems, but it undoubtedly was the basis of much of the early Buddhistic thought, the Buddhists adopting without change a considerable portion of *Kapila's* doctrine, and allowing his influence to be manifested in a changed form in other points of their doctrine. In our consideration of the other forms of the Hindu philosophies, we shall see many instances of the influence of the thought of *Kapila*.

One of the secondary, but important, theories advanced by *Kapila*, and which has been adopted by the majority of the other schools, and the religious sects of India, is that of the Three *Gunas*, or Qualities inherent in *Prakriti*. These Three *Gunas* or Qualities are held to be inherent in *Prakriti*, or

Nature, and consequently manifest in everything arising from Nature's processes, or manifestations of *Prakriti*. They are believed to be present in equal proportions in *Prakriti*—that is, that they are equally balanced in Nature. But in Nature's manifestations, or forms of *Prakriti*, some one of the *Gunas* may predominate in influence, or some two may overpower the third, and so on. To the relative predominance of one or two of the *Gunas*, and the resulting conflict among the three, the variety of manifestation, as well as the constant change in Nature, is largely due. In other words, the *Purusha* and the *Prakriti*, acted upon by the Three *Gunas*—the three often being spoken of as the "Five Great Elements"—are the basis and cause of the phenomenal universe in all of its many and constantly changing forms and appearances.

The Three *Gunas* are known, respectively, as SATVAS GUNA, also known as Truth or Harmony; RAJAS GUNA, also known as Passion or Activity; and TAMAS GUNA, also known as Indifference or Inertia (the definitions stated representing the several *Gunas* in both their mental and material aspects). As we have said, from the action and reaction, combinations and oppositions, of the Three *Gunas* the physical and mental phenomena of the universe are produced. *Satvas Guna* is considered as imponderable, luminous and agreeable; *Rajas Guna* as intermediate between ponderability and its opposite, and as both pleasant and unpleasant, or either—as a quality of equilibrium, influencing and being influenced by both the other *Gunas*; *Tamas Guna* as ponderous, dark, and disagreeable. *Satvas Guna* and *Tamas Guna* are passive, in a sense; that is, in the lack of activity, motion or velocity. The intermediate active quality—*Rajas Guna*—is the active, moving, exciting *Guna*, which in turn balanced by the harmonizing influence of *Satvas Guna* and the dead weight and inertia of *Tamas Guna*.

Tamas Guna always obstructs, retards, hinder and holds back, or endeavours to do so—in its mental aspect it manifests Ignorance, Superstition, Sloth, etc. *Rajas Guna* is the source of physical and mental activity—it sets the mind, the air, the elements, and the forces of Nature into action. *Satvas Guna* establishes harmony, wisdom, truth, right action, balanced thought, and destroys inhertia and ignorance, and in every respect is the very opposite of *Tamas Guna*. *Satvas Guna* is predominant in the Desire Mind; and *Tamas Guna* in the bodily mental processes. As the *"Bhagavad Gita"* says : "The fruit of *Satvas* is called good; the fruit of *Rajas* is called pain and dissatisfaction, and unrest ; the fruit of *Tamas* is called Ignorance, and Stupidity, and Inertia. From *Satvas* is produced Wisdom; from Rajas, Unrest and Covetousness; from *Tamas*, Ignorance, Delusion, and Foolishness, together with Sloth. The *Sankhya* teachings show that the *Gunas* are manifest on every plane, and in every instance—not only in the material, but in the mental as well, having their manifestations in every form of phenomena. The likes and dislikes of the atoms—the pain and pleasure of matter—the bliss and misery of human life—are all seen manifestations of the *Gunas*.

The *Sankhya* teaches that there are Twenty-four Principles, or *Tattvas*, proceeding from *Prakriti* under its energizing by the *Purusha*, and in accordance with the operations of the Three *Gunas*, just described. These *Tattvas*, or Principles, are as follows :

The *Buddhitattva*, or Principle of Determinative Consciousness, which proceeds from the undifferentiated *Prakriti*; and from which Principle in turn proceeds :

The Principle of *Ahamkara*, or Self-consciousness, which involves the discrimination between "I" and "Not-I"; and from this Principle in turn proceeds the following Three classes of *Tattvas*, *viz.* :

I. The Five *Tanamatras*, or Subtle Elements of Nature, namely: The Aethereal; The Aerial; The Igneous; The Aqueous; The Terrene ; and from which subtle elements proceed the Five Gross Elements of Nature, namely: *Akasha*, or The Ether; Air; Fire; Water; Earth.

II. The psychic organism manifesting in the Five Senses, respectively: Seeing; Hearing; Smelling; Tasting; Feeling. Also the psychic organs controlling the Five Instruments of Action which are named as The Speech Organs; The Hands; The Feet; The Excretory Organs; The Genitals, respectively.

III. The *Manas,* or Mental Substance or Energy manifesting as the Deliberative Function of the Mind, and including Imagination.

The above classification of the Physical, Physiological, and Psychological Principles, is regarded by modern philosophers, scientists, and occultists as rather too arbitrary for general acceptance, and the leading *Sankhya* scholars admit that it was not original with *Kapila,* nor vital or necessary to his general system, but was the classification in general vogue in his time, and for centuries before, and was naturally adopted by him to fill in the details of his general philosophical conception of *Purusha* and *Prakriti,* upon which dual-conception his system is based.

It is to be noticed in the *Sankhya* conception of Creation, that Matter, both subtle elements and gross elements, is evolved from the *Prakriti* after the development of Determinative Consciousness, and even the Self-conscious Principle, so that Matter (in the strict sense of the term) is held to be preceded by Consciousness in the *Prakriti,* and to be produced by Consciousness or Intelligence, in a sense. But this 'Consciousness' is a very different thing from the '*Manas*' or Mind of the individual, which he uses in his deliberative processes, imagination, etc., and which is but a 'thinking machine' evolved by the Consciousness in order to express material life and activities, just as were the organs of action, and the organs of the senses evolved (see above classification). To *Kapila, Manas* or Mind-Principle was an insentient, automatic energy, semi-material, and operative only by reason of the activity of the Consciousness, which in turn is illuminated by the *Purusha.* The *Sankhya* conception of *Manas,* or Mind, is very nearly akin to the Western conception of Brain, in the phases of its functioning processes.

The *Sankhyas* teach that the 'Soul' is the *Purusha*, invested with its higher principles or *Tattvas*, and must not be confounded with the *Purusha* which is 'Spirit.' The Soul is given a covering of a subtle body, or *linga sharira*, which encloses the *buddhi*; *ahamkara*; the five *tanamatras*; and the ten psychic instruments of sensation and action, and also *Manas*—the *Purusha*, of course, being at the centre of the Soul, as Spirit or *Atman*. This subtle body (*linga sharira*) is invested with a grosser body, composed of the five gross elements, and which gross body perishes at death, while its subtle counterpart survives in *Samsara*, going through incarnations and changes of physical bodies, etc.

The action of *Prakriti* is two-fold. First it has its own action inspired by the laws of its own nature which act in a more or less automatic and unconscious fashion, according to an orderly trend resembling instinctive actition. But Intelligence and consciousness it has not, nor can it have until it is illuminated by the involved *Purushas*.

The *Sankhyas* hold that the process of the creation of the material universe, with its forms of life, and energy, is occasioned by the beginning of each period of Creative Activity, or Day of Brahm, by a subtle stirring in the bosom of *Prakriti* owing to some law of its nature and influenced by the accumulated *Karma* of past creations, and whereby the *Purushas* are attracted even as the bees and flies are attracted by 'sugar-water,' or syrup. Flowing into the fluidic undifferentiated *Prakriti*, enticed by the subtle attraction of her illusory charms, the *Purushas* come—and once entrapped the results of the combination ensue. First there appears in the substance of *Prakriti* an Awareness or state of Universal Consciousness, which is called "*Mahat*, or the Great," which gradually shades into a Cosmic Determinative Consciousness on the part of the Whole Principle of the *Prakriti*. This is followed by the development of the consciousness of Separateness, or Self-consciousness, or Egoism, called by the Hindus, "*Ahamkara* and which is not, as some have supposed, a conscious realization of each *Purusha* of its own real nature and individuality, but rather a false consciousness of itself as a Personality, distinct from all else, and partaking of *Avidya*, or Ignorance concerning its own true nature as Pure Spirit, or *Purusha*. From thence on there is an Involution of Enfolding into *Prakriti* of the *Purushas*, sinking deeper and deeper into the illusory existence, and even causing the *Prakriti* to take on subtle and then gross forms of matter in order to satisfy the desires of the deluded *Purushas* for material activity and life. When the Involution has reached its limit, there then sets in the stage of Evolution, as we have stated, in which the *Prakriti* is urged into higher and higher forms, as the ascending *Purushas* rise in the scale in their upward journey toward the Blissful State.

The influence or action of the *Purushas* causes an action on the part of the *Prakriti*, and which the *Sankhyas* describe as akin to the action of particles of steel when brought into close juxtaposition with a magnet, whereupon they manifest a new action and arrangement foreign to their original custom. And so *Purusha* is the magnet which affects the *Prakriti* into which it has been attracted—for remember, that not only does the magnet attract the bits of steel, but the latter likewise attracts the magnet itself, and changes are produced upon both. From the close contiguity of the *Purushas*, the *Prakriti* is given new activities, and changes are set into operation, whereby the creative process results. In this description we have ignored the numerous technicalities and terms in which the *Sankhya* teachings abound, the strange Sanskrit terms, and the unfamiliar conceptions of the detail of the universal involutionary and evolutionary processes tending to confuse the Western mind and to divert the attention from the fundamental ideas.

And, now, this is the *Sankhya* System of *Kapila* stated briefly and as simply as possible. The student of 'The Yogi philosophy' as set forth in our previous series of lessons, and in which we have given the Inner Teachings of the

Eclectic School of the Hindu Thought, may see how the conceptions of *Kapila* fit into our own teachings, and yet how they differ. *Kapila* directs the attention of the student to the nature of the soul's immersion and entanglement in the principle of Matter in a most vivid manner, and accompanied with a degree of poetic symbology that enables the mind to take hold of the idea readily. And read in the light of the Inner Teachings, the teachings of *Kapila* are of great interest and advantage to the student in his work of assimilating the Truths of the Hindu Philosophy, and outside of their undoubted historical and philosophical interest. But the student will also see wherein the *Sankhya* System fails to express the highest conceptions, and wherein it leads one on a false by-path.

Kapila ignores, although he does not deny, the existence of THAT—The Absolute—*Brahman* and *Para-Brahm*—and devotes his attention to an examination of the 'How' of creative activity and phenomenal life and being—a most important work, surely, and yet not the most important. Moreover, he teaches that the individual *Purushas* existed before the creation of the universe, and before they became immersed in *Prakriti*—that is, existed in separate existence. Whereas our teachings are that when the Great Outpouring took place, the Absolute projected its Spirit into the manifestation called matter, and when the Evolutionary wave began, the tendency toward individual expression brought about the origin of the individual souls, which before that time had their existence only in a state of Oneness. And yet *Kapila* has given us a wonderfully clear idea of the development of the Personal Consciousness or Sense of Egoism, or *Ahamkara*, from the Universal Life Consciousness or Cosmic *Buddhi*, which in turn evolved from the Cosmic Spirit Awareness, or Universal Spiritual Consciousness, or *Mahat*, in which the *Purushas* became 'aware' of themselves in a state of Unity, or Oneness of the Many, which was their first step after they had entered into *Prakriti*, and left the state of Pure Spirit or Virgin *Purusha*. A comparison between the two teachings will show the resemblance, and the relation they bear to each other. In our own teachings we have had little or nothing to say regarding the 'Three *Gunas*' which we have described in explaining the *Sankhya* System, but we have said that the conception was familiar to all Hindu thought, and we have treated of them in a general way as forming a part of 'The Laws of Nature'; in fact the Inner Teachings hold that the Three *Gunas* are in the nature of a poetical conception of, or an idealization of, the Natural Forces, instead of being distinct principles in themselves as *Kapila* and others have taught. Strictly speaking, even *Kapila* admits that the *Gunas* are merely 'Qualities' or Forces in Nature, or *Prakriti*, and are not 'Things-in-Themselves,' as so many of the *Sankhyas* hold them to be.

SPECIAL MESSAGE III

By Yogi Ramacharaka

In our message of last month, we spoke to you of Truth. We now invite you to a consideration of the symbols whereby we seek to enter into an understanding of the nature of Truth.

I. We may consider Truth by the symbol of Substance. Substance, as you know, is the underlying or 'standing-under' Reality behind the phenomenal and relative appearances, shapes, forms and names of the physical universe. Metaphysically, the term is used to express the idea of the Real Thing-in-Itself which serves as the real foundation, basis and essence of the universe apparent to our senses and perceptions. Truth is the Universal Substance which supports the universe, and upon which all else depends. And all that is apparent to our sense perception must needs be manifestations, expressions or emanations of and from that Universal Substance, or else Untruth. There is nothing else for it to be. There is no other Substance to support anything, or from, which anything could have emanated. All else is Untruth.

II. We may consider Truth by means of the symbol of Power. And, mark you this, not only does Truth manifest Power, but it is the Essence of Power itself. Metaphysically, viewing Truth from this aspect, it may be asserted that Truth is Power. And that, other than Truth, there is no Power, and can be no Power. Truth is Omnipotence or All-Power, containing within itself all the Power there is, ever has been, or ever can be. Not only is it Omnipotent, or possessing Power, but it is Omnipotence or All-Power itself. There is no other source of Power than Truth. And all manifestations or expressions of Power must be attributed, directly or indirectly, to Truth. For there is nowhere else whence it could have come. All else is Untruth.

III. We may consider Truth by means of the symbol of Being. Being is the term used for expressing the idea of Real Existence. And Truth is not only Really Existent, but is Real Existence itself. There can be no Being or Existence outside or apart from, or other than Truth. For there is nothing else to Be or Exist. And all Being or

Existence must proceed from Truth, that is, must be manifested, expressed or emanated from it. Truth is existent, or In Being, Everywhere. It is not only Omnipresent, or present-everywhere, but is also Omnipresence, or All-Presence itself. Presence, Being and Existence belong to Truth, and are merely symbols of identity with aspects of Truth. Outside of, and apart from Truth, the terms are meaningless—Untruth.

In next month's message, we shall continue this consideration of the symbols whereby we seek to enter into an understanding of the nature of Truth.

Our meditation for the coming month is :

"TRUTH IS ALL-SUBSTANCE; ALL-POWER; ALL-BEING; AND OUTSIDE OF TRUTH THERE CAN BE AND IS NO SUBSTANCE; NO POWER; NO BEING.

Chapter IV

The Vedanta System

The leading school of Hindu Philosophy in India, at the present time, is that which is known as the *Vedanta* System, and which also bears the name of the *Uttara Mimansa,* which latter term means "the subsequent investigation," or "the investigation of the latter part," and is used in contradistinction to the term applied to another Hindu philosophical system—*i.e.,* the *Purva Mimansa,* or 'Prior Investigation.' Some hold that the terms 'prior' and 'subsequent' relate to the date of the founding of the respective schools, while others hold that the 'prior' refers to the investigation of the first part of the *Vedas,* or ritualistic and ceremonial part, while the 'subsequent' investigation is the investigation that refers to the investigation of the latter part of the *Vedas,* known as the *Upanishads.* The latter theory seems to be borne out by the fact that the popular name for the school—the 'Vedanta'—means 'the last of the *Vedas.*'

The best authorities give to one *Badarayana* the credit of having founded the *Vedanta* System, although some would dispute this claim and bestow the honour upon *Vyasa,* a legendary Hindu sage and teacher. The date of the founding of the school is not known, but it is believed to have been previous to Buddhism, and about the time of the founding of the *Sankhya* System, that is, about 700 B.C. In its teachings, the older part of the *Vedas,* which relates to the orthodox ceremonies, ritual, worship, etc., was recognized and accepted, but not dwelt upon, the attention of the *Vedanta* being principally devoted to the subject-matter of the latter part of the *Vedas,* known as the *Upanishads,* which concerns itself with the questions of "the inquiry into *Brahman*," or the Absolute, and the manifestations of the latter in the phenomenal universe.

The *Vedanta* evidently sprang into being, or rather was evolved gradually, in response to the demands of the philosophical minds of India, who desired a grouping together, or scientific arrangement of that part of the general philosophical system of the race which dealt with the One and its relation to the many, rather than with the ecclesiastical ceremonies, ritual, and religious dogmas upon which the early part of the *Vedas* laid so much stress. And from the first the new system attracted many of the brightest minds of India, and has continued to grow and prosper for about two thousand years, attracting the thoughtful minds of the race to it, and away from the more orthodox systems favoured by the priesthood. For while the *Vedanta* does not oppose the ceremonies and forms of the temples, regarding them as necessary for minds of a certain degree of development, still the system itself is far more of a philosophy of Pure Reason than a religious System of thought based upon revelation or faith. And much of its success has come by reason of its broadness and catholicity of spirit and doctrine.

The *Vedanta* has offered a friendly refuge to all shades of thought, doctrine and opinion, giving to each that which his particular development called for. Its universality is wonderful when compared with other systems. Holding as it does that there is but One Reality, and that all the rest is illusory, it can see degrees of truth in all of the doctrines, and yet recognizes all short of the One as non-truth. As Max Müller has said: "The *Vedanta* Philosophy leaves to every man a wide sphere of real usefulness, and places him under a law as strict and binding as anything can be in this transitory life; it leaves him a Deity to worship as omnipotent and majestic as the deities of any other religion. It has room for almost every religion; nay, it embraces them all." He also says : " Other philosophies do exist and have some following, but *Vedanta* has the largest."

While the *Vedanta* flourished from its conception, still its great progress has been made since about A.D. 800, the date of the great decline of Buddhism in India. Buddhism had driven many of the old orthodox dogmas from the minds of the Hindu people, and yet its doctrine of Negation and Nothingness did not satisfy the cravings of a race that always had clung close to the spiritual ideals. To return to the old forms was impossible, and yet the new, cold doctrine of *Gautama* the Buddha did not satisfy, although it had been tried for a thousand years or more. Then, in response to this need, the followers of the *Vedanta* began to do some propaganda work, in the tolerant, broad spirit that has always characterized the Hindu teachers, who would always admit Truth in the conceptions of their opponents, but at the same time would claim 'a greater Truth' in their own. And the *Vedanta,* with its broadness and willingness to admit outsiders without requiring them to cast overboard all of their preconceived and cherished ideas, appealed to the people of India at this time. The *Brahma-Sutra,* the earliest *Vedanta* work, was supplemented by the most able and brilliant commentary, called the *Sariraka-Bhasya* from the mind of *Shri Sankaracharya,* who is regarded by the *Vedantists* as one of the greatest philosophers that the world ever produced, and who was the 'second-father' of the system.

It is most difficult to state in a few words the fundamental conception of the *Vedanta* philosophy, for the reason that it has an inner and an outer doctrine—the outer, or rather several outer ones, being for the masses who are not able to grasp the higher conception of the inner, the latter being reserved for those whose rare philosophic minds enable them to grasp the Absolute Idealism of the inner teachings. As we have said, the doctrine concerns itself with the "inquiry into the *Brahman*" and the manifestation of the latter as the phenomenal universe with its individual soul. The *Vedanta* fathers found the doctrine of THAT; The Absolute; *Brahman;* firmly established in the Hindu mind— the ONE was recognized as the Source of All—or ALL itself.

Our second lesson, on the Inner Teachings, has shown you the fundamental conception, which was accepted in a general way by all, notwithstanding the many attempts to account for the manifestation of the material universe. In a general way the orthodox dogmas held merely that THAT, or *Brahman,* had "manifested" or "emanated" the universe and the individual souls, without attempting to state just "how" the transformation was effected—how the One became Many. It was recognized that the universe must have proceeded from the substance of the Infinite and Eternal *Brahman*, for the Hindu mind would never admit that "something can come from nothing"; but just 'how' this changes took place was in doubt. Many of the schools had taught that *Brahman* had in some way divided Itself up into individual souls, and the material universe, although there was here the difficulty of escaping the fundamental idea that *Brahman* was indivisible. The most favoured conception was that of an emanation, as the light from the sun; the odour from the flower, etc. *Kapila* in his *Sankhya* philosophy held to the dual-aspect of the manifestation, *viz.* (1) the innumerable individual souls, or *Purusha;* and (2) the *Prakriti,* or Nature, which supplied the material substratum, and in which the *Purushas* were entangled and involved. But there was always the general conception of a duality, or at least a dual-aspect of the One and the Many.

And at this point the *Vedantists* stepped in with the conception of Idealism, which held that the One was the Only Reality, and that consequently all else that appeared to be must be illusory, or an appearance of the One as Many, without an actual separation of the One into parts. This illusory universe was due to *Avidya*, or Ignorance, occasioned by *Maya*, or Illusory Appearance. The conception, in its last analysis, is most subtle and super-metaphysical, almost defying explanation except in its own terms. But we shall attempt it here, nevertheless.

To begin with, the *Vedanta* postulates the existence of THAT, or *Brahman*, as the Only Reality and Only Existence. It accepts the Inner Teachings (see the second lesson) regarding the report of the intellect regarding THAT, and embodies these Inner Teachings in its fundamental axioms. This One Reality, or *Brahman*, is held to be 'One and Universal'; 'Infinite and Eternal'; 'Indivisible' and incapable of separation.

This being so, the theories of 'manifestation' must be abandoned, and the term 'reflection' or 'appearance' substituted, for if the One is indivisible, and incapable of separation—and as there is nothing else but the One to manifest—then it follows that all manifestation must be illusory, and nothing but a reflection or an appearance. In other words, all outside and apart from the One must be merely 'Ideals' of the One, or else nothing at all. An 'Idea,' you know, is "the image of an object formed in the mind"; and 'Ideal' means "existing in idea or thought." So, with this bold conception, the *Vedantists* brushed away all the previous conceptions and theories, including that of *Kapila* with his individual *Purushas*, or spirits, and his *Prakriti*, or Nature, holding that even these 'aspects' or 'principles' must be merely ideals and existing merely "in the mind of the One." But at the same time it accepted all of the existing conceptions and theories of the other schools, provisionally, and allowed the converts to retain them, holding that these conceptions were useful in helping the undeveloped minds to think of the One the best they knew how, and leading up to a point when they could conceive of the One divested from these misconceptions of *Maya* occasioned by *Avidya*, or Ignorance. And so, in the end, we see that the efforts of the *Vedanta* teachers must be directed toward explaining the nature and characteristics of this baleful *Maya*, which so distorts the Truth that it is not recognized—that causes the "piece of rope on the ground to be mistaken for the snake," arousing all the terrors and horror that the real snake would have caused. For in the understanding of *Maya*, and the escape from its entanglements, lies the Road to Freedom and Emancipation of the Spirit whose eyes are blinded with the smoked-glasses of *Maya*.

Let us first consider the *Vedanta* conception of the One. *Brahman*, the One Absolute Substance, is held to be beyond qualities or attributes; beyond subject and object; to be the Source of Being; Intelligence; and Bliss. It is the efficient cause of the universe in its spiritual, mental and material appearances; creator and creation ; doer and deed; cause and effect; the underlying Truth amidst the Universe of Unreality; one; self-existent; all-there-is; all-that-ever-has-been; all-that-ever-can-be; One and Only; Alone, with Nothing within Itself, and Nothing Outside of Itself; Unique; without a Second. Since it is all there is, and cannot be divided into parts, nor subject to change, then it must follow that the Self of each of us must be in some way identical with the Self of the One, instead of being a part of or emanation of it—that the Self or Spirit in us must be the identical Spirit of the One, undivided and whole. Outside of this Self there is nothing, and therefore there is Non-Duality, the 'duality' of the other schools being held false. Surely this is a startling conception, never before equalled in the history of Hindu Philosophy, and most difficult of comprehension. No wonder that it has been called "the highest pinnacle of philosophic thought which the human mind can possibly attain"; or, as Schlegel has said: "Even the loftiest philosophy of the Europeans, the idealism of reason as it is set forth by the Greek philosophers, appears, in comparison with the abundant light and vigour of Oriental idealism, like a feeble Promethean spark in the full flood of heavenly glory of the noonday sun, faltering and feeble, and ever ready to be extinguished." And as Max Müller says : "*Vedanta* holds a most unique position among the philosophies of the world. After lifting the Self or the true nature of the Ego, *Vedanta* unites it with the essence of Divinity, which is absolutely pure, perfect, immortal, unchangeable, and one. No philosopher, not even Plato, Spinoza, Kant, Hegel, or Schopenhauer, has reached that height of philosophic thought ... None of our philosophers, not excepting Heraclitus, Plato, Kant, or Hegel, has ventured to erect such a spire, never frightened by storms or lightnings. Stone follows upon stone in regular succession after once the first step has been made, after once it has been clearly seen that in the beginning there can have been but One, as there will be but One in the end, whether we call it *Atman* or *Brahman*."

The student who, for the first time, follows the *Vedanta* teachings up the narrow path of reasoning that leads to "the highest pinnacle of philosophic thought," finds himself panting for breath in the thin, rarefied atmosphere of those exalted peaks, and feels the chill of the mountain air pervading his being. And when the highest peak of all is surmounted, he is apt to gaze affrighted at the lower peaks, and the valleys and canyons far beneath him, and he begins to wonder how he ever will be able to descend to solid earth once more. Or, dropping figurative terms, he begins to wonder how any reasoning mind will be able to explain the existence of the phenomenal universe, after having postulated a One Being that is indivisible, unchanging, and All, with the accompanying postulate that "something cannot be evolved from nothing." Surely the original Hindu philosopher who first reached this plane of thought had the courage of his logical convictions, and the fearlessness that springs from a consciousness of Truth attained. But let us see how the *Vedantist* philosophers extricate themselves from this predicament, from which there would seem to be no logical escape.

In the first place, the *Vedantist* cannot avail himself of that Principle of *Kapila*, which forms one of the dual-principles of his *Sankhya* System, namely, the Principle of

Prakriti, or Nature, which supplies the material substratum for the universe, and which is energized by the *Purushas*, or Spirits. These principles, if admitted at all by the *Vedantists*, are immediately classified with other phenomenal things, and are taken out of the consideration for the purpose before us. The *Vedantist* has nothing else but *Brahman* to start with—where does he get his phenomenal universe and his individual souls? Not from Nothing ! Not from a separation, division or change in *Brahman*, for *Brahman* is above these things. Then where else, or from what else, can they be evolved? Here are the several answers of the *Vedantins*.

I. The answer of the *Vishishtadvaita* school, or branch of the *Vedanta*, which was founded by *Ramanuga*, who lived about the same time as *Sankaracharya* the founder of the *Advaita* or Monistic school of *Vedanta*—and which school of *Ramanuga* is called the 'qualified-monistic' or else 'qualified dualism'—holds that *Brahman* contains within himself elements of plurality, or modes of existence, and which elements or modes share his reality, and are at one with himself, although apparently separate and individual. That is to say, *Ramanuga* holds that just as the individual cells of the human body, or groups of such cells, including the blood-corpuscles, may be considered as '*of* the man,' rather than as "separate parts of him," and at the same time manifest individuality, so are the individual souls of *Brahma*, and not separate from him, although apparently individuals. This school holds that the material universe is an illusion occasioned by these 'individual souls' (which are really elements of *Brahman*) being deluded by *Avidya*, or Ignorance, which produces *Maya*, the cause of the material universe. When these individual souls realize their nature and identity with *Brahman*, the spell of *Maya* is over, and the soul escapes *Samsara* and returns to its original state of Bliss.

The above explanation would seem to be a partial answer keeping fairly well within logical lines, but the *Advaitists*, or Monists, or 'non-dualists,' who compose the other great branch of the *Vedanta*, regard this explanation and doctrine as but a half-truth, and consider it unworthy of the true *Vedanta*. And, without prejudice, it must be admitted that the school of *Ramanuga* seems to attempt a compromise, and beats a retreat after having fixed its standard on the philosophic heights. It seems like a compromise with the position of the *Sankhyas*, with their individual souls, or else with the *Patanjali* school, with their individual souls and their Universal *Purusha*, as you may see in the forthcoming lessons. Or, looking at it another way, it would seem as if *Ramanuga* was changing his conception or postulate of a One Infinite, Eternal Being, incapable of change or division, into another conception or postulate of an 'Atomic *Brahman*' composed of countless 'elements' or 'modes,' which, while not called parts, still destroy the 'non-particled' conception or postulate of *Brahm* "with nothing within itself, and nothing without itself." It certainly appears that *Ramanuga's* final position is a retreat from his original one, and that he either was afraid to carry the original conception to its logical conclusion, or else feared that the people could not grasp the extreme position. This last idea seems to be correct, in part, for many Hindus who adhere to the *Vedanta* teaching are not able to grasp the extreme idealistic position of the *Advaitist* school of *Sankaracharya*, and are better satisfied with the 'qualified-monism' of the *Vishishtadvaita* school of *Ramanuga*. While it is true that it may be said that there really are *two schools* of *Vedanta*, as above stated, each equally entitled to the name *Vedantist*, it still remains true that philosophical students, without prejudice, both in India and in the West, recognize in the *Advaita* the true *Vedanta*—that is, the *Vedanta* in which the thought and argument is carried logically forward from premise to conclusion—the extreme logical consequence being admitted, and not feared or compromised. The *Vishishtadvaita* school seems more allied with some of the schools of the *Sankhya*, or the *Yoga*, than to its companion *Vedantist* school. And in our continuation of this lesson on the *Vedanta,* we shall consider the *Advaita* school as representing the original *Vedanta* doctrine to his logical and natural conclusion, believing that the facts of the case warrant the same.

Before passing to the *Advaitist* explanation of the existence of the phenomenal universe, however, let us stop a moment and consider some conceptions held by certain *Vedantists* belonging to neither of the great schools—independent reasoners, as it were, seeing a view of truth from their own viewpoint. These independent *Vedantists* hold to a conception that is an approach to a conception of a "manifestation," and yet is not such in full truth—something that may be spoken of as an 'apparent manifestation,' as it were. These views are chiefly expressed in symbols; for instance, one class will compare *Brahman* and the individual souls to the sparks arising from the blazing fire and returning thereto, but *being always within the heat-waves of the fire,* and therefore not separate, although appearing to be so. Another class favours the illustration of the perfume arising from a flower, which, while apparently apart from the flower, is still *of* it. Another class favours the illustration of the rays *of* the sun, which, while seemingly apart, are still of the sun. These illustrations all partake of the nature of 'emanations,' however, and have a resemblance to a 'manifestation.' But still another class, while very near to those just mentioned, favours a 'reflection' rather than an emanation, admitting the existence of a 'something else' as a background to, or object of, the 'reflection,' which something they call *Maya,* as do the *Advaitists,* as we shall see later. This 'reflection' class compare the relation between *Brahman* and the individual souls to the reflection of the midday Sun upon a million raindrops, each of which seems to contain a miniature Sun, the basis of which is the Sun itself, which is not affected by its countless 'reflections.' This conception has strength, is firmly held to by many, although it implies the existence of a 'something' illusory to correspond to the raindrops, and must also recognize that the 'reflection' itself depends upon an 'emanation' of the Sun's light and rays. But perhaps we are pushing the figure of speech further than perfect fairness would dictate. This idea of a 'reflection' seems to exercise a hold upon many careful minds among the Hindus. It seems to contain a hint of an underlying truth that subtly escapes the grasp of the mind that would make it its own. The figure is sometimes altered so that the illustration is that of the Sun casting a 'reflection' of itself into countless vessels or jars of water, and thus giving light and Spirit presence to the water contained within the earthen jars. The illustration of the jar as the material body, the water as the mind, and the light as the Spirit, is a beautiful poetic conception, and one that has a close correspondence with certain occult conceptions of the relations of the three.

And now for the conception and explanation of the *Advaita* school of *Vedanta*, founded by *Sankaracharya*—the True *Vedanta* of the scholars—the school of Absolute Monism—Absolute Idealism—Absolute Idealistic Monism. What is its explanation of the existence of the phenomenal universe, and the individual souls given by this great school? Let us listen to its report.

The *Advaitist* position may be emphasized by a quotation from Max Müller, who closed one of his celebrated lectures of the *Vedanta* with these words: "In one half-verse I shall tell you what has been taught in thousands of Volumes : *Brahman is true, the world is false, the soul is Brahman and nothing else.*" In other words, that instead of there being countless individual souls (either manifested, created, emanated, or reflected) being entangled in the principle of substance of *Maya*, or *Prakriti*, and losing their identity, and building up a false universe by reason thereof—instead of this, there is postulated *Brahman* itself, entangled and involved in this baleful principle of *Maya*, deluded by its illusion, involved in its glamour—*Brahman* itself *imagining* itself separated into countless individual spirits or souls and erecting an imaginary universe of the senses which serves to bind it more and more. This is a crude expression of the doctrine, but a true one, stated in its bareness and boldness. Have thinkers ever dared to say this before ? If so, the history of philosophy fails to reveal the fact.

Yes, this is the essence of the *Advaita* teaching—the Infinite involved in a figment of its own imagination, losing itself in a 'dream' of a phenomenal universe, and believing itself to be countless individual spirits or Selves, instead of the One Spirit and One Self—the All. Surely this is the most daring flight of the human mind in the thin and rarefied air of idealistic philosophy—but still it is but carrying the premise to its logical conclusion, and then escaping from the inevitable, vexatious alternative by the manifestation of the highest degree of mental courage and honesty. This is the extreme position of the *Vedanta* Idealistic Philosophy.

Brahman being the One Reality, indivisible, immutable, and alone, it must follow that the phenomenal manifestation of *Samsara* and its accompanying material universe are but illusive fictions—figments of the imagination or dream-state of *Brahman* itself—the first state of the fantasy being the illusion of Separateness; the subsequent being the illusion of the sense-universe appearing to the 'souls' (?) which themselves are but illusory fictions in the mind of *Brahm*. It is *Brahm* who *sees himself reflected* from the water-drops, or water-jars, of *Maya*, and imagines that he is Many instead of One. It is *Brahm* who sees himself through the countless eyes of the individual reflections of himself. The individual souls persist in their illusory and fictitious 'reflection' or semblance, so long as the bonds of *Samsara* hold the attention —but they are but *Brahman* himself all the while. Throughout the organisms and forms thus built up, this deluded *Brahm*, manifesting as countless unitary reflections and semblances of himself, acts, moves, and plays its many parts upon the Stage of *Maya*, identifying himself with the countless images of characters existing solely in his imagination, or dream.

Only by realizing this Unity—this Truth—may each 'soul' escape, one by one, from *Maya* and awaken from the dream of *Samsara*. Only by Knowledge may the 'soul' escape its isolation and return to a consciousness of its Real Self.

The *Advaitists* do not accept all of the Fundamental Conceptions of THAT, or *Brahman*. In fact, they discard all these conceptions as attempts to bestow "attributes or qualities" upon THAT which is above them. They refuse to consider THAT in its aspects as the Absolute Essence of Substance or Space, or in the other aspect of Absolute Essence of Motion at Rest, or in the third aspect, of the Essence of Absolute Law-in-Itself. They brush all this aside, and, claiming to rise higher than the original source of their philosophic thought, they postulate THAT, *Brahman*, as being PURE INTELLIGENCE ABSOLUTE, and which may be considered as *"Sat-chit-ananda,"* or Absolute Existence—Knowledge—Bliss.

The deluding *Maya* (which we shall consider at length presently) is held to be more than individual ignorance of the 'souls,' and is the shadow of reality, of eternal duration, and of cosmic extension and significance. Its origin is veiled in mystery and obscurity. But while it is not eternal, or real—for it passes away during the Night of *Brahm*, only to appear again when the Creative Activity once more begins—still it is something more than a manifestation. In fact, while in itself it is not real, it may be said that there is that in *Brahman* which produces it and which is real—the possibility and latency of *Maya*, so to speak, is inherent in *Brahman*. This *Maya* is regarded as the material cause of the world, just as in the *Sankhya* the *Prakriti is so regarded*—but *Maya* is not regarded as a 'something' as is *Prakriti*; for it is merely a covering or shadow of Something. And yet the *Advaitists* do not teach that the phenomenal life and universe is a 'nothing' as do the Buddhists. They regard it as an illusory appearance of an underlying reality, which appearance is unreal, and *yet real for all practical purposes*, and which must be so considered in sane reasoning and action. As Max Müller has said concerning this point: "For all practical purposes, the *Vedantist* would hold that the whole phenomenal world, both in its subjective and objective character, should be accepted as real. It is as real as anything can be to the ordinary mind; it is not mere emptiness, as the Buddhists maintain. And thus the *Vedanta* philosophy leaves to every man a wide sphere of real usefulness, and places him under a law as strict and binding as anything can be in this transitory life." And this may be understood when you consider that *even in the imagination or dream of Brahman there* Must *be an element of actuality. Samsara* is not absolutely fictitious, although illusory. Phenomena are merely indicative of the illusory appearance of an underlying reality. "Dreams are. true, *while they last*," says the poet. Therefore the phenomenal universe may be considered as true, so long as the Truth is not known. When *Brahm* awakes, the universe disappears—the souls know that they are One. The Universe and the souls are not "absorbed" into *Brahman*—but *Brahman* arouses itself, and the phenomenal appearance fades away as do the dreams of the night, or the day-dreams of the waking hour.

The *Avaita* conception regards *Brahman* as the real cause of the universe, because it all proceeds from him; and also as the operative cause, because the processes of *Maya* (which are akin to those of the *Prakriti* of the *Sankhya*) depend upon the proximity and existence of *Brahman*, inasmuch as *Maya* has no energy of its own, but acts by the energy of *Brahman* reproduced in *Maya* by induction, similar to the action of the magnetism of a magnet inducing magnetic properties in the particles of steel. Thus *Maya*, although inert of itself, becomes active by reason of its proximity to *Brahman*. The student will notice that the *Advaitists* use the same figure of speech (the magnet and the bits of steel) that is used by the *Sankhyas* in illustrating the action of the *Purushas* upon *Prakriti*. In fact, there are many points of resemblance between the *Sankhya Prakriti* and the *Vedanta Maya*, the principal difference being that the former is regarded as a fundamental principle of nature, while the latter is regarded as an illusory figment of the imagination or dream of *Brahman*—or, rather, as the imagination or dream-condition itself. As an authority says: "*Maya*, the inexplicable illusion, self-imagined, has been the unreal adjunct illusorily overspread upon *Brahman* from all eternity."

Before proceeding with our consideration of the nature of *Maya*, as stated by the *Advaitists*, let us consider the teachings regarding, the operation of *Avidya*, or Ignorance, through *Maya*. This *Avidya*, which is held to be of cosmic extent and effect, operates in two ways by means of *Maya*. The first way is in the enveloping of *Brahman* and producing the illusion of the Many Selves; the second way is the projecting of the phenomenal and material universe by reason of the first error or illusion. This projection is as follows: By *Avidya*, through *Maya*, is projected the subtle elements of ether; air; fire; water; and earth. From these subtle elements is evolved the seventeen subtle principles and the five gross elements. The seventeen subtle principles comprise the five senses, *viz*.: sight, hearing, smell, taste, and feeling; the two mental principles of *Buddhi*, the principle of understanding, reasoning, determining, etc., and *Manas*, the principle of will and imagination, respectively; also the five principles controlling the organs of action, namely, the organs of speech, the hands and feet, the organs of excretion, and the organs of generation, respectively; and the five vital airs, or vital energies, or forms of *Prana*. The five gross elements are evolved from the five subtle elements, in certain combinations and phases, and from the operation and activities of which proceed the material universe. The above classification of the principles is common to the majority of the Hindu philosophical systems, and seems to have descended from some common ancient source and to have been accepted without question by the founders of the systems, and incorporated with their doctrines and conceptions. You will notice these principles appearing in the other systems considered in these lessons. The best modern authorities do not take this classification of principles very seriously, and are apt to regard them as in the nature of worn-out systems of the past, although as the mental principles are concerned, and the psychology arising therefrom, the Hindu thinkers hold that they are much better ideas of the operation of the mind than any Western theories, or hypotheses. With the exception of the conception of the Mental Principles, therefore, the balance of the classification may be omitted from the serious consideration of the philosophies, as the fundamental conceptions of the same are not affected thereby.

The *Vedanta* adheres to the prevailing Hindu conception of the several 'principles' or 'sheaths' of the individual soul, which may be stated as follows: (1) The *Rupa*, or Physical Body; (2) The *Jiva* or *Prana*, or Vital Force; (3) The *Liṅga Sharira*, or Astral Body, or Etheric Double; (4) The *Kama Rupa*, or Animal Soul; (5) The *Manas*, or Human Soul; (6) The *Buddhi*, or Spiritual Soul; (7) *Atman*, or Spirit. The last three principles compose the reincarnating soul, while the first four disintegrate at the death of the body, or shortly after. This classification is common to the several Hindu philosophies, and the students of our own system will find them agreeing with our own classification of 'The Seven Principles.' (See our "Fourteen Lessons in Yogi Philosophy.")

The *Vedantists* hold to the teachings of Reincarnation and *Karma*, which form a part of the fundamental philosophical and religious thought of the race. To the *Vishishtadvaita* school of *Ramanuga*, *Samsara* or the cycle of existence, and *Karma*, mean the evolution and progress of the soul through the mists of *Avidya* and *Maya* back to the realization of itself as an 'element' in the nature of the One. But to the *Advaita* school of *Sankaracharya*, *Samsasra*, with its incidents of Reincarnation and *Karma*, is but a part of the universal illusion, and both disappear when the soul awakens to the fact that it is not an individual entity, but a distorted reflection or appearance of *Brahman* himself, created by him in his imagination or dream. Reincarnation and *Karma* are thus, in full Truth, held to be nothing but *Maya* arising from *Avidya*, which is annihilated by the awakening to *Vidya* or Knowledge of the Truth which informs the soul that it is *Brahman* and bids it awaken from its dream of *Samsara*, at which *Maya* fades away like the mist of the morning before the rays of the sun. But, as we have said, the doctrine holds that 'for practical purposes' the *Samsara* is true, and Reincarnation and *Karma* facts to be reckoned with, for until the Sleeper awakes the world of experience is the only real one to the soul, and its laws and rules, of which Reincarnation and *Karma* form a part, stand untouched and fully operative. Only when man becomes *Brahman* do they cease to rule him. For, at the end, says the *Advaitist*, if there is in reality nothing to reincarnate or to be affected by *Karma*, then Rebirth, Death, and *Karma* are seen to be nothing but manifestations of *Maya* itself—the machinery of the dream. And so, while holding to the truth of Reincarnation and *Karma* with firm and positive teaching, still in the end the *Advaita* denies it ultimate reality.

Among the ranks of the *Vedantists* are to be found many who cling to the idea of *Ishwara*, the Personal God, the Demiurge, or the Logos. And, notwithstanding the advanced position of some of the *Vedanta* sects, there is no opposition to this doctrine, and a place is found for it under the big tent of *Vedanta* catholicity. *Ishwara* is explained, and harmonized with the fundamental teaching, by admitting the conception that when the creative processes begin, *Brahman*, overspread with *Maya*, first manifests as *Ishwara*, and then from *Ishwara* proceeds the remainder of the creation. Thus the individual soul is held to be identical with *Ishwara*, and *Ishwara* identical with *Brahman*. Thus *Ishwara* represents the collective totality of the various principles manifested in the individual forms and units of the phenomenal universe. *Ishwara* is the Universal Soul, containing within his soul the collective totality of the three higher principles of the soul diffused among the individual souls, and containing within his body the collective totality of the four lower principles. (See the above classification of the seven principles of man.) *Ishwara* may be worshipped as a Personal God, and loved as an Over-Soul. But even *Ishwara* is but an appearance in *Maya*, and in the end must awaken to the fact that he is naught in himself, but Everything in *Brahman*. And the individual soul, seeing the Truth, may ignore *Ishwara*, and piercing his illusory nature may proceed direct to the bosom of *Brahman*. Thus does the *Vedanta* supply the want of each class of follower—satisfy the hunger of each soul, according to its nature. While postulating an abstract THAT, or Absolute, it still allows the intervention of an *Ishwara*, or Personal God, with a universal human nature and character, without being inconsistent or compromising. It willingly admits anything in *Maya*, but denies everything in Truth except *Brahman* Itself—THAT—in the words of Max Müller : "*Brahman* is true, the world is false, the soul is *Brahman* and nothing else." From the beginning to the end, *Vedanta* is consistent and logical, facing the consequences of its extreme conclusions without a tremor, and steadfastly refusing to beat a retreat. A most remarkable manifestation of human philosophical speculation—without parallel.

And now for this strange and inexplicable *Maya*—that illusion, imagination, or dream, that overspreads the being of *Brahman* and causes him to 'imagine vain things,' and to dream of strange happenings. What of *Maya*? We must confess that at this point the *Advaitists* are brought face to face with the focused energies of the argument and opposition to their system and doctrine. It is their 'heel of Achilles' —their only vulnerable point, in the opinion of outside thinkers, although they, themselves, do not admit this, and claim that the doctrine of *Maya* is as safely encased in armour as the rest of their system. From whence arises *Maya* ? There is no outside source, and it must come from *Brahman* himself—then why does he permit it? What is the cause of *Maya*?

Some of the leading *Advaitist* teachers refuse to entertain the question in this shape—asserting that to suppose the necessity of a 'cause' or 'reason' for *Brahman's* creations would be to assume something to which *Brahman* was subject—something ruling, determining or influencing the Infinite—a palpable absurdity. They say that *Maya* appears, and therefore must be in accord with *Brahman's* nature and being, and not contrary to his will or desire if such relative terms may be permitted regarding the Absolute. Therefore *Brahman*, himself, is 'the reason' or 'cause' or 'why' of *Maya*. And beyond that they refuse to go, claiming that this mystery is locked up in *Brahman* himself, and that the question can no more be answered than the 'why,' 'reason,' or 'necessity' of the existence of *Brahman*, itself. And so in the end even the advanced *Advaitist* confesses himself unable to consider and answer that great Ultimate Question that has ever perplexed the great philosophical minds that were able to realize that such a question existed—the question: "Why did God create the universe, since He is not bound by Necessity or Desire; since nothing can be accomplished by it; since there is nothing that can be that has not always been—be the universe illusion or reality; why was it created?" So it always has been—so it is now—so, perhaps, will it be always, for none but God Himself—the Absolute—can answer this question from full knowledge, for such full Knowledge is God Himself, or the *Brahman*, of Absolute Intelligence. This is indeed the Riddle of the Sphinx.

But the failure to answer this Ultimate Question, or 'Why?' does not deter the *Advaitist* from speculating concerning the nature of *Maya*. To some *Maya* is identical with a 'Principle of Nature' or a 'Creative Energy,' which is inherent in the Being of *Brahman*, and which he brings into play, willing to will it into activity, and willing to involve himself in it, temporarily. To others *Maya* is in the nature of a *Brahmic* Imagination, in which he plunges in reverie akin to the day-dream of the man. To others *Maya* is as the true dream-condition in which "the dreams are true while they last," and from which *Brahman* finally arouses himself, little by little, each individual's awakening contributing a 'little.' To others *Maya* is the mental state of Reverie or Meditation into which *Brahman* plunges himself, and objectifies universes and characters, as the artist objectifies the characters and scenes of his 'mental creation' of story, poem, drama, painting, or sculpture, from his subjective self, or 'inner consciousness.' Others hold that *Brahman* desires to express himself into relative objectivity and activity, and attempts to do so over and over again, but finding that the same is impossible, he is forced to beat a retreat, and relin-quish the effort—but this last is rather more the speculation of a *Vedantist* affected by the Buddhist or Schopenhauer like thought of an unconscious and unintelligent Absolute trying to express itself into consciousness, and being forced to a retreat by the pain arising therefrom. This idea is not true to the *Vedantist* ideal and conception, although it has been advanced by some good teachers. To others it has seemed that *Brahman* first conceived of the abstract ideas of Time, Space and Causation—the three Great Relative Principles—and in meditating upon these three relativities he began to consider himself in connection with them—through their triple glasses of thought, as it were—and thus arose the *Avidya* that produced the *Maya*, that produced the phenomenal universe, and caused *Brahman* to consider himself as the Many in Time, Space and Causation.

In all of the speculations (which concern themselves with the 'How' rather than the 'Why,' of *Maya*, remember) there is the underlying thought that *Maya* must be a mental something—that is, something prising in the 'mind' of *Brahman*, if such a relative term may be used; and also the conception that in some mysterious way *Brahman* is involved and rapt in his imaginings, dreams, or conceptions, or mental creations. These two ideas underlie all of the speculation regarding *Maya*. And all agree that pain, misery and unhappiness result from this involvement of *Brahm* in his mental creations, even though, as the teachers say, the "total period of the creation, existence, and death of universe, is as but the twinkle of an eye to *Brahman*"—that is, it is practically instantaneous, from start to finish, just as even a man may dream a lifetime in a few moments. One of the Hindu teachers gave this parable illustrating the idea of *Brahm* being involved in his creative processes : "*Indra*, one of the gods, once descended into Nature, or *Prakriti*, in order to gain experience, and so incarnated as a pig, losing all knowledge of his true nature. He wallowed in the mud, and grew fat and big, with great tusks. He took unto himself a pig-wife, and soon found himself surrounded by a brood of baby-pigs, and was very happy by reason of his pig-family. Some of the other gods, seeing his loss of recollection of his real self, and his belief in the reality of his pig-nature, sought to arouse him from his illusion, saying; 'Arouse thyself, *Indra*, thou art a god'; but *Indra* grunted lazily, 'Go away, and disturb me not—I am a pig, and am happy. What do I care for your heavens, with my mud, and my sow and baby-pigs. Go away ! ' But the friendly companion-gods, wishing to arouse him, killed his baby-pigs, and later his wife-pig; but *Indra* wept and wailed, squealed and bit, and snorted his rage and sorrow. Finally, in despair, they killed his pig-body itself, as they would any other pig, whereupon *Indra* emerged freed from his delusion, and laughed when told what a dream he had indulged in, and once more resumed his god-life. But what would have been *Indra's* sorrow, had he been compelled to work out his Freedom through the repeated rebirths and *Karma*, of *Samsara*, as do the individual souls in their road to Freedom and Emancipation?"

Those of you who have read our views regarding the nature of the manifestation of the universe by The Absolute, in our lessons on 'Gnani Yoga,' will realize that while we accept the *Vedanta* conception of the Oneness of Being, and the All being All in All, yet we do not admit or hold that The Absolute loses the knowledge of itself in its creations, but on the contrary preserves that knowledge intact. And that the reflection of The Absolute in each individual soul constitutes the Indwelling Spirit of the soul—its Real Self. And that while the nature of the Universe is that of a Mental Creation of The Absolute, and The Absolute finds itself reflected in the ideas of the universe—and that all in that universe are *ideas* of The Absolute—still the creation is deliberate and in pursuance with some design and plan of The Absolute (the reason thereof being beyond human knowledge) and is NOT the result of Ignorance or *Avidya* on the part of the Absolute, such thought being inconsistent with the fundamental conception of Infinite Wisdom. We regard *Maya*, or *Prakriti*, as the great Creative Principle emanated from The Absolute. And *Avidya* or Ignorance, we hold, is confined to the phenomenal world, and has no place or existence in The Absolute, but is itself the product of *Maya*. We must refer you to our 'Gnani Yoga' for the details of our conception, although the above will give you, briefly, an idea of the points of our agreement with, and the points of our difference from, the *Vedanta* Philosophy. Our own system is Eclectic in its nature, and has points of agreement with, and points of difference from, each of the other principal systems of the Hindu Philosophy, and, besides, advances many independent conceptions and interpretations not found in the said systems, and which are part of the great body of Eclectic Philosophical Thought in India which has refused to identify itself with any of the schools or systems.

SPECIAL MESSAGE IV

By Yogi Ramacharaka

In our message of last month, we gave you the first three of the Axioms of Truth, those symbols whereby we seek to enter into an understanding of the nature of Truth. In the message of this month, we continue the presentation of the axioms—the symbols. We invite you to consider the three following Axioms of Truth :

IV. We may consider TRUTH by means of the symbol of Creative Activity. Not only has TRUTH the Creative Energy, but it is also the Creative Energy Itself. Other than TRUTH there can be no Creative Energy. All that is, ever has been, or ever can be Created, must have been manifested, expressed or emanated by the Creative Energy of TRUTH. TRUTH is the Cause, Source and Reason for all Creation. There is nothing outside of or apart from, Truth that can Create; and, therefore, can be nothing created by anything outside or apart from TRUTH. All else is Error, Untruth.

V. We may consider TRUTH by means of the symbol of Intelligence. Not alone is TRUTH Omniscient or All-Wise, but it is also Omniscience or All-Wisdom Itself. Outside, or apart from TRUTH, there is not never has been, and never can be, any Wisdom. All the evidences of Wisdom that we see must be manifestations, expressions or emanations from Truth. TRUTH is the Source of all Wisdom and is the Fount from which all Wisdom must be drawn. All apparent knowledge outside of or apart from TRUTH is Untruth.

VI. We may consider TRUTH by means of the symbol of Good. TRUTH is the All-Good. TRUTH is Good. Our intuitive realization of the Good above us, and to which the higher part of our Being always yearns if allowed to follow its highest inclinations, informs us that there is GOOD. And TRUTH being the only Being and Reality must be that GOOD. Any other supposition is impossible and contrary to the highest intuition of the human mind. The reality of Good, and its identity with TRUTH comes to man not through his Reason alone, but also from a higher part of his being, and constitutes the Divine Message to the race. Not only is TRUTH Good, in the sense of possessing Good, but it also is GOODNESS itself ; TRUTH is the Essence of Good. And All-Good must proceed from TRUTH, for there is no other place whence it could have come. Outside and apart from TRUTH, there can be no GOOD. All else is Untruth.

In our next month's message, we shall continue this consideration of the symbolic Axioms, whereby we seek to enter into an understanding of the Nature of Truth.

Our meditation for the coming month is :

"TRUTH IS THE ALL-CREATIVE ENERGY; THE ALL WISDOM; THE ALL-GOOD; AND OUTSIDE OF TRUTH THERE CAN BE AND IS NO CREATIVE ENERGY; NO WISDOM OR INTELLIGENCE; NO GOOD."

Chapter V

Patanjali's Yoga System

The third great system of Hindu Philosophy is that known as *Patanjali's Yoga* System, or more commonly as simply 'The *Yoga System.*' (This System must not be confounded with our own "Yogi Philosophy," which is Eclectic in nature and derivation, and which differs in many respects from *Patanjali's Yoga* System, inclining far more toward the *Vedantic* idea than the teachings of *Patanjali.*) This *Yoga* System is reputed to have been founded by *Patanjali* (whose name is usually used in connection with it) about 300 B.C. Many of the best authorities regard it as a natural growth from, and an offshoot from, *Kapila's Sankhya* System, many of the tenets of the latter school being held in their original shape by *Patanjali.* In fact, with the addition of a Personal God, or World *Purusha, Patanjali* seems to have taken over the *Sankhya* System as a basis for his own, the points of agreement being too constant and numerous to admit of their being mere coincidences, and as *Kapila* undoubtedly preceded *Patanjali* there can be no counter-charge of 'borrowing doctrines.' In fact, the majority of the followers of *Patanjali* freely admit that their system is an outgrowth of the *Sankhya*, and 'an improvement' thereupon. The '*Mahabharata*' says : "He is wise who sees the *Sankhya* and the *Yoga* as but one." The prime distinctions between the two systems are the 'improvements' of *Patanjali*, which are in the nature of certain methods of psychic development, mental control, and occult development, which are generally known as the '*Raja Yoga* methods,' and which are used also by many of the followers of the other systems, and the most desirable and 'saner' of which are sometimes taught in connection with some of the branches and cults of the *Vedanta*. From these '*Raja Yoga* Methods' the System of *Patanjali* takes its name. '*Yoga*' is the Sanskrit term meaning "contemplation, concentration, and conjunction"; and also used in another sense of a 'yoking up' or 'union,' implying a union, by means of these methods, between man and the higher planes of being—even of *Brahman*. There are many forms of *Yoga* in the philosophies, '*Gnani Yoga*,' or the *Yoga* of Wisdom being the form preferred by the *Vedantists* who strive for Attainment, or Emancipation, by means of Wisdom, Understanding, and Knowledge acquired by the exercise of Pure Reason and Right Thinking. The followers of *Patanjali*, or a large number of them, prefer the road of '*Raja Yoga*,' or the *Yoga* of Mental Control, Psychic Development, Unfoldment of Latent Forces, etc. The *Purva Mimansa* system, and the followers of the many religious sects and cults in India, seemingly prefer the road of '*Karma Yoga*' or the Yoga of Work, Duty, Action, Devotion, etc.—the Path of Right Living and Devotion to Duty and God. And so, in our consideration of '*Yoga*' in connection with *Patanjali's Yoga* System, we shall hold ourself to its favourite phase of *Raja Yoga*. But before passing on to a consideration of its *Yoga* Methods, let us examine the system in its philosophical and metaphysical aspect.

Patanjali, like *Kapila*, does not dispute the existence of THAT, or *Brahman*, but like his predecessor he "takes THAT for granted," as we have heard the matter stated. He accepts the *Sankhya* doctrine of the *Tattvas*, or Principles of Creation, and holds to the *Sankhya* conception of the basic principles of the phenomenal universe, *i.e.*, the two opposing but interacting Principles of *Purusha* and *Prakriti* respectively. Like *Kapila*, he postulates a great universal principle of *Prakriti*, from which has evolved "all this side of Spirit," including Mind. And like *Kapila*, he postulates the existence of innumerable spiritual entities, Souls, or *Purushas*, whose entrance into *Prakriti* energizes the latter and produces the creation of worlds, and the manifestation of the life forms and activities.

But, as also in the *Sankhya*, the *Purushas* are held to be merely and purely passive in their inner nature and being, and their activity (if such a paradoxical term may be allowed us in this connection) consists in illuminating and awakening of the processes and energies of the *Prakriti*, particularly in its form of *Chitta*, or Mind-Stuff, which principle represents an intrinsically material activity, or phase of evolving *Prakriti*, and *which, while unconscious in itself, becomes conscious by reason of its association with the Purusha*, through being subjected to its illumination—the action being similar to the particles of steel becoming magnetized by proximity to, and association with, a true magnet—in short, through 'induction.' In its original state *Purusha* dwells in a blissful state of unconscious knowing and being, and awakens to the pain of self-consciousness only when involved in *Prakriti*. Finally, when it escapes the embraces of *Prakriti*, and cleanses itself from the stick-sweetness of its poppy-made honey, the *Purusha* gains Perfect Emancipation (*kawalva*), and is freed from the activities, work, illusions, and sufferings of the *Prakriti*-caused self-consciousness, and dwells again for eternity in undisturbed blissful transcendental repose.

But leaving *Kapila* at this point, *Patanjali* goes further, and postulates the existence of a World *Purusha*, Universal Soul, Personal God, or *Ishwara*, which he teaches is infinite, formless, omniscient, and free from desire, rewards, pains, or activities. This Lord, Personal God, *Ishwara* or Universal *Purusha*, is defined by *Patanjali* as: "A particular *Purusha*, or Spirit, who is untouched by affections, works, the result of works, or deserts; in whom the germ of omniscience reaches its extreme limit; who is the preceptor of even the first, because He is not limited by time ; and whose appellation is 'OM,' the term of Glory." The student will recognize that this Universal *Purusha*, of *Patanjali*, is more than a Principle of *Purusha*, and in fact is truly '*Ishwara*,' the Personal God of the Hindu philosophies. But still *Patanjali* makes a shadow of a distinction from the orthodox ideas of *Ishwara*, when he teaches that the Universal *Purusha* differs from the Individual *Purushas* not in nature, but in degree only—and that the difference principally manifests itself in the fact that the Universal *Purusha* remains apart, outside and above Time, while the Individual *Purusha*s are involved in Samsara, or the 'course of existence.' Devotion to Him is held to uplift and aid the worshipper and devotee who "makes over his activities to Him"; but He takes no active part in the world of *Samsara*, or embodied life or things. "He ever remains apart." He did not create the universe, neither is He involved in it, nor is He responsible for it. Such is the teaching of *Patanjali* regarding the *Ishwara*, or Universal *Purusha*.

Some of the best authorities hold that *Patanjali's* original teaching was not that this Universal *Purusha* was a Personal God, but rather that it was the united beings of the liberated and free spirits, souls, or *Purusha*s, independent of *Prakriti*—a Union of Units, as it were, to which Union the individual *Purusha* should strive and aim for, by the road of Liberation through the *Raja Yoga* methods. But, so it is held, this teaching rapidly assumed a changing phase, and there manifested an evolution of this Union of Units into an *Ishwara*, Personal God, or Universal *Purusha*, until the latter doctrine became firmly established in the system. Accordingly *Patanjali*'s 'Union with God' does not mean the 'Return to THAT' of the *Vedantists*—the Absorption into the Absolute—nor a return of the Unit to the Union, along the lines of the *Sankhya* teachings—but rather an Absorption into, or a Union with the Universal *Purusha* or Personal God. So *Patanjali's* conception of 'Union with God' has a literal meaning to his followers, and does not mean a passing into the plane of the Absolute THAT, but rather a blending with the Divine nature of God—a Union with God in a strict sense, and akin to the conception of the *Sufis* in Persia (see later lesson on *Sufiism*).

Some of the authorities hold that this Universal *Purusha* is eternal, and does not return into THAT or *Brahman* at the close of a Day of *Brahm;* while others claim that, like *Ishwara,* this Universal *Purusha,* or Personal God, must return along with the individual *Purushas,* and the principle of *Prakriti,* and all else that has been emanated or manifested, into the nature of THAT or *Brahman.*

Patanjali, of course, teaches that the *Purushas*, entangled in *Prakriti,* and entering into the long journey of *Samsara,* undergo many and repeated successive incarnations or rebirths, just as all Hindu philosophies and religions teach. The general teachings of this system regarding Rebirth agrees almost precisely with that of the other systems—in fact, there is but little difference in this fundamental teaching among the various philosophies. This is also true of the teachings regarding *Karma,* or Spiritual Cause and Effect, the teachers holding that the law of causation binds all things in *Samsara,* from atom to man, and that each precedes sowing and reaping, effect following cause. The *Yogin* is taught to concern himself little about past lives, but to dismiss them as outlived tasks, the memory of which will serve only to bind him to material life. He is urged to divest himself, one by one, of the material sheaths that are holding him, that in the end he may awaken from his nightmare of material existence, and pass to the blissful state of freedeom and emancipation, gaining liberation from 'the pairs of opposites'; the '*gunas* or qualities'; from time and space and causation—thus gaining Liberation in Truth.

As will have been seen, the animating principle of *Patanjali*'s teaching is the Method of Deliverance of the Individual *Purusha* from the bonds of *Prakriti,* or material existence, by means of the knowledge of the Truth, and by the exercise of proper methods and exercise, practices and work, which lead to Union with God, or an absorption of the Individual *Purusha* with the Universal *Purusha,* Ishwara, or Personal God—or as some hold, instead of the Union being an 'absorption' it is in the nature of a 'drawing together' or 'yoking-up,' or true *Yoga*. This union is held to be possible of attainment by several roads, the principal and best of which is that of the Absolute Concentration of the *Raja Yoga* methods—which *Yoga* is called the Royal *Yoga*, or the King of *Yoga*. And therefore, the study of the *Yoga* System of *Patanjali* becomes a study of the principles of *Raja Yoga* as expounded by *Patanjali* and his followers, to which subject our consideration now passes.

Patanjali's principal work was not in the direction of building up new theories and doctrines concerning the nature of the One, and its relation to the Many. As we have said, he accepted the *Sankhya* doctrine almost without change, and built his own system thereupon—the development of the Universal *Purusha* idea following. He devoted his attention principally to building up a *Raja Yoga* system of 'methods,' 'practices,' etc., whereby man might be able to unfold certain latent forces within himself, and to raise himself by such unfoldment to a higher perception of universal laws and principles, to the end that he might escape the thraldom of material life, and rise to a higher state, and then on to the ultimate 'Union with God.'

In his *Raja Yoga, Patanjali* has much to say regarding the subject of Chitta, or Mind-Stuff, which both he and *Kapila* conceived of as being material, rather than spiritual; holding it as evolved from *Prakriti*, and being entirely distinct from the *Purusha* or *Atman*, which is considered the Real Self and which uses Mind as an instrument. *Patanjali* taught that *'Chitta'* or Mind-Stuff was the finer material out of which Mind, as we know it, is created—the more subtle element which manifests as operating Mind. The Organs of Sense; the Mind of Thought (*manas*); the determinative faculty (*buddhi*); the Self-consciousness (*ahamkara*); form a class called the *Antakharana*, the 'Internal Instruments,' and are considered as but various modifications of *Chitta*, or elemental Mind-Stuff. What are called *'Vritti,'* are 'whirlpools' or 'vortexes' in the *Chitta*. To restrain these whirlpools of Mind, or *Vrittis*, and to compel a calmness in the ocean of Mind, or *Chitta*, is the object of the *Yogin*, and forms an important part of the *Raja Yoga* of *Patanjali*.

Patanjali in his *Raja Yoga* taught that there are eight stages of approach—Eight Steps—leading to Attainment. The Eight Steps are as follows : (1) Self-control (*yama*); (2) Religious Duty (*niyama*); (3) Postures (*asana*); (4) Control of the *Prana* or Vital Forces (*pranayama*); (5) Control of the Senses (*pratyahara*); (6) Control of the Mind (*dharana*); (7) Meditation (*dhyana*); (8) Transcendental Contemplation or Ecstasy (*samadhi*). These eight steps are described as follows :

(1) Self-control (*yama*) consists of right relations and justice toward living beings; mercy; kindness; love; non-injury; non-stealing; truthfulness ; chastity; non-covetousness; and non-acceptance of gifts.

(2) Religious Duty (*niyama*) consists of inward and outward purity—that is, purity of thought as well as of action; contentment; avoidance of luxury, sensuousness and worldly vanity; performance of the religious duties of the individual's sect; and earnest and constant love of the Lord.

(3) Postures (*asana*) consisted of the control of the body, and the assuming of certain bodily postures, which were thought to be valuable in the following Steps.

(4) Control of *Prana* or Vital Forces (*pranayama*) consists chiefly of certain methods of Psychic Breathing, principally Rhythmic Breathing, having three forms, namely, inhalation, exhalation, and retention of the breath.

(5) Control of the Senses (*pratyahara*) consists of the absolute mastery of the senses, under the control of the Will, whereby they may be withdrawn from their respective and customary objects of sense, and either held in abeyance or else transmuted to certain psychic functions. This step is regarded as preparatory to the following ones.

(6) Control of the Mind (*dharana*) consists of divesting

the Mind of the influence of the senses, desires, emotions, etc., so that it may be held firmly and under perfect control. *Patanjali* gives many methods whereby this control may be acquired, but such are not apt to appeal to the Western mind, being more or less in the nature of auto-hypnotization which is not desirable or helpful. The more rational methods of the occultists by which the mind is naturally controlled, instead of 'hypnotized-byself,' are far preferable. (We have given these latter methods in our work on '*Raja Yoga*," in preference to those of *Patanjali*, which we consider undesirable and partaking too much of certain reprehensible psychic methods and practices).

(7) Meditation (*dhyana*) consists of the fixing and concentring of the mind on some one object of knowledge, preferably the Universal Soul, or *Purusha*, so as to exclude every other consideration, object or thought. *Patanjali* gives many methods of bringing about this condition, some of which are akin to the practice known to Western 'New thought' people under the various forms of "Going into the Silence," while others are rather too much inclined to the production of abnormal, negative psychic conditions to appeal to advanced occultists who have given the subject careful consideration. We do not advise the following of many of these methods, believing them to be undesirable, and because we believe that the end may be obtained more naturally and normally.

(8) Transcendental Contemplation, or Ecstasy (*samadhi*) consists of the production of, or entering into, the transcendental state known to all Mystics, of whatever age or country they may belong, and which we have described in our 'Fourteen Lessons' and in our 'Advanced Course' as 'Spiritual Consciousness,' and which others in the Western world have called 'Cosmic Consciousness'. This state is a mystic phase of consciousness, and cannot be well described to those who have not experienced it, even by those who have, it being beyond words. We feel, however, that many

of the cases claimed to be 'Spiritual Consciousness' are merely certain lower forms or phases of psychic phenomena, depending more or less upon the emotions. And we feel that many of the Hindus claiming to have attained *Samadhi* by means of the *Patanjali Yoga* methods, are mistaken, and have experienced merely some of these lower stages mentioned. The attainment of *Samadhi* is rare, and almost always brings in its train a subsequent spiritual illumination, and mental advancement, which is typical of the experience, but which is sadly lacking in many of these cases of psychic experiences. The latter are as but the pale and sickly glare of the Moon, as contrasted with the bright, warm, radiant beams of the Sun—in fact, occultists use the terms Sunlight and Moonlight to distinguish between real spiritual illumination and the mock-phenomenon of psychic astral experiences.

The first principle impressed upon the mind of the student of *Patanjali's Raja Yoga* is that the Mind is not the Soul, nor the Self. The Self is the *Purusha*, or Spirit, of which you have been informed in our lesson on the *Sankhya* philosophy—the Soul is the *Purusha* surrounded by its *Tattvas* or Semi-material principles including Mind—and Mind, or *Manas*, is the instrument of the Self and used by the latter for impression from, and expression in, the phenomenal world. The *Yoga* Philosophy follows the *Sankhya* in teaching that all perception of the outside world comes from the sense organs, and all action in the outer world is performed by the organs of action. And back of the organs of sense and action, there are the Psychic Faculties controlling physical organs. And, starting with this fundamental conception, *Patanjali* builds up a system of Mental Control whereby the organs of action, the organs of sense, the deliberative faculties, the emotions, the imagination, and in fact the whole mental organism may be controlled and mastered. In our own work on *Raja Yoga* we have given the phases of the Mental Control and Mastery which will appeal more strongly to the Western mind. We shall now give the phases that attract the majority of the Hindus to the philosophy, practice and methods.

Let us begin with the Fourth Step—*Pranayama*— Control of the *Prana*, or Vital Forces. *Prana* is the Universal Principle of Energy, manifesting in all forms of Energy, including, Vital Force. And *Pranayama* is the Control of this Universal Energy, particularly in its form of Vital Force. The *Yogins* consider this control, if acquired to a high degree, gives one the mastery of the other manifestations of *Prana*, and is the Secret of Power. The first step toward Control of *Prana* is the control of the portion of *Prana* manifesting in our individual bodies and minds—so this is the natural place at which to begin, says the *Yogin*. The *Prana* within you is the little inlet from the great ocean of *Prana*, and here is where you are to begin your Control of it. But there is a more subtle form of *Prana* within your organism than even the Vital Force in its manifestation of bodily activity. There is a Psychic *Prana*, which is manifested in mental action, nerve force, etc. And as the mental and nervous energies are nearer to the 'I' than are the bodily forces, the student is taught to begin at this point in his *Pranayama*. And here is the method prescribed.

The *Yogins* teach that there are two currents of *Prana* (called *Pingala* and *Ida*) travelling along the spinal column, moving on either side of a canal or tube in the spinal column which the Hindus call Shusumna, and which is at the centre of the substance of the spinal cord. At the lower end of the *Shusumna* is a triangular form of subtle substance called by the Hindus "The Lotus Chamber of the *Kundalini*," which contains a stowed-up and latent force called *Kundalini*. This *Kundalini* is held to be a wonderfully potent occult force, which, if it is aroused and induced to ascend the *Shusumna*, will produce wonderful psychic effects, opening up many planes of psychic activity undreamed of by the ordinary person, and which, when it finally reaches the brain, tends to free the soul from the bondage of matter, and causes the *Yogin* to become a Superman.

The *Pingala* is the nerve-current running along the right side of *Shusumna*—the *Ida* is the left-side current. Along the *Shusumna* are several 'lotuses' or centres of psychic activity, beginning with one at the base, called *Muladhara,* and ending in the brain is the chief lotus, called the *Sahasrara,* or thousand petalled lotus in the brain. This *Shusumna,* with its storage-batteries of lotuses, is regarded as a great psychic battery of force, which may be set into motion by and regulated by certain *Yoga* systems of Breathing, particularly along the lines of Rhythmic Breathing. And this Rhythmic Breathing is held to arouse the latent forces of the *Kundalini.* And from the arousing of the *Kundalini* and its controlled action and direction is said to rise the Supernatural (so-called) Powers claimed by the *Yogins,* of which we have spoken in another part of this lesson. And the science of arousing this *Kundalini* is known as *Pranayama,* the Fourth Step of Attainment of *Patanjali.*

The primal point in the exercises of *Pranayama* is the arousing of rhythmic vibration by means of controlled breathing, thus setting into motion the vibrations which arouse the *Kundalini,* by which certain psychic phenomena are produced—and at the same time to control, direct and concentrate the *Prana,* or nerve-force, with which the system is filled, and which the various ganglia, or plexi, in the body, particularly the great Solar Plexus, serve to store as great storage-batteries.

In connection with *Prana,* which the *Yogins* call the Fourth Step, there is put into operation the practice of the Third Step, known as Postures (*asana*), upon which the *Yogins* place great attention and to which they ascribe great merit. There are a great variety of these Postures used by the *Yogins,* and there have been a number of Hindu books written for the purpose of explaining the details of them. Some of the Postures are very intricate, the strained and unnatural positions usually ascribed to the gods in the Hindu Pantheon, and which are shown by their images, pictures, etc., giving an idea of the difficulty of assuming them. In fact, one would have to be a trained and developed contortionist in order to assume them. Some of the ascetics carry this idea of the Postures to an absurd extent, and spend their lives with their bodies twisted and contorted into abnormal and unnatural postures—deeming the same a mark of piety, holiness, and attainment—much to the sorrow and disgust of the philosophical Hindu.

The simple Posture usually taught to the student who wishes to acquire the science and method of *Pranayama,* is that of the 'Yogi Seat,' which consists in the person seating himself on the ground, or floor, easily and well balanced, the spinal column being kept upright and straight so that the spinal cord be allowed to hang freely and unrestricted within its natural channel. The head, neck, and chest must be so held that a straight line would pass directly through the centre of each.

Then the Breathing is taught, beginning with the cultivation of the natural measured breath, inhaling slowly, retaining a moment under control, and then exhaling slowly, carrying the sacred word 'Om' in the mind, and accompanying the inhalations and exhalations, thus serving as a rhythmic accompaniment to the incoming and outgoing breath.

The next step is the Single Nostril Breath—the *Ida* current being held to pass through the left nostril, while the *Pingala* current passes through the right nostril. The student is taught to close the right nostril, and then, breathing through the left nostril, he directs the *Ida* current down through the spinal cord by concentrating his attention upon the descending nerve current, the operation tending to arouse the basic lotus in which is stored up the *Kundalini.* When the *Ida* current has been inhaled, and the nerve force direct to the *Kundalini* storehouse, the breath is retained for a few moments, with the thought that you are passing it through the lotus and over to the right side or the channel of the *Pingala* current.

Then exhale it slowly through the *Pingala* channel, through the right nostril, closing the left nostril while so doing. The favourite method taught beginners is to close the right nostril while inhaling through the left; then to pinch both nostrils tight while you are passing the current through the *Kundalini* store-house; then release the right nostril as you exhale. Then the process is reversed, the breath being inhaled through the right, held a moment with nostrils closed, and then exhaled through the left nostril.

The centre of the spinal cord contains the channel which the *Yogins* call the *Shusumna*, of which we have spoken, and which is the channel through which the central current flows, the *Ida* and *Pingala* flowing on each side of the *Shusumna*. The *Shusumna* channel is closed to the ordinary person, for when it is opened the person becomes a *Yogin*, with psychic powers. Through the opened *Shusumna* the *Kundalini* arises and lifts the mind to the higher planes, say the *Yogins*. And so the 'stirring up' of the *Kundalini* in the basic plexus tends to cause it to mount, and thus open up the *Shusumna* a little each time, gradually and slowly. As the *Kundalini* mounts it arouses the activities in the several lotuses along the spinal column, connected with the *Shusumna*. The lowest of these lotuses—the one situated at the base of the column—is called the *Muladhara*; the one next above is called the *Svadhisthana*; the next is called the *Anahata*; the next is called the *Visuddha*; the next is called the *Ajna*; the last, which is in the brain, being called the *Sahasrara*, or 'the thousand-petalled lotus.' In the lowest, or *Muladhara*, the *Kundalini* is stored up; and the highest, or the *Sahasrara*, is used to distribute it to the brain, in the production of certain forms of mental phenomena.

Then the student is taught of the virtues of the *Ojas*, which is a highly concentrated form of energy stored away in the brain, or that lotus called the *Sahasrara*. This *Ojas* is held to be the energy that manifests in intellectual power and spiritual force. *Ojas* is held to be the source of the subtle power known to the Western world as 'Personal Magnetism.' But *Ojas* is not confined to the brain, but a certain amount of it is distributed all over the system. The lower forces of the body may be transformed into *Ojas*, says the *Yogin*, particularly the energy of the Sex Nature, and so he devotes much attention to this transmutation—hence the advocacy of celibacy among many of the *Yogins* and ascetics.

The next grade in the instruction is that of *Pratyahara* or the process of making the mind introspective—that is, turning it back upon itself, and releasing it from the power of outward impressions. This is a form of Mental Control, of course, and requires much practice and perseverance. The student is taught by various, tedious and complicated exercises to get perfect control of his mind, so that he may inhibit the impressions from the outside world at will.

The next step in the class is that of *Dharana*, which is the acquiring of 'One-Pointedness,' whereby the mind may be concentrated to one particular point of thought—focused like the sun in a sun-glass. This is what is known as "Concentration" in the West. This step is also gained only by long and persistent practice, extending over years, and with attention to details that are distracting to the average Westerner who attempts them. This *Dharana* or Concentration is held to be the basis of the higher *Yogin* powers, and psychic states, and until this is mastered there can be no further progress.

The higher *Yogin* states, as taught by *Patanjali*, are known as (1) *Dhyana*, or Meditation, which is called the Seventh Step of *Patanjali*, and which consists of the fixing of the mind in the most profound meditation, upon some one object of knowledge, preferably the Universal Soul or *Purusha*; and (2) *Samadhi*, or Transcendental Contemplation, or Ecstasy, which produces what the Western World calls "Cosmic Consciousness," and which we have described in previous series of lessons, under the term of 'Spiritual Consciousness,' and which is *Patanjali's* Eighth Step. This mental state has been described as a state of Super-consciousness, and is quite difficult of description or definition. It is an exalted state of ecstasy, such as has been sought after by mystics of all times and lands, and which is regarded by them, and the *Yogins*, as almost akin to 'Union with God,' nothing but the last material sheath remaining between the worshipper and the object of his devotions.

The Three Higher Steps, *viz.*, *Dharana*, *Dhyana*, and *Samadhi*, together, are called *Samyama*. In *Samyama*, the Mind is first taught to concentrate absolutely *(dharana)*; then to meditate profoundly upon some higher plane or object or thought (*dhyana*); then to rise to the super-conscious state (*samadhi*). And this three-fold *Samyama* is what the school of *Patanjali* makes a prime object of life—the attainment of *Samadhi* being regarded as the Supreme Goal of the Living *Yogin*—the final step toward absolute Union and Freedom.

And the above, together with the performance of good works; the observance of duties; morality; austerities; self-denial; the repetition of sacred *Mantrams*; and the performance of the fundamental religious precepts of the Vedas, is what constitutes *Patanjali's Raja Yoga*, which is the embodiment of the 'practical' part of his system.

The followers of *Patanjali* claim that the absolute mastery of the 'Eight Steps' causes the *Yogin* (or advanced student of the philosophy) to reach the stage of 'Superman,' developing in him certain latent powers of mind which enable him to transcend the experience of the ordinary individual. Among other results claimed by them, as being in the possession of the *Yogin*, are the following : A knowledge of Past and Future Events (clairvoyance); a knowledge of the language of the animals, so that he may converse with, understand, and be understood by, them; knowledge of one's past incarnations, and those of others; prophecy and foresight as to future events; ability to send the mind to distant worlds and perceive the events transpiring there—a form of travelling in the astral; the clairvoyant ability to see into one's own body, the bodies of others, and into the ground. And, in short, the majority of functions and 'powers' which are generally grouped under the head of 'psychic phenomena,' and many of which are possessed by persons of merely abnormal psychic development, possessed of but little spirituality or spiritual power, in the true sense of the word.

While there is much of real value along the lines of true *Raja Yoga* in *Patanjali's* System, there is undoubtedly much of the false *Raja Yoga* there also, the latter producing not Mental Control and Mental Power, but merely Abnormal Psychic Development, which is condemned by all true occultists. This fact has brought the system into more or less disrepute among true occultists and students of the spiritual philosophies of India, and which has caused many of them to avoid '*Yoga* Methods' as a poisonous thing. But it is scarcely just to condemn the entire system far the weeds it contains—it is better to destroy the weeds, and allow the flowers and wholesome fruit to grow the better for the elimination.

In addition to the 'powers' above mentioned, claimed to be possible to the *Yogin* who practises the methods and who masters the practice of *Samyama*, or Restraint, there are others, known to the followers of the system as "The Eight Superior Powers," which are given as follows : (1) The Power of Shrinking to the Size of the Smallest Atom; (2) The Power of Becoming Extremely Light; (3) The Power of Becoming Extremely Heavy; (4) The Power of Unlimited Extension of the Sense Organs; (5) The Power of Irresistible Will; (6) The Power of Obtaining Unlimited Dominion Over Everything; (7) The Power of Control of the Powers of Nature; (8) The Power of Transporting Oneself Anywhere at Will. We shall not enter into a discussion of these claims, and content ourselves with saying that many of these claimed powers are possible only to the most advanced Adepts, who have risen to exalted spiritual heights, and who may have passed beyond the limits of experience and life of the ordinary man. Whether or not these magnificent powers may be developed and acquired by an ordinary individual, by the practice of certain 'methods' without regard to the acquirement of high spiritual knowledge and attainment, we leave to the judgment of our students. Certainly India shows us no examples of mere Method-*Yogins* manifesting any such godlike powers. Adepts there are in India, but they are not Method-*Yogins*, but great souls, developed and unfolded spiritually, who smile pityingly upon these so-called *Yogins* who spend their time endeavouring to "break into the Kingdom of Heaven" by means of Postures, Exercises, and Methods.

Another set of powers claimed by the *Yogins* of the *Patanjali* school is that of "seeing all things at once," which power is said to be derived from the practice of Concentration upon the smallest division, in thought, of Time and Space, and the combination of these divisions into larger groups of 'time and units' and 'space units,' etc., by which means. Time and Space are annihilated, and all things appear simultaneously in Time and Space. As to this, we would say that the highest Hindu Philosophers teach that there is no limit to the mental subdivision of Time and Space, and that the process is infinite; therefore there can be no such thing as an absolute 'unit' of Time or Space, for if such unit could be thought of, the next thought would be able to divide it into two, or into a million parts, and so on to infinity and eternity. Thought of this nature, as to Time or Space, inevitably leads the thinker back to THAT, or the Absolute, wherein Time and Space vanish. Moreover, the best Hindu Teachings hold firmly to the idea that "seeing the universe as One in Time and Space" is an attribute of Deity, to whom Time and Space are as *Maya*, Illusion; *Avidya* or Ignorance— therefore the claim of the: *Yogins* is slightly presumptuous, unless the "seeing" is admitted to be a mental realization of the Illusion of Time and Space, as the *Vedantists* teach, whereupon the "miracle" vanishes.

We do not wish to appear as in any way hostile to this part of *Patanjali*'s teachings, nor to be captious in our criticism of them, but, nevertheless, we feel that we should endeavour to point out what we consider the erroneous part of the philosophy, that it may be distinguished from that part which is undoubtedly good and helpful, so that the entire system may not be condemned for certain of its parts. That it is in danger of such condemnation is only too apparent to those who are familiar with the current trend of occult thought and opinion, and who are in touch with the best channels of thought along these lines at the present time. There is much that is very good in *Patanjali's* methods and system—particularly those portions of it in which the control, mastery of and development of the Mind is concerned—the methods by which the mind may be developed and shaped into a perfect instrument of impression and expression, by the Self, or "L" In our work on "*Raja Yoga*" we have endeavoured to bring out these parts of *Patanjali's* teaching, combining them with the teaching of many eclectic Hindu *Yogis*, and blending them with some of the methods of the Western schools of Occultism—but omitting the 'abnormal' and 'psychic' practices and methods. In the same way we endeavoured to purify the system of '*Hatha Yoga*,' which, strictly speaking, is the 'Science of Physical Well-Being,' but which many of the *Yogins* in India have prostituted by adding certain abnormal and revolting physical methods and practices, including the terrible excesses of ascetic self-torture, posture, etc., which are still more reprehensible than even the lower forms of the false *Raja Yoga* as favoured and practised by the Fakirs of India, posing as *Yogis* and Masters, and imposing upon credulous Western travellers as, the "real *Yogis* of India."

These absurd claims, abnormal conditions, unnatural

methods, and Moon-phenomena of Psychism, have tended to bring about the steady lack of philosophical interest in, and adherence to, the system on the part of educated Hindus. Many have passed on to the *Vedanta* for these reasons ; and others, who do not favour the *Vedanta*, have forsaken the school of *Patanjali* for the *Sankhya* System of *Kapila*. In this connection we bid you remember that *Patanjaii's Yoga* System does not include the entire *Yoga* Teachings of India. Far from it, for the entire Hindu Philosophy is permeated with *Yoga*, which means 'Union,' or methods leading to that Union—and also methods of attaining Mental Control. *Patanjali's* System is called the "*Yoga* System" merely because of the importance he placed upon the *Yoga* methods as laid down by him. And in justice to him it should be said that the decline of the, importance of his system is due not so much to his original teachings, or the change of public opinion, but to the additions and changes wrought by the more extreme and unphilosophical of his followers, as above described. To read the Aphorisms of *Patanjali* one may see how different a thing may become from the original plans of its architect. The *Yoga* System of *Patanjali* to-day is kept alive in India principally by reason of the interest in certain of its methods, exercise, and practices—its philosophical importance has departed, and outside of the schools of its teachers one hears but little of its original philosophy, which, after all, was merely *Kapila's*—plus a Personal God, and with a super added System of Methods. And, by the irony of Change, much of the really valuable part of the *Yoga* Methods was afterward absorbed into the body of the *Vedanta* System, which finds room for all that is valuable and useful—which 'takes its own wherever it finds it.'

'Yoga' in its formerly generally understood and commonly accepted meaning in India meant 'union'; 'yoking-up'; 'joining,' etc., being symbolic of the union of the individual soul with the divine—the relative with the real—the finite with the infinite—that is the original meaning

of *'Yoga'* and *'Yogi'* in the Hindu Philosophies. But the prevalence of *Patanjali's Yoga* System, and particularly the methods and practice enjoined therein, has caused the term to acquire a secondary meaning among the Hindus, and it is now commonly used in the sense of "effort; exercise; exertion; concentration," etc., the spirit being lost sight of by reason of the consideration of methods, and means. In *Patanjali's* First Aphorism, the term is used in the sense of : "The control, or suppression, of *Chitta* (mind-stuff or mental principle)."

And, as we have said, *Patanjali's Yoga* System has lost much of its original philosophical significance, and is being regarded more and more in its aspect of a system of exercises, methods, etc., and is being studied by many for the purpose of the attainment of psychical powers, often for the purpose of selfish use and employment, although this use of the powers supposed to attend the practice of the methods is expressly condemned by *Patanjali* himself, as is also the acquirement of these powers for show purposes, public exhibitions, vainglory, notoriety, etc. The founder's teachings were that the practices, exercises, and methods are to be employed solely for the purpose of developing the mind so that it could contemplate clearly, and freely receive, the Truth which leads to Emancipation and Freedom of the Soul—as a means of subduing the body, and mind, that the Spirit might overcome the material restraints, obstacles, and confining and restraining sheaths, and come once more to its own blissful condition of rest and peace above and beyond the storm of the world of *Samsara*.

But, nevertheless, the fact remains that the teachings have been allowed to be overshadowed by the practices, and exercise, and methods, until now *'Yoga'* means the latter instead of the former, to the minds of many in India and in the West. As a standard work of reference says on this subject : "The great power which the *Yoga* System of Philosophy has at all periods exercised on the Hindu mind, is less derived from its philosophical speculations, or its moral injunctions, than from the wonderful effects which the *Yoga* practices are supposed to produce, and from the countenance they give to the favourite tendency of orthodox Hinduism, the performance of austerities." And, indeed, this is true, in its latter sense, as well as the former, for there is not a self-tortured Fakir (or false *Yogi*) in India who does not claim the authority of *Yoga* for his revolting practices and terrible self-tortures—his sitting in one position for years; his fasting and emaciated condition; his withered arm held erect for years; his finger-nails growing through the palms of his hands; his matted locks serving as a bird's nest; his indescribable filth and squalor—for such are among the forms of the prostitution of the *Yoga* by the fanatics and self-deluded enthusiasts, whose name in India is legion. And there is not a juggling and conjuring Fakir in India, whether his tricks be performed by pure imposture, or whether by developed powers of concentration and hypnotic methods (see our lesson on Hindu Wonder-Working), who does not claim the authority of Yoga as the basis of his work. Could *Patanjali* have seen the perverted application and consequences of his teachings—could he have foreseen the prostitution of his valuable methods, exercises, and practices—he would have hesitated to give them to the world. He warned against such perversion and prostitution, so far as he thought it necessary—but see the result of telling people "how to do things," even from the best motives and intent. And still people ask why the Adepts do not give their higher teachings, and instructions as to the attainment of occult power, to the general public. The Fakirs and false *Yogis* of India, and the dark practices of some of the Western dabblers in occult practices—these are the answers to that question.

And even aside from these things, and viewing the higher aspect of the case, it must be admitted that the so-called 'practical side' of *Patanjali's* teachings has caused his philosophical doctrine to be overlooked, as we have said, and as says a well-known authority: "The *Yoga* is in truth *a system of practical discipline* for effecting the ultimate release of the *Purushas* from the entangling bondage of matter"; and his philosophy is described and dismissed, with the conclusion so well expressed by the same authority, who says: "The *Yoga* theories of knowledge, cosmology, physiology, and psychology are essentially those of the *Sankhya;* and the goal of final deliverance is conceived originally in the same manner." And so *Patanjali,* the great Hindu teacher and philosopher, is now regarded in philosophical history as "the man who gave us the *Raja Yoga* methods, exercise, and practices in his Aphorisms." So much for "being practical," even in India, that land which the West believes to abhor the practical side of things.

SPECIAL MESSAGE V

By Yogi Ramacharaka

We continue this month the consideration of the Axioms of Truth, those symbols whereby we seek to enter into an understanding of the nature of Truth. By the employment of these symbolic Axioms we may be partially able to picture to ourselves more clearly the nature of Truth, in our relation to it. We now invite you to consider the two following Axioms of Truth and what follows.

VII. We may consider TRUTH by means of the symbol of Love. We know that there is an All-Love, just as we know that there is an All-Good. The highest regions of our being convey to us this report and message. And TRUTH, being the only possible source of Love, must be the All-Love. There is nothing else to be the All-Love but TRUTH. TRUTH is more than All-Loving it is All-Love itself. There can be no real Love outside of, or apart from, TRUTH. All real Love must proceed from, be exprssed, manifested or emanated by TRUTH. All else is Untruth.

VIII. We may consider TRUTH by the means of the symbol of Life. We know that there is life in the universe, for we see it on all sides, and our reason informs us that it must proceed from a common source. TRUTH being the only Being, Existence and Substance, must be the only thing that can possess the All-Life. TRUTH is more than the possession of All-Life ; it is All-Life itself. There can be no Life outside of or apart from TRUTH for there is nowhere else or anything else, from which Life could have proceeded. And all the Life apparent to our perceptions must have been manifested, expressed or emanated by or from TRUTH. All other Life is Untruth.

The above statements concerning TRUTH are what is known as The Axioms of TRUTH. That is, they are Statements of Truth, which are self-evident to any mind that will earnestly consider them, and do not need proof or argument. These Axioms contain the report of the highest planes of the Mind of Man, as well as of his Reason. They constitute the Basic Principles of the Science of Truth, and as we proceed we shall have frequent need to refer to them. So we advise each student to ponder carefully these Axioms, and to commit them to Memory, so far as is possible.

In our message of next month we shall give you the Axiomic Summary, whereby you may be enabled more readily to fix in your mind and memory the fundamental principles of the symbolic axioms.

Our Meditation for the coming month is :

"TRUTH IS ALL-LOVE; TRUTH IS ALL-LIFE. OUTSIDE OF TRUTH THERE CAN BE NO LOVE; NO LIFE. ALL-LOVE AND ALL-LIFE PROCEED FROM TRUTH, AND ARE ASPECTS AND SYMBOLS OF ITS ALLNESS."

Chapter VI

The Minor Systems

Of the six principal philosophical systems of India, the *Vedanta* is by far the most important, judging from the careful attention to the details of thought, the height of speculative reasoning attained, and the growing popularity of the system in modern times among the educated classes of its native land. Next to the *Vedanta* comes the *Sankhya* System, which still has many influential followers in India, and which is interwoven into many of the native religious systems and teachings, and which has had a profound influence on certain phases of the Western thought, notably the school of Schopenhauer and his followers. The *Yoga* System of *Patanjali*, once so powerful, has diminished in power and influence, until to-day it exists principally in its forms of *Yoga* practices and methods, its philosophical aspect having been obscured. And as for the remaining three systems—the *Vaisheshika* System of *Kanada*; the *Nyaya* System of *Gotama*; and the *Purva Mimansa* System of *Jaimini*, respectively, it must be admitted that they have rapidly diminished in influence, and have dwindled away in the number of their followers, until to-day they remain as but shadows of their former selves, the remaining systems having proved more fit to survive by reason of the greater vitality of their doctrines, and by the adaptability of their teachings to the requirements of the modern Hindu mind. But as any work on the Philosophical Systems of India would be incomplete without a reference to, and a consideration of, these three minor systems ; and as the general philosophical system of India may be better understood after an examination into the principles of these dying systems, we now invite your attention to them, considered severally, in the present lesson, in which we will endeavour to present the vital, fundamental principles of each in a concise, clear form, without wandering into the by-paths of the details of the doctrines.

The Vaisheshika System

The first and by far the most important of these Three Minor Systems is that known as the *Vaisheshika* System of *Kanada*, which is believed to be older than the *Vedanta* System, the exact date of the forming of the school, however, being unknown. It is believed to have been-founded by *Kanada* several centuries prior to the Christian Era, and since that time has had many influential teachers and commentators, many voluminous works having been written on the teachings in the early centuries of our era. Its name is derived from its doctrine of atomic individualities (*visheshas*), which is one of its fundamental doctrines. The system has been called the 'Philosophy of Discrimination.'

Kanada, the founder of the system, taught that the phenomenal universe was composed of Six Categories (*padarthas*)—a 'category,' as we know, being a term employed in the science of Logic, and which Webster defines as "One of the highest classes to which the objects of knowledge or thought can be reduced, and by which they can be arranged in a system; an ultimate conception"; the term implying something absolute in nature, and not hypothetical or relative, or admitting of exceptions—something final. The *Vaisheshika* doctrine is that after the period of Cosmic Rest, or the Night of *Brahm*, in which cosmic activity ceases—and at the beginning of the period of Cosmic Activity or the Day of *Brahm*—the new universe is begun by the operation of the 'stored-up *Karma*' or 'essence of Activities' arising from previous universes, and which energy has lain dormant throughout the Night of *Brahm*. Like other systems, the principal aim is to teach the Science of Deliverance from material life—an escape from *Samsara*, or the Wheel of Rebirth, and an entrance into the state of Pure Being, which exists 'Behind the Veil.' This Deliverance, *Kanada* teaches, is to be gained only by the perception of the real nature of the Soul, and the unreality of Matter; and this perception depends upon the knowledge of the truth summed up in the *Vaisheshika* doctrine of the Six Categories. Hence the importance of these Six Categories of *Kanada*, which we shall now consider, and upon which the distinctive character of this philosophy depends.

Kanada based his philosophy upon the fundamental basis of the existence of Six Categories and ultimate classes of phenomenal objects or things, qualities or principles. These Six Categories are as follows :

I. *Drava*, or Substance, which is described as "the innermost cause of the aggregated, collective effect"; the fundamental substratum of phenomena, in which all properties and qualities, inhere, and in which all action occurs. This *Drava*, or Substance, is held to be nine-fold, *viz.*: (1) Earth; (2) Water; (3) Light; (4) Air; (5) Ether; (6) Time; (7) Space; (8) Soul or Self (*atman*); (9) Mind (*manas*).

II. *Guna*, or Qualities (which must not be confounded with the Three *Gunas* of Qualities, of the *Sankhya* Philosophy of *Kapila*, as stated in our Third Lesson), which inhere in Drava, or Substance, and which give rise to the differences in the latter. *Kanada*, in his system, enumerates seventeen *Gunas*, or Qualities, as follows : (1) Colour; (2) Taste; (3) Odour; (4) Touch; (5) Number; (6) Dimension; (7) Individuality; (8) Conjunction ; (9) Priority; (10) Posteriority; (11) Understanding; (I2) Pleasure; (13) Pain; (14) Desire; (15) Aversion; (16) Volition; (17) Gravity. Later teachers of the *Vaisheshika* added the following seven additional *Gunas* or Qualities : (18) Disjunction; (19) Fluidity; (20) Viscidity; (21) Sound; (22) Merit; (23) Demerit; (24) Self-restitution. The teachers of the *Vaisheshika* hold firmly to the theory that these

Gunas or Qualities are inherent in and belong to the substance of the Soul, as well as to the substance of matter, which is directly opposed to the teachings of the *Sankhyas* and the *Vedantists* (see lessons on these respective Systems), who hold that the Self or Soul is free from the Qualities, in its real nature, and only becomes subject to them by its entanglement with *Prakriti*, or *Maya*, according to the respective teachings.

III. *Karma*, or Action, which is held to consist of Motion only, and to be inherent in and manifested by Substance, or *Drava*, alone, and which must not be confounded with *Karma* in its other meaning, *i.e.*, as Spiritual Cause and Effect. This *Karma*, or Action, of the *Vaisheshikas*, is divided into Five Motions, as follows: (1) Upward Motion; (2) Downward Motion; (3) Contraction; (4) Expansion; (5) Change of Position.

According to the *Vaisheshikas*, all objective knowledge consists in the perception of things in their three Categories, or *Padarthas*, *i.e.*, of *Drava*, or Substance; *Guna*, or Quality; or *Karma*, or Action, respectively—these three Categories, or *Padarthas*, being basic and fundamental, universal and general. The three remaining Categories, or *Padarthas*, are as follows :

IV. *Samanya*, or Generality, which relates to a genus, or kind, and which the *Vaisheshikas* hold abides in Substance, Quality and Action, and which is of two kinds, viz. : (1) the Higher, or Genus; and (2) the Lower, or Species.

V. *Vishesha*, or Atomic Individuality, or Separateness, which is held to abide in the Eternal Substances, by which is meant Mind, Soul, Time, Space, Ether, Earth, Water, Light, and Air (see first Category—*Drava*, or Substance). This *Vishesha* is the distinguishing feature of the *Vaisheshika* Philosophy, and from whence its name is derived. Its theory and doctrine is that all Substances are composed of countless minute, invisible Atoms, from the combinations of which all forms of substance, physical and mental, arise, and from the operation of which all phenomena are occasioned. These Atoms are held to be so minute that they may be said to lack physical and spacial dimensions, when alone, and even when combined in pairs; but when three combine they form a larger atom, or molecule, and then acquire dimensions and may be said to occupy space. These Ultimate Atoms are held to be homogeneous, that is, "of the same kind and nature," but are exclusive in nature, and can never 'blend' with each other, but may only form combinations in which the separate atomic individuality of each is preserved. These combinations of the Ultimate Atoms are merely temporary, and are subject to change, destruction and alteration, so far as the combinations are concerned, but the individual Atoms, of course, can neither be destroyed nor changed nor altered in their nature. The student of philosophy must see in this *Vaisheshika* teaching the fundamental ideas which were afterward advanced by Democritus, the early Greek philosopher, who is generally regarded as the father of the Atomic Theory; and which are now advanced and held by the most advanced modern Western scientists. Even the destruction of the former Atomic Theory of the West, and its replacement by the Corpuscular Theory, is in accordance with *Kanada's* teaching, in which he held that the Ultimate Atoms were invisible and without dimensions, while in combination they became visible and acquired dimension—the Ultimate Atom of *Kanada* being similar to the Corpuscle, Ion, or Electron of Twentieth Century Western Science in its last conclusions and theories.

VI. The sixth and last of the Categories, or *Padarthas* is that of *Samavaya*, or Coherence, whereby the parts of certain inseparable things are held together in their respective places. These 'Inseparable Things' of *Kanada*, for which this Sixth Category is required, are rather abstract in nature, the following 'parts' in 'coherence' being mentioned as examples of the nature of the Category, *viz.*: The Parts and the Whole; Quality and the Object Qualified; Action and Agent; Atoms and Substance; Subject and Object, etc., etc.

In addition to the Six *Padarthas,* or Categories, the Later Teachings of the *Vaisheshika* add a Seventh Category, or *Padartha,* which is called *Abhava,* or Non-Existence, and which is divided by the teachers into four classes, *viz.* : (1) Non-Existence which is without beginning, but which has an end; (2) Non-Existence which has a beginning but no end; (3) Non-Existence which has neither beginning nor end; and (4) Non-Existence which is the negation of identity. Many of the *Vaisheshikas* vigorously oppose this Seventh Category, claiming it to be unwarranted and unnecessary, and also unphilosophical and contrary to the trend of Hindu thought and common sense. We mention it here merely for the purpose of calling the attention of the student to it, for we feel that it has no real place in the *Vaisheshika* System. It is about as non-understandable as some of the most difficult propositions of Hegel, the German metaphysician.

Kanada teaches that 'Understanding' is the Quality, or *Guna,* of the Soul, and that the Instruments of Understanding are Perception and Inference. He holds that the Ultimate Atoms were not created by the Logos, *Ishwara,* or Personal God of the Universe, but are co-eternal with Him; but that He holds the power which forms the combination and aggregates of the Ultimate Atoms, and from which all the phenomenal forms, shapes and varieties of 'things' in the universe arise. This God, however, must not be mistaken for THAT, or *Brahman,* but is in the nature of a Personal God, *Ishwara,* or Logos, which in turn is an emanation from and manifestation of THAT, or *Brahman.* The Hindu Philosophies which admit the existence of this Personal God, or *Ishwara* are called 'theistic'; while those who deny it are often called 'atheistic' by their opponents. But the term 'atheistic,' as used by the Hindus, has an entirely different significance and meaning from that of the Western world, and refers simply to the Personal Deity—for both 'theistic' and 'atheistic' philosophies in India admit the existence of and are, in fact, based upon the idea of the existence of THAT, or *Brahman,* from which All proceeds. *Kanada* teaches the existence of this Personal God, *Ishwara*, Logos, or Demiurge, who is regarded as the Lord and Ruler of the Universe, but who is destined to pass away with His universe when the Day of *Brahm* ceases, as He emerged from *Brahman* when the Day of *Brahm* began.

You must remember that the *Vaisheshika* teaches the existence of countless atomic individual Souls, or Selves (*Atman*)—see the First Category—and these Souls are eternal with *Ishwara* or the Personal God, and were not created by Him, although He rules them. These Souls incarnate in other forms of substance, and work their way upward toward Freedom just as do the *Purushas* of the *Sankhya* System of *Kapila*—in fact, the teachings on this point are almost identical in the two systems. Mind is held to be composed of Ultimate Atoms, as is everything else, according to this philosophy, but it is entirely separate from the Souls which use Mind as their instrument of expression. The *Atman*, Self, or Soul, however, is regarded as possessing Qualities, or *Gunas*, which oppose the teachings of the *Vedanta* and the *Sankhya*, which hold that the Soul is above qualities, which arise only from the Soul's descent into material life and activity. As we said at the beginning of the lesson, the *Vaisheshikas* teach that the soul's Liberation from Bondage is attained by the perfection and freedom arising from a comprehension of the nature and causes of the phenomenal world—and that a comprehension of the same is to be obtained only by an understanding of the truth of the Six Categories—and as the Six Categories are taught only by the *Vaisheshika* School, it would follow that one must be a *Vaisheshika* in order to win Emancipation, Perfection and Freedom, which renders the System rather more narrow than its companion systems, and which, in spite of its many excellent qualities and phases of excellent scientific truth, has caused it to be rejected as too narrow by the thinkers of India, which has contributed to its losing popularity and strength. Its principal field of usefulness now is in the sense of giving to other systems, particularly to the Eclectic Systems, bits of philosophical, metaphysical and scientific truths, which may be assimilated with their own truths. As a separate system the *Vaisheshika* has not proven its fitness to survive and flourish, and it seems to be on the decline in India, and attracts but little interest in the Western world.

The Purva Mimansa System

The second of the Three Minor Systems of Hindu Philosophy is that known as the *Purva Mimansa* System of *Jaimini*, which is based upon the attainment of the Freedom of the Soul by means of the observance of the orthodox rites, ceremonies, worship, prayer, etc., as taught in the *Vedas*, or great religious works of the Hindus, principally along the lines of *Karma Yoga*, or the Philosophy of Work and Action, which is one of the Three *Yoga* Paths of Liberation of which so much is heard in all of the Hindu Teachings and Religions. The first of these Three *Yoga* Paths is that of *Gnani Yoga*, or the *Yoga* of Wisdom, which is the Path favoured by the *Vedantists*, and which consists in the understanding of the great underlying Truths concerning THAT and the Universe, and which is also the favourite Path of the *Sankhyas* and of the *Vaisheshikas*, of whom we have just spoken—the Vedantists paying more attention to the understanding of THAT, while the *Vaisheshikas* devote their principal attention to the understanding of the Universe in its phases of Soul and Substance; the *Sankhyas* also devoting more consideration to the question of the 'How' of the phenomenal world, and universal life, than to the subject of THAT in the abstract as apart from the universe. The second of these Three *Yoga* Paths is that of *Raja Yoga*, which consists in the mastery of the Mind and Body by the Self or Soul, by the operation of the Will, and according to certain methods, including Rhythmic Breathing, etc., and which also has its phases of the development of Psychic Power. (See our works on *Raja*

Yoga, and The Science of Breath, as well as our lesson on the *Yoga* System in this series, and which is the Path favoured by *Patanjali* in his *Yoga* System). The third of the Three *Yoga* Paths is that of *Karma Yoga*, or Liberation through Works and Action, and which, as we have stated, is the Path favoured by *Jaimini* in his *Purva Mimansa* System, which we are now about to consider.

The term *Purva Mimansa* is derived from two Sanskrit words, the first, 'Purva,' meaning 'prior, former, or previous,'; the second, '*Mimansa*,' meaning "investigation, research, or examination." The term is used in contradistinction to "*Uttara Mimansa*," or "subsequent, final, or last investigation, research, or examination," and which is one of the original names applied to the celebrated *Vedanta* System. So, you see, the very name of this system implies a certain orthodoxy and conservatism at variance with the latter and more advanced forms and systems of philosophy. And the name of the system is not a misnomer, for the *Purva Mimansa* is indeed an 'orthodox' system, and is favoured by the orthodox schools of religion in India, particularly the less progressive denominations and cults, who adhere to the old forms and ceremonies, deeming them sacred by reason of their antiquity, and resisting any new ideas or interpre-tations as "meddling with the ancient sacred teachings of the *Vedas*." *Purva Mimansa* is naturally the philosophical system favoured by the more conservative of the orthodox priesthood of India, for it is settled and not calculated to disturb the minds of the people with argument and investigation and 'thought'—for it is a philosophy of ritualism, form, ceremonies, creeds, dogmas, rites, and all that goes with that form of thought, or absence of thought, and which finds complete satisfaction in the contemplation of the observance of centuries-old ceremonies and ritual, in accordance with centuries-old formalized and crystallized creeds.

Purva Mimansa claims the divine inspiration of the *Vedas*, or Sacred Books of India, and also claims to be the philosophy based upon the ancient interpretations of these books. While the majority of the Hindu philosophies proudly boast that they are not "religions founded upon a book," *Purva Mimansa* comes very near to being such a school of thought. The majority of the Hindu philosophies claim to be based upon Pure Reason, and while they take pleasure in showing that their teachings are supported by passages in the *Vedas*, they do not claim that their systems of thought are founded upon the same, and many of them expressly teach that if the text of the *Vedas* conflict with the report of Pure Reason, the latter shall be given precedence and the *Vedas* dismissed as either error, or truth not correctly stated, or perhaps misunderstood. But not so with the *Purva Mimansa*—this system does not attempt to place Pure Reason at the head and front of its system—it pushes to the fore the Sacred *Vedas*, as interpreted by its own teachers, and claims to be the Mouthpiece of the *Veda*, and the ancient source of interpretation and authority. Hence it is that it rightly is what it claims—extremely orthodox and having the weight of authority of ancient interpretation—it is indeed the 'Old School' of Hindu Philosophy.

Jaimini, the founder of this school, or rather the one who established the system under its present name by gathering together the ancient and most orthodox interpretations and collating them into a system, lived many centuries ago, the exact date having been lost, but it is believed that his system, even under its present name, has been in existence perhaps longer than many of the other systems, although some authorities hold that the system was established by him because of the rise of the *Sankhya*, the *Vaisheshika*, the *Yoga*, and the *Vedanta*, particularly the early stages of the latter; and for the purpose of counteracting the influence of the newer and heterodox schools of philosophy—a reactionary movement "back to first principles," as it were. From the beginning the system has been associated with extreme ceremonialism, and technical interpretations of the various rites, ritual, and forms prescribed in the various *Vedas*. It always has insisted upon the divine inspiration of the Sacred Books; their literal interpretation; their infallibility; their absoluteness as the Source of Truth; their completeness—all that was Truth was in the *Vedas*—all in the *Vedas* was Truth—and all that was not in the *Vedas* was not Truth; that the very words of the *Vedas* were sacred, not alone in the sense of expressing sacred truths, but in themselves as words; that man's only hope of freedom, salvation, and emancipation must come from a strict study and understanding of and an absolute belief in the *Vedas*, and their divine origin, as well as by the exact following of the precepts and injunctions contained therein, in accordance with the doctrines of the teachers and the 'letter of the law.'

The precepts of the *Vedas* were held to be the direct revelations and explicit teachings of God, and to be accepted as such without doubt, alteration, free interpretation, or "higher criticism." *Jaimini* insisted upon the sacred virtue of the words, before alluded to, holding that their presence in the *Vedas* was sufficient proof of the existence of the objects which the words symbolized. For instance, there are the Sanskrit words for "Sun, Moon and Stars" in the *Vedas*, consequently the sun, moon and stars exist—if the *Vedas* did not contain these words, there would be no such objects—the conception of "the word" and "the object" in the mind of God being correlated, simultaneous, and connected-in-action. Things not expressed in words in the *Vedas* were untrue, and non-existent. Consequently the *Vedic* "words" were of divine origin, as well as objects—both the "words" and the "relation of the words" are of divine origin, and eternal, and not the work of the mind of man. This idea of the eternal relation between thought, word, and object is gone into at great length in the writings of the *Purva Mimansa*, and while it is carried to the extent of absurdity, nevertheless it possesses an interest for the philosophical mind, when divested of its narrow association with "the sacred books," etc.

The *Purva Mimansa* philosophy has been exposed to the strange charge of 'atheism' on the part of some of its opponents—a strange charge surely for an 'orthodox' system which undoubtedly recognizes an *Ishwara* or Personal God, as well as *Brahman* or THAT which is at the basis of all Hindu Philosophy. The charge, which is absurd and unfounded, arises from the teachings of this system, to the effect that *Karma*, or Spiritual Cause and Effect, operates according to fixed and unchangeable laws, acting automatically and without reference to the will or wishes of *Ishwara* or God—that "works produce their fruit directly, without superhuman interference," instead of by the will of God exerted in each case according to His inclinations, desires, response-to-prayer, or other temporary inclination—in short, that *Karma* was a 'natural law' instead of an arbitrary dictate of Deity. To charge the *Purva Mimansa* with 'atheism' is so absurd that it seems almost that the accusation was made in an ironical spirit, and in derisive mockery, and in a tantalizing spirit toward the ancient authority. Its analogy in the Christian world would be the accusation of the old Presbyterian Church of 'atheism' because of the doctrine of Predestination.

The phase of the *Purva Mimansa* which is regarded as the most worthy of respect and philosophical interest is its teachings regarding '*Karma Yoga*'—the *Yoga* of Action and Works; and the corresponding teaching regarding *Dharma*. The 'Philosophy of Work,' in relation to the effects resulting therefrom, is discussed at great length in the *Purva Mimansa*. The various doctrinal points regarding 'the fruits of *Karma*' are gone into with a wonderful degree of clearness and wealth of detail and analysis, it being the boast of some of the old teachers of this system that by it they were able to point out the exact consequences of any single act, carried forward through a hundred incarnations. They would take up some little action, and show how, flowing from it, would emerge results of the greatest consequence to the individual and the world. Every tiny event and action became the parent of millions of results and consequences in the ages to come, so that one should observe the utmost care to perform proper actions and to generate good *Karma*, thereby avoiding the opposite, which would produce the most direful results. Anyone familiar with this line of reasoning from Cause to Effect, according to the great Law of Causality, may imagine to what great lengths these old teachers carried their doctrine and theories—and that without fear of successful contradiction. For instance, one might show how the fact of a dark-eyed maid raising her eyes and glancing at a passer-by in her village, a thousand years ago, set into motion a chain of cause and effect—action and consequences—which after the passage of nine centuries resulted in the birth of Napoleon Bonaparte, whose existence was productive of destructive wars, involving the death of hundreds of thousands of men, and the destruction of thousands of homes, and the production of many thousands of widows and orphans, and the expenditure of millions of treasure, and so on and on, with the numerous branches of subsequent effects resulting from Napoleon's life—all from the little roguish glancing of a pair of dark eyes on a warm summer day a thousand years ago. Verily these old *Purva Mimansa* teachers must have caused terror to the souls of their students and followers, who would be afraid to breathe, less a chain of cause and effect should thereby be started which might result in all sorts of trouble in the years to come. For such is the result of any doctrine when carried to its extreme limits of logical conclusion—a *Reductio ad Absurdum*, or reducing a proposition to an absurdity, or, in the common parlance, "carrying a good thing too far."

To the philosophical mind which has the inclination and time to delve into the extreme lengths of reasoning, and speculation, indulged by these old *Purva Mimansas*, the works of some of these old teachers would be a source of the greatest joy, and it is a pity that so little of their work is obtainable in translations. They built up a system appalling in its details, all dealing with "the Fruits of Action." Colebrook says of their work: "Each case is examined and determined upon general principles, and from the cases decided the principles may be collected. A well-ordered arrangement of them would constitute the philosophy of law; and this is, in truth, what has been attempted in the *Mimansa.*"

The real merit in the study of *Karma Yoga,* which is the Path of Liberty best suited for the everyday person who has not the mind for the higher Paths and studies, lies in the Essence of the Teachings, which is to the effect that the 'Fruits of Action' may be avoided in their *Karmic* effect, by the recognition of the nature of the Soul, and its relation to the Universe and to THAT. This recognition leads to the understanding of the performance of "good work, for work's sake," and the virtue of "performing action without hope of reward or fear of punishment"—the observance of the best that is in one—the doing of the best you know how, "without bribe of heaven, or fear of hell," from the pure joy of the doing. The Hindu teachers of *Karma Yoga* point out to the student that while seeds in their natural state always sprout and bring forth fruits, so do all actions bring forth *Karmic* fruits of effect. But that as the 'fried seeds' used in the Hindu cookery have the 'fruit-quality' killed within them, so are actions performed as a duty, and right, in accordance with the highest impulses of one's nature, and without hope of reward or fear of punishment—so are such actions 'fruitless' of a chain of binding consequences, which attach the soul to their *Karmic* results in future lives, but which, on the contrary, enable it to rise above the plane of desire and cause and effect resulting therefrom, and, spreading its wings, soar to higher planes of being as the eagle soars above the low-lying clouds of the lifting fog. As the old Hindu aphorism says: "Kill out Desire for Fruits of Thy Work—yet Work as do those who are consumed with the Desire for Fruits." Do the Best you

Know How—but leave the consequences in the hands of the gods, without any further concern on your part—wash your hands of the results of Work well Done in accordance with the Best That is In You. Such is the advice of the Wise of all Lands and Ages. Or, in the colloquialism of the American business man—"Do your very best, and let it go at that!" Or, in the words of the Persian poet:

- Do what thy manhood bids thee do, from none but self expect applause.
- He noblest lives and noblest dies who makes and keeps his self-made laws.
- All other life is living death, a world where none but phantoms dwell;
- A breath, a wind, a sound, a voice, a tinkling of the camel-bell.

In connection with *Karma Yoga*, the *Purva Mimansa* naturally takes up the subject of *Dharma* at great length. '*Dharma*' is the Sanskrit term, similar in meaning to "virtue; duty; law; righteousness; etc.," but none of which words convey its precise meaning. In a previous writing on the subject, we defined the term as follows: "*Dharma* is the rule of action and life best adapted to the requirements of the individual soul, and best calculated to aid that particular soul in the next higher step in its development. When we speak of a man's *Dharma* we mean the highest course of action for him, considering his development and the immediate needs of his soul." It is the Hindu Science of Ethics—the Philosophy of 'Right and Wrong'—the Rule of Conduct. It is a peculiar Rule of Action, viewed from our Western position, inasmuch as it does not claim to establish absolute positions of Right and Wrong, but rather adopts the idea which every thinking man has considered at some time—the position of things right "in their time and place, or under the circumstances and conditions"; or else wrong, from the same reasons and conditions. It is a science of the Evolution of Ethics, and inasmuch as it is so, it is in accordance with the teachings of the highest Western philosophy, although perhaps contrary to certain religious dogmas which persist in theory although abandoned in practice. The Hindu idea of '*Dharma*' includes Ethics based on Revelation, Higher Teachings, Intuition, Conscience, or Spirit, and Practical Utility—the system is catholic, eclectic and all-inclusive, you see, and is a study worthy of the attention of any and all students of philosophy, whether of the East or of the West. We cannot go into the subject here at greater length, and such would be beyond the scope and field of this series of lessons. (We must refer the student to our two lessons on '*Dharma*,' and the one lesson on '*Karma Yoga*,' in our work entitled "Advanced Course in *Yogi* Philosophy," published by the house that issues the present lesson).

And so this is the *Purva Mimansa* System of *Jaimini*, in its general outlines. Passing from view, as it is now in India, still its influence for the good has been apparent, and its 'fruits of good work' will live after it. Freed from its narrowness, and formalism, it contains many important truths, and emphasizes many points that the other systems were prone to overlook in their interest in others. And none need hesitate to give the system its proper place as one of the Six Great Pillars which support the great structure of the Temple of Hindu Philosophy.

The Nyaya System

The sixth, and latest in point of actual crystallization, of the Six Systems of Hindu Philosophy, is the *Nyaya* System formulated by *Gotama*; the history of the founder and the details of the formation of the school, as well as the exact date thereof, being unknown; the general opinion, however, being that the school was founded in the early centuries of the Christian Era, being based on older teachings, as indeed has been the case with all of the Six Systems in their present forms. *Gotama*, the founder of the *Nyaya* System, must not be confounded with *Gautama*, the *Buddha*, the founder of Buddhism—there is very little chance for this mistake, yet it has been made by Western writers and students, the similarity of the names having led them to believe that the two men were identical.

The term '*Nyaya*' is the Sanskrit word meaning 'Analysis,' and is bestowed upon this system by reason of the latter's analytical trend and nature. In fact, so much of the *Nyaya* teaching is devoted to the exposition of a system of logic, and an enunciation of the methods whereby Truth may be ascertained by logical process of examination and analysis, that many Western writers have assumed that the system was a school of Logic, ignoring the philosophical and metaphysical aspects of the teaching. The system, indeed, is dual, partaking of the nature of a school of Logical analysis, and also of philosophical and metaphysical reasoning and pronouncement of doctrine. Let us examine it in its Logical phase first, and then in its philosophical aspect.

Gotama, the founder of *Nyaya*, was distinctly a logician, and careful students of his work have accorded to him high rank in his class. By some he has been called the Aristotle of India, and he developed a distinctive system of Hindu Logic which compares very favourably with the Grecian systems. Davies says of his school of logic: "The right methods of reasoning have been discussed with as much subtlety as by any of the Western logicians." Some are inclined to the view that the Greek schools were indebted to the early Hindu systems, which were afterward combined, purified and crystallized by *Gotama*. Dutt says: "Comparing dates, we are disposed to say of this as of many other sciences, the Hindus invented Logic, the Greeks perfected it." *Gotama* eliminated many of the non-essentials and elaborate details of the previous Hindu logicians, and concentrated his attention upon forming a logical system in which "right reasoning and correct inference" was the keynote. Accordingly he devotes much time to the forming of scientific syllogisms, or logical forms of arguments in their parts or propositions. The Western syllogism consists of three parts, or propositions, viz., the two Premises (or presumed conditions) which form the basis of the argument; and the Conclusion, or the inference derived from the premises, and which follows them logically, and which concludes the argument. The Hindu syllogism of *Gotama* consists of five parts or propositions, *viz.* (1) the Premise; (2) the Proof ; (3) the Illustration; (4) the Application of the Proof; (5) the Conclusion.

Gotama held that the logical method of ascertaining Truth was by the application of the Sixteen Categories or *Padarthas*, sometimes called 'The Topics for Discussion.' These 'Topics' are as follows: (1) Means of Knowledge; (2) Objects of Inquiry; (3) Doubt; (4) Purpose; (5) Illustrative Precedent; (6) Dogma; (7) Syllogistic Premise; (8) Confutation; (9) Ascertainment; (10) Discussion; (11) Wrangling and 'Hair-Splitting'; (12) Cavilling; (13) Fallacy; (14) Prevarication; (15) Futile Objections; (16) Illogical Argument. The student is trained and drilled until he thoroughly understands the nature and use of each of these Sixteen Topics, and then only is he considered capable of conducting an examination into the subject of Ascertaining Truth, and rejecting Error. *Gotama* also held that the Channels of Knowledge were four, as follows: (1) Perception through the Senses; (2) Inference; (3) Analogy; and (4) Testimony of Others, according to the Laws of Evidence. The Twelve Objects of Knowledge, as stated by *Gotama*, are (1) The Soul; (2) the Body; (3) the Physical Organs of Sense; (4) Perception of the Objective World; (5) the Higher Consciousness; (6) the Mind; (7) the Will; (8) Error; (9) Disembodied States; (10) Karmic Law; (11) Pain; and (12) the Freedom, Emancipation and Deliverance of the Soul. *Gotama's* system laid especial stress upon the consideration of the nature of the Intellect, and the relation of articulate sound to objects, the latter being somewhat along the lines of the *Purva Mimansa* System of which we have spoken; and also to the consideration of the subjects of genus, variety, species, and the individual manifestations.

In many respects the *Nyaya* System is complementary to, and in almost perfect agreement with, the *Vaisheshika* System, of which we have spoken in the first part of this lesson. Together the *Nyaya* and the *Vaisheshika* systems may be said to form a philosophical group, although the *Nyaya* also has some affiliations with the *Purva Mimansa* in certain minor points of doctrine and teaching. Together with the *Vaisheshika*, the *Nyaya* adheres to the Atomic Theory of the Universe, and to the general logical arrangements and classification of ideas and subjects of thought. It holds that the Material Universe is atomic, and that the Souls are countless and become involved and entangled in Matter, just as do the other systems of Hindu philosophy, in one form or another. The Way of Liberation, Freedom and Emancipation is held to be attained only through the thorough knowledge of the *Nyaya* philosophy and methods, and the application of the same according to the principles laid down by the teachers; or as one writer has expressed it : "Final Beatitude arises from a proper comprehension of the Truth, as summarized in the Sixteen *Padarthas* of the *Nyaya*." Originally, the *Nyaya* System did not admit the existence of an *Ishwara*, Personal God, or World Soul, but afterward there crept in the doctrine of an *Ishwara* or Supreme Soul (*Para-Atman*) which regulated and maintained the Universe, creating and directing the formation of the combination of Atoms, and often taking an active part in the affairs of His universe, but who was not the Creator or Cause of the Souls or Atoms, the two latter being held to be co-existent with Him, although under His control and direction, subject to the higher Law, and all emanating from *Brahman* or THAT, and being destined to return to the Source from which they originated, at the close of the Day of *Brahm*.

Miscellaneous Systems

In addition to the Three Minor Systems which we have just considered there are several other minor systems with a number of followers, but which are but little known outside of India. These systems are rather more of religious systems, or systems of theology, than systems of philosophy, and advance no new conceptions or ideas, their efforts being in the direction of advancing certain theological dogmas, or the claims of certain priestly cults. To this class belongs the school founded by *Anandatirtha*, known as the *Purnaprajna* cult, and which is really a *Vishnuitic* sect or school of theology, devoted to the advancement of the worship of *Vishnu*. Similar in nature are the four schools of theology devoted to the worship of *Shiva*, the names of which sects are the *Nakulisa-Pasupata*; the *Pratyabhijna*; and the *Rasecavara*, respectively. All of the above mentioned five systems, schools or sects superimpose their theological teachings and dogmas upon a fundamental basis of philosophical thought derived from the *Vedanta* and *Sankhya* conceptions. There is also a sixth school, that claims rank as a philosophical system, namely, the school of *Panini*, which is really a system of grammatical science, coupled with an inquiry into the internal and external significance of sounds and the inner meaning of words, the latter resembling some of the tenets of the *Purva Mimansa* System considered in this lesson, and which holds that the word is merely the vehicle for the indwelling 'spirit' of thought, which is an eternal, indivisible, unitary Idea. Other religio-philosophical systems will be mentioned in our two lessons on 'Hindu Religions.'

Agnostic and Materialistic Systems

In addition to these metaphysical systems, there have existed from time immemorial various agnostic and materialistic cults in India, strange as the idea may be to the West. And, in fact, these Hindu agnostics and materialists, like their metaphysical brethren, have anticipated their Western counterparts by several centuries, and nearly every modern school of materialistic and agnostic Western thought can find its predecessor several centuries before the Christian Era in India. The early Buddhistic writings show that there were several schools of this kind in existence in India about the time of *Buddha* (B.C. 600). Among the early teachers of this kind may be mentioned the following contemporaries of *Buddha* :

Sanjaya, who founded a school of Agnosticism, holding that there was no basis of knowledge warranting the doctrines of Reincarnation and *Karma*, or survival of the soul;

Ajita, who founded a materialistic school, the tenets of which were that the universe had a purely material basis, no spirit being involved therein, and everything consisting of fire, water, air, and earth, from which everything was evolved, and into which everything would return;

Kassasapa, who founded a school of Indifferentism, the doctrine of which was that morality and immorality were but names, and that the laws of the universe were unmoral, that is neither moral nor immoral, and that the latter terms were inventions of men, and changed from time to time in their meaning and application; and that there was no such thing as merit or demerit for actions or deeds, as claimed by the current religions and philosophies, particularly the school of *Buddha*;

Makkhali, who founded a school of Determinism, holding that *Samsara*, or the Cycle of Existence, proceeded according to fixed and invariable laws, allowing of no voluntary choice or action, and therefore making of *Karma* a mechanical law instead of a moral one; and holding that everything and every individual worked out its own nature according to its inherent laws, without possibility of modification or control; the operative cause of all action being *Niyati*, which means Destiny, Fate or Logical Necessity.

The Charvakas

In addition to the above minor non-metaphysical schools, we find from the earliest days a school of Materialism in India, supporting various phases of that thought, the *Charvakas*, named after its founder, and which school is often called the *Lokayatika*. This school was founded nearly three thousand years ago. It was not only Materialistic, but also manifested various forms of Hedonism, with a tendency toward the "eat, drink, and be merry, for tomorrow we die" idea. The *Charvakas* held that Reality consists of the Principle of Matter, which is composed of the four elements of fire, air, water, and earth, respectively, from which the body is evolved, and the mind also. The soul was held to be merely the faculties of the mind, which perish at death. They held that perception is the sole means of knowledge, and experience the only basis. All future existence was denied by the *Charvakas*, and the believers in the current creeds and philosophies were derided for their credulity. The irony and sarcasm of the *Charvakas* was directed especially at the priests and the ecclesiastical machinery of the Hindu religions; the priests and Brahmins being derided as rogues robbing the people of their sustenance; the ritual was regarded as a farce, and sacrifices and offerings as clever means of the priests to subsist upon the ignorance of the masses; the *Vedas* were derided as wordy masses of drivel and falsehood and vain imaginings ; and the philosophers as cheats who "palm specious promises for gold"; God or *Brahman* was denied, and Matter was raised to the altar. Such was the ancient school of the *Charvakas*. The modern Hindu Materialistic school has softened the *Charvaka* teachings somewhat, and its doctrines and writings are now very similar to those of the Western materialistic school of the Nineteenth Century. A number of modern Hindus now affect the prevalent Agnosticism or Naturalism of the West, claiming to have 'advanced' beyond metaphysics and spiritualistic philosophy. But these dissenting thinkers are lost to sight among the millions of adherents of the old schools of thought.

SPECIAL MESSAGE VI

By Yogi Ramacharaka

In our messages of the past three months we have given you the Axioms of Truth—those symbols whereby we seek to enter into an understanding of the nature of Truth. We have given you these Axioms, as symbols for the reason that by reason of them our spiritual understanding is aided in unfoldment. We are unable to grasp the idea of the nature and essential Being of Truth, and must rest content with the statement that it is identical with Spirit, which also is ineffable and incapable of being expressed in relative terms. And only by the employment of symbols are we able to picture to ourselves the aspects of the nature of Truth, and our relation thereto. And so we have invited you to consider hese several symbolic axioms, from month to month. We have now given them to you in full. Meditate over them often that the Message of the Truth may sink into your consciousness, and there serve as the seed from which shall spring into being, and blossom and fruit, the glorious plant of the Spirit.

In order to give you the essence of the Axioms in a form that may be readily committed to memory, we herewith attach the following :

Axiomic Summary

Truth *IS*.

TRUTH is Real.

TRUTH is Spirit.

TRUTH is All-Substance.

TRUTH is All-Power.

TRUTH is All-Being.

TRUTH is All-Creative Activity.

TRUTH is All-Wisdom; All-Intelligence.

TRUTH is All-Good.

TRUTH is All-Love.

TRUTH is All-Life.

TRUTH is All That is; All That Can Be; All That Ever Has Been; and all else is Untruth, having no existence in TRUTH.

He or she who perceives TRUTH as the All-in-All has found Truth; he or she who fails to perceive this, is in the bonds of Untruth.

The opposite of TRUTH is Untruth, which has no real existence, but which masquerades as Reality and deludes the minds of those who are in Error, not having found TRUTH. Untruth is but the shadow of TRUTH. When TRUTH is discerned, Untruth disappears.

Our Meditation for the coming month is :

"TRUTY IS THAT WHICH IS; SPIRIT IS THAT WHICH TRUTH IS: TRUTH IS SPIRIT; SPIRIT IS TRUTH; TRUTH SPIRIT IS ALL THERE IS—ALL ELSE IS UNTRUTH."

Chapter VII

Buddhism

The term 'Buddhism' is applied both to the philosophy of *Gautama Buddha,* and also to the vast system of religion which has been evolved from his teachings, with its accompaniment or elaborate ceremonial and ritual, and which counts its followers to the number of perhaps three hundred million (300,000,000), principally in China, Japan and Thibet, and including about ten million (10,000,000) followers in India, chiefly in Burmah—the number of Buddhists in India proper, the land of its founder, having decreased until the religion is practically dead in the land of its origin, its philosophy being kept alive principally by its influence upon the surviving philosophies. In India, it still numbers followers among the Northern tribes, and is quite flourishing in the whole Indo-Chinese Peninsula, Burmah, Ceylon, Nepal, etc., but is almost unknown in the centre of India. It claims millions of followers in China and Japan, which are its great strongholds, and it has another great centre north of the Himalayas, in Thibet, where it is the prevailing religion, under the name of Lamaism. It is the popular religion among the entire Mongolian sections and peoples of Asia, and is found to the extreme north of Siberia, and even in Lapland. But the present form of the Buddhist religion, particularly as it appears among the Japanese and Chinese, and in Thibet—and the North generally—has very little resemblance to the original teachings of *Gautama*. The Buddhists of Burmah adhere more closely to the orthodox teachings, but even there Buddhism is held more as a religious system and 'church,' than as a philosophical system.

And yet the original philosophy of *Gautama Buddha* exerted a wonderful influence on the philosophical thought of India—and having played its part, it passed from the scene and now lives only in the shape of 'a religion,' and as the basis for the philosophical conceptions of others, East and West.

Buddhism dates back to about 600 B.C., the time of *Gautama* its founder, and has for its birthplace India. *Gautama*, the *Buddha*, was a prince by the name of *Siddhartha*, who was also known by the name of *Sakyamuni*, the term meaning "the solitary one of the family of *Sakya*." The term '*Buddha*' means the 'illumined mind,' or 'enlightenment,' and is a term bestowed upon *Gautama* by reason of his Spiritual Illumination. The titles of *Bhavagat*, or 'the Blessed one,' and the *Bodhisat* are also frequently used in reference to *Gautama*.

There is a great mass of legendary lore connected with the early life of *Gautama*, which has been carefully combined and beautifully stated in the poem entitled 'The Light of Asia,' by Edwin Arnold, the English poet. According to the legends *Gautama*, the prince *Siddhartha*, in his boyhood developed a tendency toward philosophical thought and speculation, and his father who desired him to become a famous warrior hastened him to an early marriage, and placed him in environments calculated to keep his mind away from the misery and pain of the world, and surrounded with the luxury and sensuous splendour of an Oriental court. All sickness, disease, and death was kept from the sight and knowledge of the prince, and nothing but brightness and joy was allowed to enter into his life. But, notwithstanding this, the young prince began to tire of the perpetual round of pleasure which palled upon him, and led him to declare that 'all is vanity' and idle dissipation, satisfying not the mind or the soul. One day, escaping from his bounds, he discovered that misery, pain and disease are the common occurrences of life, and that Death the Reaper ever stands ready to mow down man as the grass of the field. Behind all he heard ever 'the tinkle of the camel-bell,' as the Persian poet has called it—the warning of approaching death. He therefore determined to forsake all and become an ascetic, and in that life to seek the peace which the world had failed to give him. He escaped from his father's palace, and fled to the jungle. He met the various Brahmin philosophers, and studied their doctrines, but still peace evaded him. Asceticism and self-punishment also failed to bring the coveted reward. And so at last he came to the conclusion that Peace can come only from Within, and he began a life of meditation and mental self-examination, with concentration upon the idea of the Source of Pain and Sorrow.

He determined to conquer the difficulty by sheer force of Mind. And so he sat beneath the famous Bo-Tree for weeks at a time, plunged in the most profound meditation, and abstract thought. At last *Nirvana* or Transcendental Illumination came to him, and he saw clearly the cause of phenomenal life and the pain attendant thereupon, and also the Way of Escape. He saw that in *Samsara*, or the Cycle of Existences, is to be found the Source of Pain. For, he reasoned, if we were not born and reborn, we should not be subject to pain, sickness, misery, old age and death. And then reasoning backwards, he finds that the cause of *Samsara* lies in Desire, and its continuance upon Ignorance. Therefore, he who masters Ignorance, and who is strong enough to kill out Desire, may escape the bonds of *Samsara*, the Wheel of Life, and attain *Nirvana* or Peace. And then came the final stage, in which he set himself mentally free from *Samsara*, and attained *Nirvana* on earth, to be followed by *Para-Nirvana* after he passed from the body—the chain of Rebirth being broken, and *Samsara* being defeated. And then *Gautama* went forth as a teacher of Freedom and Emancipation, and the founder of his school of system, which afterward developed into the Buddhist religion and church. He made many and important converts, and firmly established his philosophical system, and his system of morality which rose therefrom, before his death, which occurred in *Kusinagara*.

Let us first examine the fundamental conceptions of the Buddhist system of philosophy. In the first place a reference to many of the English books upon Buddhism will give the student the impression that *Gautama* taught an atheistic philosophy, which closely approached materialism, denying any Reality back of phenomenal life, and refusing to admit the existence of *Brahman*; and that also he denied the existence of the 'soul,' although he explained Reincarnation under the 'desperate expedient' of *Karma*, which afforded a connecting link between the lives of the successive beings in the Chain of Rebirth or *Samsara*. On both of these points Western discussion has raged fiercely, some holding to the above ideas, while others attempted to combat them. We think that when the Fundamental Principles of the Inner Teachings of the Hindu Philosophies are applied to the teachings of *Buddha* order may be brought out of chaos. Such is the opinion of the advanced Hindu teachers (non-Buddhists, remember) who would protect *Gautama* from the attacks of his orthodox Hindu opponents, and the Western writers on Buddhism. Let us examine into the matter.

In the first place *Gautama did not deny* the existence of *Brahman*, but simply refused to speculate regarding Its nature, character and being, holding that the concern of man was with the phenomenal world and the escape therefrom—and that speculation upon *Brahman* was useless and a waste of time—"Enough to know that THAT is" was his idea. He denied the existence of *Ishwara*, the Personal God, of the Hindus, and thus brought upon himself the reproach of Atheism, which had also been visited upon the heads of *Kapila* and other philosophical teachers. But *Gautama did not deny* the existence of THAT—*he merely took it for granted without argument* as a fundamental axiomic truth. Nay, more, in his system he clearly indicated the existence of a *Para-Brahm*, or Supreme *Brahman*, that is a *Brahman* in the aspect of Non-Being, or Non-Manifestation.

Gautama has been described as postulating a 'Nothing'

from which the phenomenal universe emerged, and into which it would return. Now, anyone at all familiar with the fundamental conceptions of the Hindu philosophical thought knows that the one positive position from which the Hindu mind refuses to budge, is the idea that "Something never can come from nothing—nor can something be resolved into nothing "; or, as it is often expressed, "From nothing, nothing comes." And, moreover, to suppose that the *Nirvana*, or Soul Freedom, of *Gautama* was a state of 'nothingness' or annihilation, shows a profound ignorance of the fundamental conceptions of the Buddhist philosophy, as well as of the general Hindu, or even the general Oriental, thought, through all of which the thread of an Ultimate Universal Consciousness runs unbroken. And yet you will find the majority of Western writers on Buddhism assuring you that *Nirvana*, the goal of the Buddhist, is a "state of nothingness," or "a state of annihilation." *Nirvana* is "the annihilation of *Maya*"—a "blowing-out of *Avidya*, or Ignorance"—and a state of Universal Inner Consciousness, rather than an extinction of consciousness. And if these Western writers fail to grasp even this important point of the Buddhist teachings, how can you expect them to grasp the subtle minor points of doctrine ?

As we have said, *Gautama* refused to speculate upon The Absolute, THAT, *Brahman*, or the Noumenal. But instead of denying its existence, he merely treated it as an existent Unknowable, a position very similar to that of Herbert Spencer, the great English philosopher, whom men mistakenly call a 'materialist,' although he clearly and positively postulates an 'Unknowable' upon which the entire phenomenal universe or 'The Knowable' depends and is sustained. *Gautama* admits this Unknowable, and although he treats it as a Nothing, he does not claim it is Nothing—it is simply that which is entirely "Different from and Antecedent to Things." So subtle is *Gautama's* conception and analysis that it is no wonder that his meaning escapes the observation of the Western examiners of his teachings. For not only does he consider the Absolute-in-Action, or THAT Manifesting, as the Unknowable; but he also perceives to exist a *Para-Brahm*—that is THAT in its aspect of Rest and Not Activity—*Brahman* divested even of *Maya* and the Illusory Universe. To use Western terms *Gautama's* highest and ultimate conception was that of 'The Thing-in-Itself' with all of its manifestations vanished—the Absolute as Non-Being, as distinguished from The Absolute as Being. But as all advanced Western students of philosophy know full well, 'Non-Being' does not mean 'Nothing,' but is the term used to designate Reality in Pure Essence, as distinguished from Reality manifesting Relativity.

And so we state positively that a careful study of the original teachings of *Gautama* will reveal the fact that he *did not* teach the doctrine of Ultimate Nothingness or Nihilism; but that his 'No-Thing' was identical with the Western conception of Non-Being, which is really the highest conception of Reality 'beyond-Being'; and that he recognized THAT in its purest essence as the fundamental reality underlying all that is in appearance. Without this basic conception, the entire philosophy of *Gautama* would fall to the ground—would be meaningless—would be a doctrine of Something proceeding from Nothing and to Nothing returning in order to gain Freedom—a palpable absurdity lacking all sanity, and opposed to every principle and instinct of Hindu thought. *Gautama* indeed taught the Nothingness of the phenomenal life, or *Samsara*, even surpassing the *Advaitist Vedantists* in his conception of the nature of *Maya*, which he denounced as the purest Ignorance lacking even a shadow of Truth or Reality; a Lie in the mind of The Absolute. But upon THAT he founded his teachings—upon THAT which is ever present in all Hindu thought—THAT which if removed would bring all Hindu thought tumbling in shattered bits beyond possibility of repair or restoration. *Gautama* was considered as an iconoclast—an infidel—an 'atheist' even, in the eyes of the orthodox church of India—but he was not a Fool, claiming a NOTHING as a basis for All-Things. Surely the "interpreters" of *Buddha* have inverted his pyramid of thought.

While *Gautama* forbade all speculation regarding the nature of the Unknowable, holding that the ultimate questions could not be grasped by the human mind, although "all would be understood" when the state of *Nirvana* was reached, still from the sidelights which he threw upon his doctrines from time to time, it may be stated that his Inner Teachings (arising from his transcendental knowledge gained in his state of *Nirvana* or Illumination) were that the Fundamental Reality of THAT, in its Essence, was equivalent to NON-BEING, when contrasted with BEING as the human mind understands the latter term. Non-Being is *not* Non-Existenee, but rather *Existence in a state devoid of attributes, qualities, or activities, so far as manifestation is concerned, although all possible manifestation must be latent therein*—in fact the meaning of Non-Being may be stated as "*Being, in Latency.*" The distinction is highly metaphysical, but some of the Ancient Grecian philosophers, and those of the modern West, have recognized the distinction, and embodied it in their metaphysical systems; as for instance Hegel, who states that "Non-Being and Being are One." This conception of Non-Being is also recognized by certain Hindu metaphysicians who postulated a *Para-Brahm*, or Supreme *Brahm*, or Essential *Brahm*, beyond the *Brahman* in its phase of the Active Cause of the Universe. It is one of the very utmost tenuities or refinements of subtle distinction in metaphysical thought. And it is no wonder that *Gautama* was charged with advancing a doctrine of the 'Nothingness' of Reality, for to the average mind Non-Being must seem to partake more of Nothingness than of 'Thingness.' But *Gautama* saw the distinction, and indeed upon it depends his distinction between *Nirvana* and *Para-Nirvana*, as we shall see presently.

From Non-Being, or *Para-Brahm*, proceeded Being or

Brahman (although *Gautama* avoided the use of these customary terms, wishing to free his teachings from the conceptions attached to the old terminology). Non-Being was THAT—All that Is—and besides it was Nothing. And from Non-Being, or THAT, arose or proceeded Being or a manifestation as Universal Consciousness or Creative Mind, or Universal Soul. *Gautama* positively refused to explain, or to allow discussion upon the nature or 'reason' for this proceeding of manifestation of Being, claiming the ordinary mind could not grasp this Truth, but that it would be made plain and clear when the state of *Nirvana* was reached. Then Being proceeded to manifest the 'Lust-of-Life,' which corresponds closely to Schopenhauer's 'Will-to-Live' except that the latter is conceived as being a Thing in itself, while the 'Lust-of-Life' is merely a phenomenal manifestation or appearance. This Lust-of-Life arose from Being according to the 'Chain of Consequences ' or 'Causal Evolution,' which is stated as follows: first from *Avidya* or Ignorance arose Illusory Ideas or the Consciousness of Separateness; the Lust-of-Life, or Desire for Objective Experience; then the psychic basis for the Sense Organism; then the Contact through these sense organs with outside objects; then Vague Perception or Feeling; then Desire for Things; then Attachment to Objects then human Birth; and then the circumstances of Life, *viz.*, life, old age, death, grief, pain, etc.; the *Karma* arising from the life; then Rebirth, and—*Samsara*, until Emancipation or Freedom is gained. And *Avidya* or Ignorance was the beginning of the Chain and is the Final Enemy to be overthrown. And the prime form of Ignorance is the Illusion of Separateness.

The Lust-of-Life, judging from the many allusions to it on the part of *Gautama*, and the early Buddhist teachers and commentors, may be considered as a fierce, lustful longing, hunger or thirst for objective existence, acting along unconscious or instinctive lines, which afterward manifested consciousness in some of its forms of creation or manifestation; and which was manifested in everything from the atom to man, including the plant life, and the animal forms—in fact in all living things. Some have defined it as Life itself, as we understand it, in all of its manifestations and forms. Some have called it by the name of 'the Creative Will'; while others have identified it with 'Nature.' To all, however, it is recognized as meaning that instinctive, persistent, craving, striving, acting, doing, longing, changing, LIVING FORCE, that is ever manifesting through all the phenomenal shapes and forms in the world, creating, preserving, and then destroying each form. Constant change, and becoming—nothing remaining intact—building up, and tearing down—being born, growing, becoming old, dying—to be succeeded by other forms—new life springing from the very bodies of the dead forms. And this is the Lust-of-Life.

Gautama taught that the very Essence of the Lust-of-Life was *Kama*, or Desire. DESIRE was the moving spirit of the Lust-of-Life—its motive-force and inciter to action. Everything comes from Desire in one form or the other, and it is impossible to escape it except by killing it outright, taught *Gautama*. Renunciation of Desire is the only hope, said he to his disciples, and his entire teaching is bent toward this Renunciation of Life, by the Killing Out of Desire. This is the Keynote of *Gautama's* teaching, from first to last.

Arising from the Lust-of-Life, with its motive-force of Desire, arises *Samsara*, or the Cycle of Existence, which constitutes the world of error; guilt; sorrow; death; birth; decay; disappointment; suffering, and (unless escaped from) the endless, ceaseless cycle of rebirth, and re-embodiment under the Law of *Karma*. *Samsara* is held to be really naught but the result of Ignorance brought about by the Lust-of-Life, and the Desire for Expression in objective existence. But while it lasts it is terribly real—a Nightmare of the Self—and it will ever last until Desire is renounced, and Emancipation gained. Desire holds all in the embrace of *Samsara*, from the unconscious atoms, minerals, plants, and animals, until in man Desire culminates in manifestations of sensuality; striving for personal gain; selfish aims; personal desires, aversions, and inclinations—in short in all of the attributes of Personality, from which arises Selfishness, and Separateness.

The student will notice the similarity of *Gautama's* conception of the Lust-of-Life with the *Sankhyan* principle of *Prakriti*, and the *Vedantic* idea of the *Maya* overlying Reality, and from which spring the phenomenal life with its *Samsara*, or Cycle of Existences, from which the soul struggles to escape. This idea is ever present in the Hindu philosophies—the soul far from home, striving and struggling to find its way back to the shelter of Home. Even New-man, in his hymn, 'Lead, Kindly Light,' voices this intuitional conviction : " For I am a stranger, far from Home; Lead Thou me on!" Buddhism follows closely upon the older *Sankhyan* conception of the Spirit entangled in *Prakriti*, and striving to escape, although *Gautama* differs materially in his interpretation of the 'soul,' as we shall see presently. Prof. Garbe says in his "Philosophy of Ancient India": "The *Sankhya* system supplied, in all main outlines, the foundations of Jainism and Buddhism, two philosophically embellished religions, which start from the idea that this life is nothing but suffering, and always revert to that thought. According to them, the cause of suffering is the desire to live and enjoy the delights of the world, and in the last instance the 'ignorance' from which this desire proceeds; the means of the abolition of this ignorance, and therewith of suffering, is the annihilation of that desire, renunciation of the world, and a most boundless love toward all creatures."

And now, before proceeding to consider *Gautama's* plan for the escape of the suffering soul from *Samsara* let us first consider the second heresy of *Gautama* (according to his critics), namely, his denial of the existence of the soul, of which grave offence he has been charged by Hindu followers of opposing systems, who considered *Gautama* 'heterodox';

and also by the Western critics who failed to grasp the fundamental ideas of his doctrine, and who accuse him of inventing a mechanical *Karma* to connect the different lives, under the law of Reincarnation, in absence of the 'soul.' If there is no soul, objected these critics, how can rebirth occur?—what is there to reincarnate ? And yet see how easily the matter straightens itself out, when understood in the light of the general Hindu philosophy. Just as *Gautama* was called an 'atheist' because he refused to acknowledge *Ishwara*, so is he called a teacher of soullessness, because he will not admit the 'individual *Purushas*' of *Kapila*, although adopting the *Prakriti* conception of the latter teacher.

In the first place *Gautama*, holding that all the phenomenal world was *Maya* or Illusion, in its strictest sense and carried to its final logical conclusion, refused to admit of the existence of the individual soul, claiming that the sense of separateness was due solely to Avidya, or Ignorance, or Maya, or Illusion, and that there could be no such thing as an individual entity, or soul, in reality—as All was THAT and nothing else. Consequently, the individual soul was regarded as a part of the figment of an illusory phenomenal world. When examined carefully, it will be seen that *Gautama* claims nothing more, in this respect, than does the *Advaitist Vedanta* with its "*Tat tvam Asi*"—"THAT Thou art"—the individual soul being considered merely as the result of "the One appearing as the Many." But *Gautama* really goes a little further, and refuses to admit even the appearance of an individual soul, or spirit-entity, claiming that the same is not necessary to account for the sense of 'Personality,' or to explain Reincarnation. Critics have claimed that *Gautama* used 'the desperate expedient' of the principle of *Karma* to carry the effects of the causes of one life over into the next, which idea was held to postulate a great injustice, because it would be the bestowing upon one individual of the effects of causes generated by another individual. But this is not so, because the only 'individual' affected is the same in both cases, just as is the man of sixty the same 'individual' as the man of twenty, or the child of six, although appearing differently to an observer. The whole trouble arises from the understanding of the word 'soul.'

To the *Sankhyas* the 'soul' was the individual *Purusha*—an entity gathering to itself certain "qualities and attributes" from the mental evolution of the *Prakriti*—that is that a 'soul' was something different from its mind—being the 'spirit' or permanent thing, animating the mind or impermanent thing—the soul being a persistent Principle. Now *Gautama* would not admit this Principle of the individual 'soul,' even as being a manifestation of and one of the dual-principles emanated by THAT. Instead, he held that the only Spirit in man was the animating reflection or, manifestation of the undivided One Spirit of THAT; he holding that there was no separate 'soul' other than the 'CHARACTER' of the individual, which character consisted of the Attributes and Qualities of the man—his personal nature, or characteristics considered as a whole. This 'Character' he held was the only 'soul' that man had, or could have, and that it was that 'character' which reincarnated in a new body, under the laws of *Karma*. In other words, this Character was the essence of the man's thoughts and actions, held together firmly, and constituting an 'I' which was individual but which was not a real and eternal entity.

In discussing this point with the Brahmins, and he had many opportunities so to do, *Gautama* would illustrate it by comparing the 'soul' with a chariot, which was composed of wheels, body, axle, floor, tongue, etc., but which was 'nothing in itself' when these parts were taken away from it. So he held that if all the attributes were taken away from a man, there would be no 'soul' left. Or, another illustration, man's soul was like an Indian bulb akin to an onion, which when stripped of its successive layers of skin in search for the 'real onion' or 'the onion-in-itself,' resulted in nothing being left. His opponents would answer: "Yes, but there would remain the *Purusha*, or Spirit !" But *Gautama* would answer saying: " There would be naught remaining but the Spirit of THAT, the Unknowable—divest the man of his attributes or character, and there is nothing left but THAT which is No-Thing, and which is Unknowable!" And this is why they claimed that *Gautama* denied the immortal soul ! They overlooked the fact that this stripping away of the 'attributes' or 'characteristics' is just what *Gautama* sought to accomplish by killing out Desire, and thus resolving man back to THAT, or Non-Being, which indeed, in reality, was all that man was. Read this over, carefully, and you will see the finesse of *Gautama's* logic and reasoning, and why he out-reasoned the Brahmins.

A word here regarding the reason that *Gautama* and Buddhism always have been regarded as heterodox, and outside of the pale of the 'orthodox' Hindu philosophical systems. You will notice that Buddhism is always treated as 'an outside system.' You will notice that the 'Six Systems,' differing as they do from the orthodox religious dogmas of the Brahmins, and differing from each other, are still considered 'orthodox,' even though they deny the existence of every god in the Hindu Pantheon, as does *Kapila*, even to the extent of denying *Ishwara*, the Personal God of the Universe. And *Gautama's* Buddhism, which denies but little if anything more, is regarded as 'non-orthodox.' The reason is simple, when understood. And here it is: In India, among the Brahmins, or priestly caste, there exists a wonderful degree of liberty of philosophical or theological speculation, without the danger of being read out of the fold, or excommunication. No matter how bold the speculation, or how startling the doctrine, it is not opposed or considered non-orthodox, *providing always that the teachers recognize the inspiration of the Vedas; and providing still more strongly that they recognize the caste system of India*, particularly the high-nature of the Brahmin, or priestly caste, the members of which are considered to be 'twice-born' and almost sacred, and who take precedence of even Kings and Rulers, who are generally of the *Kshatriya* or warrior caste. The Brahmins were considered as little less than gods. Some of the old works contain sentences like this :—"There be two classes of gods—the real gods, and the Brahmins who expound the *Vedas*"; "The Brahmins are even more than gods, for do they not protect and supply with sacrifices the gods themselves ?" etc. And so it may be seen why adherence to the doctrine of the semi-divine priesthood, and the inspiration of the *Vedas* was considered a requisite to even this broad 'orthodoxy.' It is as if the Christian Church of the Middle Ages (or even later) were to have said, "Teach any philosophy that you wish, providing you always assert the inspiration of the Holy Scriptures, and the Virtue and Infallibility of the Church and Priesthood."

Now, while the teachers of the 'Six Systems' taught doctrines in direct variance with the orthodox teachings to the masses, still they never disputed the virtue of the *Vedas*, and were free with the texts from the same—in fact they built up their systems on the teachings of the *Upanishads*, as interpreted by themselves. And they always bowed to the Caste System, and the Virtue of the Brahmins, and so were considered 'orthodox.' It was more of an acknowledgment of the authority of the Brahmins than any agreement to the teachings of the Church. But *Buddha* would have none of this. He taught Universal Brotherhood, and did much to weaken the hold of the Caste System. He neither denied nor affirmed the infallibility of the *Vedas*—but largely ignored them, and built up his system on human reason aided by Transcendental Illumination. *Gautama* opposed the system of sacrifices, and denounced the ceremonies and the ritual as of no avail. He also condemned the practice of austerities and self-torture. He taught Democracy and Universal Brotherly Love. All men were his brothers, *Sudra* and Brahmin alike. Is it any wonder that he was considered 'non-orthodox' by the priestly caste, and denounced for 'atheism'; and 'denying the existence of the soul'—even when he went no further in those directions than did many others of 'orthodox' tendencies ?

Gautama has also been charged with 'materialism,' and 'earthliness,' because he refused to encourage speculation regarding subjects outside of the earth life and the duties concerning the same. This course he followed because he saw that the Hindu people had lost sight of 'works' by dwelling too much upon doctrine, and he sought to awaken them to an activity Here and Now. Not only did he teach them 'to do things' in the direction of attaining Freedom and Emancipation, but he inculcated new truths regarding human duties toward one's fellow men, comparable only to the teaching in this direction of Jesus of Nazareth, who followed him six hundred years later. Prof. Jackson says: "The element in Buddhism which more than any other, perhaps, gave it an advantage over all surrounding religions, and led to its surprising extension, was the spirit of universal charity and sympathy that it breathed, as contrasted with the exclusiveness of caste. In this respect, it held much the same relation to Brahminism that Christianity did to Judaism. It was, in fact, a reaction against the exclusiveness and formalism of Brahminism—an attempt to render it more catholic, and to throw off its intolerable burden of ceremonies. Buddhism did not expressly abolish caste, but only declared that all followers of the Buddha who embraced the religious life were thereby released from its restrictions; in the bosom of a community who had all equally renounced the world, high and low, the twice born Brahmin and the outcast were brethren. This was the very way that Christianity dealt with the slavery of the ancient world." And Max Müller says : "The *Buddha* addressed himself to all castes and outcasts. He promised salvation to all; and he commanded his disciples to preach his doctrine in all places and to all men. A sense of duty, extending from the narrow limits of the house, the village, and the country, to the widest circle of mankind, a feeling of sympathy and brotherhood to all men, the idea, in fact, of humanity, were first pronounced by *Buddha*."

Gautama held that the Fundamental Cause of Suffering and Unhappiness in *Samsara* was the Sense of Separateness by which the 'I' was deluded or hypnotized. This sense of Separateness brought in its train Selfishness, Greed, Strife, Conflict, and all the other evil manifestations that make of life in *Samsara* a nightmare of suffering. In other words, Separateness is the Root of Evil, and all manifestations of evil may be traced back to its common source. And therefore all of *Gautama*'s teachings were directed toward escape from this illusion of Separateness, by means of killing out the Desire which was its very life energy. And all of the vague longing that possesses the human soul arises from an intuitive realization that it belongs to a Larger Life, and that Separateness prevents it from realizing Itself. The essence of the doctrine seems to be the following conception, although its original purity has been clouded by the additions of the 'church' which has arisen from the teachings, and which has covered over the light of the true teachings by the coloured shade of ecclesiasticism. But this seems to be the original teaching :

That, from Not-Being, or THAT, emerged a portion, or aspect of Itself which manifested as Being, which in turn manifesting the 'Chain of Consequences,' evolved the Lust-of-Life, the moving principle of which is *Kama* or Desire, and from which arose *Samsara*, or the Cycle of Existences—the Wheel of Life. The *Avidya*, or Ignorance, from which arose the Lust-of-Life and Desire, had as its essence the illusion of personality, or separateness—the breaking up of the Cosmic Consciousness into countless 'personalities' or centres of consciousness of qualities which men call 'souls.' The 'souls' are not entities but merely aggregates of qualities and attributes, composing 'characters,' which are illumined and energized by the One Spirit of THAT, which appears as the Many Spirits of the 'souls,' by reason of the illusion.

Intuitively every 'soul' feels that it is really identical with the universal life and soul, and experiences unhappiness and uneasiness by reason of its isolation, and yearns to return to its original state of Oneness. And the selfish life, aims, thoughts and actions engendered by this illusion of Separateness brings into existence Evil, with its multitudinous train of manifestations and consequences. Each Desire brings forth a brood of new Desires, and the soul is bound fast in the entanglements of *Karmic* Cause and Effect. The only escape is by first learning the Cause of Evil, and then proceeding to eradicate it, working from the manifestation back to the cause, and then back until Freedom is obtained. Thus by killing out all Desire, one strips the Lust-of-Life of its power, and renders it easy to be overcome. The Lust-of-Life once overcome, the 'soul' realizes that it is not a personality or separate entity, but that it is Being itself—that is THAT in the state of creative activity. Thus the 'soul' as a personality disappears, for when the soul perceives that it is the Universal Being, then all sense of separateness is dissolved—"the dewdrop slips into the shining sea"—the 'character' dissolves and the Spirit alone remains. And then still there is another stage, when finally the liberated soul, surrendering all—even its Cosmic Consciousness or Being—retires into the very heart of THAT—into *Para-Brahm*—the Abysmal Abyss—or Non-Being—and attains *Para-Nirvana*, the Bliss Absolute. Such is the Essence of Buddhism.

Gautama taught the Four Truths of Salvation, which must be grasped by all Seekers of Escape : (1) The Truth of Suffering, or the realization that Life is indeed Suffering; (2) The Truth of the Cause of Suffering, or the Lust-of-Life fed by Desire; (3) The Truth of the Cessation of Suffering, or the knowledge that in the overcoming of the Lust-of-Life lies the cessation of *Samsara*; (4) The Truth of The Path that leads to the Cessation of Suffering, or the methods of killing out

Desire, whereby the Lust-of-Life is overcome and Freedom gained.

Gautama taught that if the Desires were killed out, then the 'character' or 'personality,' which is composed of the qualities and attributes engendered by Desire, must dissolve, leaving the Spirit intact and unclouded, no longer deluded by the sense of Separateness, and realizing its identity with The Whole—THAT. Therefore anything that tended to kill out Desire was a step on The Path. He had experienced, in his own life, the sense of the futility of ceremonialism and ritual, and had tested asceticism and austerities, and proved them worthless. Therefore all that remained for the Seeker after Freedom to do was to 'kill out Desire.' Here is where *Gautama* struck a new note in India. Not by violent repression of Desire was it killed, he argued—for that only fed the appetite of the beast by arousing an internal hunger. But by avoiding all Selfish acts and devoting one's life to unselfish deeds, and acts of service to one's fellows—by Love for All Living Things. *Gautama* held that by thus turning the Life Energies out towards others, Selfishness was dissolved and disappeared and the mind was purged of Desire and the Lust-of-Life was overcome, and *Nirvana* reached. This was The Path of the Cessation of Suffering.

It will be noticed that in the majority of the Hindu philosophies, Freedom and Emancipation were held to be gained by the ultimate absorption of the Individual Soul in the Universal Soul or *Brahman*. The *Advaitist Vedanta*, not believing in the absolute existence of the Individual Soul, holds the Emancipation comes from the individual (who is really *Brahman* in disguise—deluded by *Maya*) awakening to a realization that he is not an individual, but is *Brahman* himself. Buddhism, not recognizing an Individual Soul, or even the temporary phenomenal separate entity called soul—the Buddhist 'soul' being but a bundle of desires, habits, etc., called 'Character,' illumined by the One Spirit—does not lead the 'soul' to Recognition of the Real Self in the manner of the

Advaitist Vedanta, but instead reaches the Emancipation by leading the mind to a knowledge of the true state of affairs; teaching it that it, as a soul, does not exist ; and then bidding it to deliberately destroy and dissolve itself by the burning out and destroying of Desire—to the end that finally when all Desire is burned out and destroyed, then the 'soul' will vanish and the Real Self alone will be left in its place. *Nirvana* is the state of actual realization of the Oneness of Life—and that the Many are One. *Para-Nirvana* is the withdrawal from Activity entirely, and dissolving into *Para-Brahm*, or Non-Being, to return no more in incarnation—*Samsara* entirely escaped. *Nirvana* is attained in the flesh, and is not an 'annihilation' as has been taught, but a state of Cosmic Consciousness—a glimpse of the *Sat-Chit-Ananda*, or Existence-Knowledge-Bliss Absolute—a Desireless Being. The soul may pass out of the body after Nirvana, and may dwell on certain planes of Being, helping the race to escape its bondage—such are the Masters and Adepts, of which we have heard—the Elder Brethren of the Race, who forego the Bliss Absolute for aeons in order to render service to the race. But beyond it all is the entrance into *Para-Nirvana*—dissolution into *Para-Brahm*—sinking into the Abysmal Abyss—Eternal Peace and Rest Absolute.

Gautama's Way of Escape comprised Eight Points, namely: (1) Right Faith; (2) Right Judgment; (3) Right Speech; (4) Right Purpose; (5) Right Action; (6) Right Endeavour; (7) Right Thinking; (8) Right Meditation. These Eight Points in the Way of Escape, may be understood only by a comprehension of *Gautama's* 'Concatenation of Causes,' or 'Chain of Causation,' which is based upon the fundamental idea of the Second Truth of Salvation, namely, The Cause of Suffering, which holds that the Cause of Pain and Suffering is the Lust-of-Life and Desire; the immediate Cause of Pain is Birth, for were we not born we would not suffer; Birth, in turn, is caused by the *Karma* of previous existences, of which it is a continuation and effect, and the 'character' or soul is the result of the experiences of the past; Reincarnation and *Karma*, in turn have their cause in previous Desire; Desire is held to be caused by Perception; and Perception by Contact; and finally Ideas are held to be an early Cause; and Ideas are held to be the result of *Avidya* or Ignorance, which mistakes the illusory and transitory for the real and permanent; therefore *Avidya* or Ignorance is the Root of Causes to be attacked. And *Avidya* is destroyed by opening the windows of the mind and letting the Sunshine of Truth pour in, which will dispel the darkness of *Avidya—Vidya* or Knowledge is the antidote for *Avidya* or Ignorance. Destroy *Avidya* or Ignorance, and the resulting 'Chain of Consequences,' *viz.*, Illusory Ideas; Distinction of Forms; Sense Impressions; Contact; Perception; Desire; Attachment; Existence; Birth; Misery; Old Age; Death—*Samsara, Maya*, Illusion—all vanish, and *Nirvana* is attained.

We shall not take up space to enumerate the exhaustive moral code of Buddhism. Enough to say that it formulates a moral code going to the extreme detail of conduct, embracing the world-ideas of honesty, chastity, kindness, unselfishness, morality, benevolence, truth, etc., etc. The greater part of this code is the work of the teachers who followed *Buddha*, and the various later Church Councils arising from the crystallizing of *Buddha's* teachings into a 'Church.' As usual in such cases, the Church has invented many new forms, ceremonials, and dogmas, and has had many schisms and subdivisions in denominations. In the South, the division of the Buddhists which is called 'Southern Buddhism' has held nearer to the original teachings than has 'Northern Buddhism,' which has added and changed materially, particularly in the direction of altering *Gautama*'s original conception of the 'soul' as 'character,' and replacing it with an individual soul or *Purusha*. The Church has added many 'heavens and hells,' particularly the latter, of which there are several hundred; the period of sojourn in some of these hells being as high as ten millions of years, and being as full of torture as the orthodox Middle-Age Christian Hell. In some of the highest heavens, the happy soul is held to dwell for as long as ten billion years. And so it goes, as 'churches' and priests have ever gone—building up an edifice of dogma and creed, ritual and ceremonial upon simple philosophical teaching. The doctrine of *Karma* has been so distorted that it now forms the most effective ecclesiastical weapon of rule ever invented by the mind of man. The Church teaches that a man is born blind because he looked too much upon the things of sense in past lives; that he is deaf because in past lives he would not listen to the teachings of the doctrine and creeds; that he is dumb because in a past life he mocked and reviled the priests—and so on, according to the custom of the Church everywhere. In the North, Buddhism is taught under the name of *Lamaism*, with elaborate ceremonialism and ritual. Northern Buddhism is so rich in ritual and ceremony that the early Jesuit missionaries, finding the ritual and forms bearing such a remarkable resemblance to some of the ceremonies and ritual of their own church, reported that it was undoubtedly the work of the Devil, who had invented Buddhism as a mockery of the True Church. Northern India, and Thibet, is filled with hordes of mendicant Buddhist monks, who subsist by begging from the people, living in monasteries endowed by the faithful. Images of *Buddha* abound, and he is regarded as a Deity, although the teachings expressly hold otherwise.

Is it not an irony of Fate, that *Gautama*, whose work was in the direction of undoing the work of priests and established religions, and whose teachings were directed toward aiding the race to escape vain forms, creeds, and ceremonies, and to make them think and act for themselves—that his teachings should have served as the basis for a 'Church' an Creed, whose followers rank second, if not first numerically, in the list of the Churches ? Like Jesus, *Gautama* came as a teacher without temples, organizations or creeds—and like Him, he unwittingly became the founder of a great "Church," with creeds, dogmas, theologies, forms, ritual and ceremonies; priests and ecclesiasticism, Wherever form and dogmas supplant the spirit of the Truth, then churches crystallize and the living faith burns low. It ever has been so, and ever will be so. In the East, so in the West.

But *Gautama* taught, as did the *Krishna* of the Hindus, that when the spirit is almost extinguished, then comes a new Messenger of Spirit, to revive the Truth. *Gautama* is held to be but one of a line of Buddhas, or great Spiritual Teachers—*Avatars* of Divinity—who have come, and will come to save the race from rank materialism and darkness of *Avidya*. *Gautama* said: "Whenever the pure doctrine threatens to fall entirely into disuse, and mankind again sinks into sensual desires and mental darkness—then a new Buddha is born." *Krishna*, in the "*Bhagavad-Gita*" makes a similar promise. While Christians regard *Buddha* as a 'heathen' teacher, whose teachings were amazingly akin to those of Jesus, and whose Moral Code "for pureness, excellence, and wisdom, is second only to that of the Divine Lawgiver himself," the Buddhists freely acknowledge Jesus as a Divine Messenger sent to teach the 'heathen' of the Western worlds—a Buddha of the West, in fact.

× × ×

Our students, familiar with the Inner Teachings of the Hindu Philosophy, have been able to read into Buddhism the Fundamental Truths, according to the interpretation of *Gautama*, and to trace the differences and correspondences between it and the several other systems. The point of the greatest difference between our own teachings and those of *Buddha* is regarding the extremely Pessimistic view of the universe—the dwelling upon the Pain, and overlooking the Joy. Life is neither joy nor Pain, but a commingling of both. He who puts on the blue spectacles of Pessimism sees everything 'blue'; while he who dons the rose-coloured spectacles of Optimism sees everything 'rosy'—the pure clear glasses of Understanding sees neither colour, but everything in its relation and true colouring. Another great point of difference is that in which *Gautama* pictures THAT allowing itself to be the subject to illusion and *Avidya*, and involved in the baleful *Samsara* existence—this being a tendency among the majority of Hindu Philosophies. To us, The Absolute—THAT—*Brahman*, is not deluded or fooled by *Avidya* or *Maya*, but is pursuing a Divine Plan of Manifestation and Mental Creation, in full knowledge and wisdom, for purposes and ends unknown to man, but satisfactory to the Divine Knowing, and which has always Ultimate Justice and Absolute Good in view—guided by the Light of Infinite Love. This is the antidote for Pessimism.

SPECIAL MESSAGE VII

By Yogi Ramacharaka

For this month we invite you to participate in the contemplation and consideration of the following gems of Spiritual Truth, gathered from the inexhaustible mines of the Hindu Thought :

"This is the Truth. That is the Truth. All is in Truth, and Truth is in all. Truth cannot be added to, nor subtracted from. Add all to the Truth, and the Truth remains. Subtract all from the Truth, and the Truth remains."

"The Truth is that which when gained, there is naught else to gain; the bliss of which experienced, there is no other bliss to be experienced; which, when seen, there is naught else to be seen; which once known, there is naught else to be known."

"As the sun contains all Light, and in itself there is neither play nor night—so in Truth, which is all Wisdom, there is neither knowledge nor ignorance."

"Truth is beyond sound, touch, form, taste, and smell; beyond beginning and ending; beyond involution and evoution Those who realize this saying, also escape these attributes of ignorance."

"Eye cannot see, nor mind know truth. And yet there is that within each by which It may be seen, and may be known. None can this riddle see, unless he hath both seen and known."

"There is a state of Bliss Absolute, wherein one does not see another, nor does he hear another, nor does he know another. States in which one sees another, hears another, knows another are not Bliss Absolute. Bliss Absolute is Immortal Mind. Aught else is Mortal Mind. Where is Bliss Absolute to be found? Everywhere, or Nowhere, say the sages."

"Where is the Truth? Above, below, north, south, east, west, up, down, high, low, without, within. Many who seek it, find it not; many who seek it not, find it. He knows and sees the Truth, becomes filled with Bliss Absolute, and becomes a Lord. To him is opened the door or doors that lead to worlds above and worlds below."

"The Truth is ever awake, even when asleep. As the sun lighteth many things not resembling it, so does the Light of the Truth illumine many minds, high and low, each thinking the light its own. Only, the wise perceive that in the mind there is no light, other than the light of the Truth shining therein."

Our Meditation for the coming month is :

"THE TRUTH IS TO BE SOUGHT EVERYWHERE, FOR EVERYWHERE ABIDETH IT."

Chapter VIII

Sufiism

'Sufiism' is a term applied to the philosophical and religious system of a large body of Mystics sheltered beneath the wing of the Mahommedan religion, to which they owe temporal allegiance, but among whom they are a 'strange people.' Although the *Sufis* are to be found in Turkey, Arabia, Egypt, and principally in Persia—India not knowing them at all except through the chance visit of one of their number—still *Sufiism* is a direct offshoot of the Hindu Philosophy, in its *Vedantic* interpretation and *Bhakti* manifestations, and justice requires that we should include it in our consideration of the Philosophies and Religions of India. Just as Buddhism, which is almost extinct in India; outside of the far northern regions and in Burmah and surrounding places, its principal following being in the foreign lands, is still considered as a Hindu Teaching because of its origin in India—so do we attribute *Sufiism* to India, although her borders enclose but few *Sufis,* and their great following is in Persia, and other Mahommedan lands. Without India there would be no *Sufiism*—without the Hindu Teachings the Sufis would be orthodox Mahommedans. And as you consider, herein, the doctrines of the Sufi, you will agree with us that their origin must be found in the *Vedanta* and *Bhakti Yoga* of India—they tell their own tale.

The word *'Sufi'* is derived from the Persian word *'suf'* (derived from the Arabic) meaning *'wool,'* the connection being evident when it is remembered that the early *Sufis* discarded their former costly robes of silk and costly materials, and adopted a plain garb of coarse undyed wool—the plainest and cheapest material in the land, corresponding to the cheap cotton robe in which the Hindu ascetic wraps himself. Consequently these men became known as 'wool-wearers,' and from the term '*Suf*,' meaning wool, the words '*Sufi*' and '*Sufiism*' arose. It is difficult to determine the date of the origin of *Sufiism*, in absence of historical data, and we are compelled to fall back upon the legends for information and clues. The *Sufis* themselves hold that it is thousands of years old, the saying being that: "The seed of *Sufiism* was sown in the time of Adam; germinated in the time of Noah; budded in the time of Abraham; began to develop in the time of Jesus; and produced pure wine in the time of Mahommed," but this saying is in line with other claims common among the Mahommedans who indulge in characteristic flowery speech, and the best authorities believe that *Sufiism* had its rise in the early centuries of the Christian Era.

One of the first recorded mentions of the word '*Sufiism*' is in connection with one *Abu Hashim*, who lived and taught about 750 A.D., while about a half-century later the sect sprang into prominence in Persia, *Abul Said, Abul Khair, Dhul-Nun-al-Misri*, and other leaders spreading its teachings vigorously. Some of the best authorities trace it back to the very time of Mahommed himself, claiming there is historical evidence to prove that Ali, the Favourite Disciple of the Prophet, was a *Sufi* and really founded the sect in an Inner Circle of the new religion. But there are numerous legendary fragments tending to prove that the teachings of *Sufiism* existed in the lands conquered by Mahommed, long before his advent, having been taught there by wandering *Vedantists* from India, and which secret teachings were adopted by those of Mahommed's followers who were mystically inclined, and who were not willing to part with their favourite philosophy in spite of their adherence to the doctrines of the new Prophet. At any rate, it may be said safely that Mahommed had no share in keeping alive the germ of mysticism, for he was opposed to it, and taught positively against it.

While there are many apparent points of difference between the *Sufi* doctrines, as now taught, and the doctrines of the *Vedanta*, still one familiar with both may see many points of resemblance, and easily may reconcile the points of divergence. Both hold to the One Reality which they declare is 'All that Is,' although the *Vedanta* conception is more metaphysical and abstract in its conception of THAT without attributes and qualities, while to the *Sufis* the One is God, warm, personal and living—but this is merely a difference in the temperament, training and environment of the two races—the Hindu and the Persian—and still more the influence of the particular form of *'Yoga'* manifested by the two schools. The Vedantists prefer the *Yoga* of Wisdom —*'Gnani Yoga'*—while the *Sufis* adhere tenaciously and earnestly to the *Yoga* of Love—*Bhakti Yoga*. And there is but little difference in the teachings of the Hindu *Bhakti Yoga*, and the Persian *Sufi*. To both Love of God is the best Path of Attainment, and the *Moksha* or *Nirvana* of the Hindu is almost identical with the 'Union with God' of the *Sufi*. And as the Hindu *Yogi* has his state of Samadhi, or Ecstasy of Spiritual Consciousness, so has the *Sufi* his state of Ecstasy of the 'Sight of the Beloved'—both being identical in nature, and both being forms of the world-wide state of Illumination of the Mystics. Just as the *Yogis* have their teachers known as *'Gurus,'* so have the *Sufis* their teachers known as *'Pirs,'* the same reverence being shown in both cases, and the same methods of initiating the neophytes into the esoteric mysteries being observed. Some authorities have pointed out correspondences between the Neo-Platonists and the *Sufis*, and have held that the latter owed their teachings to the former. But when it is remembered that the Neo-Platonists themselves obtained their germ-thoughts from the Hindus, it is not to be wondered that resemblances may be traced between the Grecian followers, and the Persian followers, of the same root-teachings. Undoubtedly later *Sufiism* has been influenced by thought from many sources, but it shows its direct descent from the Hindus too plainly to admit of doubt.

The great *Sufi* teachers lived in the early days of the Mahommedan era. The authorities gave the names of *Dhun-Nun* (A.D. 859); *Sirri Sagvait* (A.D. 867); *Junaid* (A.D. 910); *Al-Nallaj* (A.D. 980); *Gazali* (A.D. 1111); *Jalal-ud-Din Rumi* (A.D. 1273); as being the great teachers of their times. And among the great poets who have versed the *Sufi* teachings under the familiar disguises should be mentioned *Omar Khayyam; Nizami; Farid-ud-Din Attar; Sadi; Shamsi; Hafiz; Anvari; Jami;* and *Hatifi*. *Sufiism* flourished under the teachings of the early sages and poets, but about the Sixteenth Century it began to yield to the overwhelming influence of the orthodox Mahommedan church, and a decline set in, from which the sect never has entirely recovered. But although the sect suffered this reverse in point of numbers and popularity, it has recently experienced a new life, not drawing to itself great numbers, but in the sense of attracting to it many Orientals of education and culture, to whom its mysticism proved ccngenial. For about the last fifty years it has been malting quite a headway among the cultured Persians and Turks, and among a few in Egypt and Arabia, the work, however, being conducted in secret and being in the nature of secret-society work rather than religious ceremony or worship. A few Europeans and Americans have been attracted to the sect, particularly those who have been able to read between the lines of *Omar Khayyam's* 'Rubaiyat,' seeing the mysticism appearing behind the apparently materialistic expressions as interpreted by Fitzgerald, which interpretation is generally held to contain more of Fitzgerald's expression than *Omar's* conceptions—but still, the mystic teaching may be discerned when one has the key, as we shall see presently.

In Persia, Egypt, Arabia, and Turkey, the word '*Sufi*' has

been as much abused as has the word *'Yogi'* in India. Both words originally meant "wise men" and spiritual teachers, whereas in India the term *'Yogi'* has been applied by Westerners and some Hindus, to the hordes of ignorant fakirs who are on a very low plane of mentality and spirituality as well as of social standing; while the term *'Sufi'* has been applied to a similar class of mendicant beggars, dervishes, fanatics, and wonder-workers, infesting the Mahommedan lands. There is a vast difference between a Hindu fakir, and a real *Yogi*; and there is the same vast difference between a Persian, Egyptian, Arabian, or Turkish fakir or dervish, and a true *'Sufi.'* As an old *Sufi* writer once said: "He who forsakes the world is a *Sufi*—he whom the world forsakes is a mendicant." So in considering the *Sufis*, we must ask you to distinguish between the true and the false, just as we once asked you to do in the case of the *Yogis*, before you were familiar with the subject.

Passing on to the philosophy of the *Sufis*, we would say that the original teachings did not go deeply into metaphysics or philosophical subtleties, but contented themselves with affirming the Oneness of Reality—the Omnipresence, and Imminence; Allness and Oneness, of God—and the fact that He might be reached by Love and Devotion. The rest of the doctrine was left to be developed as the sect grew and the philosophical interest developed. Briefly, the teaching was that God was the Supreme Good. That He was the Source of all Things. That He was Self-Existent, and Uncreated. That the Universe was created by a reflection from, or emanation from God's own Being. That, therefore, He was imminent in, and permeated all Nature. That Matter was but an appearance, being temporary and. changing, and in the nature of an illusory screen whereupon God could manifest his Universe. That. by Ecstasy and Contemplation and Meditation upon this All-Good, the soul could and would rise to its source and be merged therein at the last. That in the return to the Source—the All-Good—man must pass through many incarnations, rising ever higher and higher. This was the essence of the teaching, and the essence of that essence was that God was within Man—that Man contained the Divine Spark within his inner nature, and that that Inner Divinity, or Spirit, was the Real Self. Surely this was closely akin to the *Vedanta*, even to its Inner Teachings. And we feel sure that after reading the above paragraph, every one of our *Yogi* students may be able to recognize the *Sufi* as his brother.

There are many interesting legends connected with the realization of the doctrine by the early *Sufis*, and the natural extremes to which their new thought carried them, and the opposition the idea aroused among the people who had always considered God to be "Somebody away off." A few of these instances may interest you, so we will relate them. One of the most celebrated of the early *Sufis* was a woman, by name *Rabia al Adawiyya*, also known as *Rabia of Basra*. One day *Rabia* was asked if she hated the Devil (of the orthodox Mahommedan church, of course) and she replied: "No, not at all. My love for God occupies all my mind, all my time, so that I have neither time nor room to hate anything, even the Devil." When asked why she did not marry, she replied: "I am already wedded to my Lord by the bonds of Divine Wedlock. I am not free, for am I not my Lord's spouse, and must I not be faithful to Him ?" *Rabia* exerted a great influence on the early *Sufi* sect, until the time of her death in Jerusalem, in A.D. 753.

Of another one of the old *Sufi* 'saints' or sages, named *Bayazid*, the following is told: One day the old sage passed into an ecstatic condition, in which he attained Cosmic Consciousness, Union with God, Ecstasy, *Samadhi*, Illumination, or by whatever name men chose to call that wonderful state. Awakening therefrom, and still under the spell of his vision of Oneness, he cried aloud to his disciples : "Lo ! I myself am God Almighty. There is none other God beside Me !" His disciples were horrified, and when their Master had fully recovered, they told him of the blasphemy he had uttered. *Bayazid* replied: "Oh ! woe is me ! If I blaspheme again, straightway slay me !" And his disciples sharpened their knives for their holy task, for so they considered it. Once more the Master passed into *Samadhi*, and cried aloud. "Within my robe there, is none but God—wherefore seek you him or heaven or earth ?" The disciples, overcome with horror, and in accordance with the Master's orders, straightway plunged their blades into his body. But, the legend concludes : "their knives were turned back upon their own bodies, and they perished, for they had raised their hands upon the Divine Spirit within the Master which inspired the speech." And then *Bayazid* explained to the remaining disciples that his Personality had vanished during his ecstasy, and he saw that his Form was but "a mirror faintly reflecting the form of God," and that when the disciples wished to strike him with their knives, they saw only the Mirror reflecting their own faces (not seeing God, and *Bayazid* having vanished) and so their knives struck themselves.

Many of the early *Sufis* fell into the same error that has carried away so many of the modern Western students of advanced metaphysics—that supreme foolishness which would call the 'reflection' by the name of THAT which causes it—and which voices itself in the strident, raucous cry of : "I Am God !" We find instances of this throughout many of the early records of the sect, particularly as the doctrine of the Indwelling Spirit was argued out to its extreme possibilities, and the difference between the Reality and the Reflection faded away, and in the *Sufi* terminology : "The Beloved and the Lover are known to be One." One *Mansur al-Hallaj* became renowned by his claims that "I am God !" which nearly caused a schism in the sect. In this teaching he was rivalled by one *Akbar*, who modestly refrained from founding his own God-ship, but who inspired his followers to do so, one of his poet-disciples singing enthusiastically : "See *Akbar* and you see God !"

Al-Hallaj at one time was crucified by the orthodox Mahommedans, remaining suffering on the cross for four days, on both sides of the Tigris river. He bore his sufferings with noble courage, saying : "From His own cup He bade me sup, for such is hospitality "; and, "I am receiving only what is mine, for by God, I never distinguished for a moment between pain and pleasure !" also uttering one of his characteristic sayings : "The Way to God is but two steps : one step out of this world, and one step out of the next world—and lo, you are there with God." The legends have it that he did not die on the cross, but was released after the four-days' crucifixion and lived for ten years more, being finally stoned to death, the legend being that, expiring, he wrote with his finger, with his own blood, on the stones, the words: "I am God !" But these are instances of the extreme of the thought, and the body of the *Sufis* did not hold to these claims, but instead, regarded every man's soul as a mirror in which was reflected the Image of God, and which image constituted the Spirit with each man, and which was his true Self. There is a great difference between the conception of the Indwelling Spirit—the Immanent God, and that of the "I Am God" teachers.

One of the most confusing points about the *Sufi* teachings, to the Western mind, is the symbology of the writers, and the corresponding fact that many of their sacred writings seem to be mere voluptuous and bacchanalian rhapsodies, filled with references to 'the grape,' or 'the vine,' or the 'red wine, and wine-cup,' as well as praises of 'the Beloved Damsel'; the 'Beloved'; the 'Embrace of Love'; the 'Nuptial Couch'; and much other imagery which to the Western mind is connected with subjects far removed from religion and devotion. But when one has the key, and recognizes, as does the Persian, that in these verses there is to be seen two separate meanings, besides the five mystical meanings, which are claimed for all mystic poetry there may be an understanding.

The cause of this peculiar style lies in the fact that outside of the natural exuberant imagery of the Oriental mind, which the West finds difficult to understand, there always has been the necessity of the *Sufi* veiling his inner meaning beneath the form of current poetical subjects. Surrounded on all sides by the hordes of ignorant, bigoted, fanatical orthodox Mahommedans, the *Sufi* has been compelled to take refuge in this peculiar symbology. To the Persian, and particularly to the *Sufi* mystic, there must always be a 'veil' before the outer and vulgar meaning of the verses, which veil must be pulled aside by the elect before they may see the beauties which lie behind the covering—the vulgar see nothing but the painted veil with its gross, sensual figures appearing thereon, which veil is boldly pulled aside by those who Understand, and who would see the truth Behind the Veil.

This symbolism is based upon the Ecstasy of the Recognition of the God. Within—the Presence of the Indwelling Spirit. And accordingly, 'The Embrace' means the ecstasy of the conscious Union with Divinity; the 'Wedding' the entrance into the Knowledge; the 'Wine' the *Sufi* Mystical Teachings; the 'Vine and the rape' the source of the 'Wine," hence '*Sufiism*' ; the 'Tavern' the Temple or *Sufi* secret "lodg of instruction"; the "Beloved" is the symbol for "The All-Good," or God; and the "lover" is always the *Sufi* gazing at his Beloved—the term "the Beloved Damsel' is oftn used as a cloak for the Divine One, in the sense of being the object of the ardent love of the 'Lover' or *Sufi*; and the terms the 'Red Roseī which is beloved by the 'Nightingale,' are used in the same sense of beloved and the lover. Many Western writers have considered this symbology far-fetched, and have preferred to read nothing but sensualism and bacchanalian rioting in the verse of the inspired poets of Persia, but the *Sufis* know better, and a careful reading will disclose the hidden meaning—will pull aside t'e veil. For instance, read the apparently riotous verses of the 'Rubaiyat'with the above interpretation, and see if it does not agree with the Inner Teachings :

And David's lips are lockt; but in divine
High-piping *Pehlevi*, with "Wine! Wine! Wine!
Red Wine! "—the Nightingale cries to the Rose
That sallow cheek of hers t' incarnadine.

A Book of Verses underneath the Bough,
A Jug of Wine, a Loaf of Bread—and Thou
Beside me singing in the Wilderness—
Oh, Wilderness were Paradise enow !

You know, my Friends, with what a brave Carouse
I made a Second Marriage in my house;
Divorced old barren Reason from my Bed,
And took the Daughter of the Vine to Spouse.

And lately, by the Tavern Door agape,
Came shining through the Dusk an Angel Shape
Bearing a vessel on his shoulder; and
He bid me taste of it; and 'twas—the Grape !

The Grape that can with Logic absolute
The Two-and-Seventy jarring Sects confute :
The sovereign Alchemist that in a trice
Life's leaden metal into Gold transmute.

And much as Wine has play'd the Infidel,
And robb'd me of my Robe of Honour—Well
I wonder often what the Vintners buy
One half so precious as the stuff they sell.

Before the phantom of False morning died,

Methought a voice within the Tavern cried,
"When all the Temple is prepared within,
Why nods the drowsy Worshipper outside ?"

Come, fill the Cup, and in the fire of Spring
Your Winter-garment of Repentance fling ;
The Bird of Time has but a little way
To flutter—and the Bird is on the Wing.

So much for old *Omar* and his Wine, and Tavern, and Spouse, and Roses—how different it all seems when one has the key! How many of us can voice with him his praise of the 'Wine' which intoxicates the soul with the Bliss Ineffable ! How much the old *Sufi, Omar,* resembles Spinoza, whom people have called "the God-intoxicated philo-sopher" ! How much is the *Sufi* like the ecstatic Hindu *Bhakti Yoga,* filled with the Wine of Spirit, who fills the air with his rapturous cries of : "Oh, my Beloved—my Beloved One !" You who think that this is a mere coincidence, and that old *Omar* is still a materialistic, cynical, sceptical; old wine-bibber and libertine epicurean—wait a while, until you learn "The Secret of *Omar.*"

The *Sufi* philosophy is very simple. There is very little more to it than the fundamental principles we have already stated. The *Sufis* do not concern themselves with hair-splitting metaphysical discussions regarding the 'How' phase of the universe—enough for them to know that God is, and that His Reflection and Image is in themselves—they hold that in this realization there is "a knowing of That, which when once known causes all to be known." They believe in Reincarnation, and have some vague teachings regarding States of Rest, in Heavens and Hells, between Incarnations, but some of the advanced *Sufis* pay but little attention to these teachings, deeming them at the best but discussions of inferior phases of existence but little above or below the earthly life—holding that there is but one life looking forward to—Union with God. Some of these advanced thinkers, in their writings and verses, speak of the highest heavens of their brethren as "those petty villages, filled with hovels, called Heavens—at which we will tarry not, but shall hasten on to the Mansion of our Beloved One, wherein our Wedding Feast is awaiting us, and our Nuptial Couch is spread with the finest silks and most costly adornments—wherefore shall we dally with the petty villages and the hovel-like resting places"; and again: "What terror shall the lowest Hell have for him who knows that eventually, yea, even at the end of many aeons, he shall be clasped in his Beloved's arms?—"tis but a foul nightmare fantasy, and awakening, the Lover shall find his Beloved gazing longing into his eyes." Surely, heaven can hold no reward, nor hell any punishment, for souls like these.

The general philosophy may be summed up as follows : God is Pure Being—the Necessarily Existent (*Wajibul-wujud*)—the Absolute Good (*Khayr-imahz*)—the Absolute Beautiful. In His aspect of the Absolute Beautiful, He desired to witness Himself in reflection—wished to realize His own beautiful nature and being—and so caused His divine image to fall on the mirror of 'notreality' (*adam*), the reflection thus caused being the cause of the phenomenal world, or 'appearance of Being' (*imkan*), which reveals the divine image of the Creator but does not partake of His Substantial Being, and which is, on the contrary, in truth but a phantasy and an illusion. Man is the Eye of the phenomenal world, when he is able to see God as the One and Only Reality behind the phenomenal universe of appearances; and to see the illusory. nature of the latter; then he is able to escape from the bondage of the shadow-world—the phantasmagoria of the world—and attain absorption in the Divine (*fana fillah*). By the study of the Mystic Teachings (*shariat*), and the following of the Mystic Path (*tariqat*), the mystic student and Seeker of Truth arrives at his goal, and sees and realizes the Truth (*haqiqat*).

Evil is held to be but a negation of Good, and therefore has no real being. "There isno absolute Evil in the Universe—Evil is but relative," says the old *Sufi* mystic *Jalal-ud-Din Rumi.*

There is little or no doctrine or dogma in *Sufiism*—it is taken up with statement of the existence of the Lord, and his abiding Spirit within the soul, and with instruction whereby one may plant his feet firmly on The Path that leadeth to Paradise. The whole aim is toward Union with God, in which there are two stages, *viz.* (1) the Recognition of the Union in consciousness, during earth-life, by means of Spiritual Consciousness, Ecstasy, or Illumination; and (2) the final and complete Union with God, in which the individual Spirit returns to the bosom of the Great Ocean of Spirit and loses itself in the One—or as the Buddhists put it, "the dewdrop slides into the shining sea." The first stage is akin to the Hindu *Samadhi*, the higher phases approaching *Nirvana;* while the second stage is akin to the Buddhist *Para-Nirvana*, or Complete Absorption. There are but two Truths known to the *Sufi*—(1) The One; and (2) the Way to the One. The first is called *'Ahad'*—the second *'Tariqat.'*

The first Truth (*ahad*) is that which we have stated, *i.e.*, that there is naught but God in Reality—that all is delusion and illusion, untruth, a phantasmagoric puppet-show, operated by 'the Master of the Show,' so long as it pleases his fancy to allow it to remain in his view—God made the Universe as a passing show, because: "I was a Hidden Treasure, and I wished to be known, so I created The Universe that I might be known, and know that I am known" —God is not only Absolute Being, but also Absolute Truth, Absolute Love, and Absolute Beauty. The Second Truth (*tariqat*) or the Way to the One, is akin to the Hindu teachings on the subject. Instructed by his *'Pir,'* teacher, or *Guru*, the disciple ascends the Steps of the Ladder of God, discarding his material ideas, desires, tastes and attachments—freeing himself from illusion—regenerating himself anew, and sanctifying himself by devotion, contemplation, meditation, and right thinking and right living. There are many mystic practices familiar to Hindu, Ancient Greece, and some of the Modern Western cults and mystic orders—dances there are, rhythmic and graceful motions accompanied by chants—"silences" there are also, in which the soul may enjoy mystic communion with higher planes of being—ecstatic states are frequent, and Cosmic Consciousness frequent among the higher students.

The *Sufis* hold that man is miniature God, in relation to his body, which is his miniature universe—hence the statement of the authorities that *Sufiism* teaches that Man is both, and at the same time, a *Microtheos*, and a *Microcosmos*. They hold that there are Five Planes of Being, namely: (1) The Absolute Invisible; (2) The Relatively Invisible; (3) The Plane of Similitudes; (4) The Plane of Visibility; and (5) The Plane of Below-Visibility. These Planes are sometimes roughly classified as 'The Three Planes,' styled, respectively, the Invisible; the Intermediate; and the Visible. The uneducated and simple followers after the advanced teachers, speak of but 'Two Planes,' the Visible and the Invisible, respectively, so that there seems to be an esoteric as well as an exoteric doctrine concerning these Planes. But this is not all—the most advanced speak of a Plane vastly higher than even the Absolute Invisible, which they speak of as above words or thought, and which one authority has compared to Dante's 'Spaceless Empyrean.' The Spirit, or as some call it 'the soul,' is of course conceived of as immortal and pre-existent, in the sense that before it started on its round of incarnations it was in the Bosom of God. It is held to retain a memory of its former blissful state, and the natural appreciation for Beauty is held to be due to a faint recollection of the Beauty of the Spiritual Existence in the One. The Universe, as we have said, was conceived of as a panoramic phantasmagoria, the scenes and actors constantly changing, making their appearance, playing their part, and passing off the scene. Man's Spirit was an emanation of God, and his body was but an incidental covering, created for the purposes of the show-world, and therefore of but little value except as a part of the play. Fate and Destiny are the directions of the Divine Stage Manager—the Divine Purpose and Will, which may not be avoided or disobeyed. But the Spirit was always homesick, repining, and longing to be reunited with its Beloved. As *Avicenna*, the *Sufi* poet, hath sung in his great poem on the mourning soul seeking its Beloved :

> **Lo, it was hurled**
> 'Midst the sign posts and ruined abodes of this blessed world.
> It weeps, when it thinks of its home and the peace it possessed,
> With tears welling forth from its eyes without pausing or rest,
> And with plaintive mourning it broodeth like one bereft
> O'er such trace of its home as the fourfold winds have left.

Strictly speaking, then, *Sufiism* is the Philosophy of Oneness—of all-Godness, in the strictest sense of the word. And *Sufiism*, as a religion, is the Religion of the Love of God, in the strictest sense of the term. Even the most radical and advanced *Vedantist* can conceive of no more absolute Godness, than the *Sufi*; and even the love-stricken *Bhakti Yogi* of India can claim no more 'divine love-sickness' than the *Sufi*. And therefore *Sufiism* is Love-of-God in its most active form—therefore let us consider this Love-of God and the *Sufi* expression of it, in verse and action, and in connection with the Hindu *Bhakti Yoga*.

It is difficult for the Western mind to understand the Oriental conception and expression of the 'Love-of-God' of which we find many references in the Hindu and Persian poems, hymns, and epics. The Western mind recognizes a quiet and repressed expression of the love of the creature toward the Creator, which expression seldom goes beyond a quiet earnest expression of the love of the child toward the Father. In some cases the expression of love toward the Christ and Saviour is expressed with rather more fervour and human feeling, and terms such as 'the Beloved' are not uncommon in this connection. Some Western religious writers have even hinted, in poetical form, of the relationship of the Creator and creature as the love of the Mother for the babe, etc., but even such instances are rarer. It is true that under the excitement, ardour, and fervour of the old-time revivals, we often heard ecstatic and passionate expressions of love of God, which, at times, faintly approached the Oriental form of expression, but even this extreme voicing of the feeling seems to be dying out.

But in the Eastern lands it is quite different—the warm, poetical natures of the people express themselves in the use of the most ardent terms of endearment addressed to Deity, and (to the Western mind) the most extravagant forms of expression of the Divine Relationship are freely indulged in. The *Bhakti Yogis* of India—and the majority of the followers of the religious creeds profess this form of *Yoga*—make the expression of this Love-of-God one of their principal religious ceremonies and duties. On all sides are heard the voices of the faithful raised in prayers and praise of Deity, in which the most endearing terms are used. It is quite frequent for the Hindu *Krishna-Vaishnava Bhakti* to address his Lord as "Beloved; Darling; Sweetheart; Precious One; Light of my Heart; Beautiful One; Being of Rapturous Bliss," etc., etc. Some who find a nearness in considering the Lord in the aspect of Mother-Love (not uncommon in Eastern countries) are heard addressing prayers to 'My Blessed Mother Divine,' with references to the "Divine Breasts which have ever suckled thy Infant," and so on. Instances are common in which Hindu women, whose conception of the greatest love was that of the mother-love toward the child, are found in rapturous devotion before the picture of the Infant *Krishna*, addressing the Deity as "Oh! my Beloved Baby—My Darling Infant—Thou whom I suckle at my breast for ever and always," etc., etc. And Western travellers in India, who have had some of the religious prayers and ecstatic addresses translated for them, are shocked to hear the terms of ardent endearment, usually applied in cases of intense love between man and woman, being used in addressing the Deity. To the Oriental God is not only a Father but is also a Mother, a Brother, a Sister, a Child, a Friend, a Husband, a Wife, a Sweetheart, a Lover—in fact, to him the Lord answers every worthy and pure human cry for love and affection, and responds to it by a return of the love—to him every human love relation (of a pure kind) has its transcendental counterpart and pattern in the Divine, and he feels no hesitancy in calling upon his Lord giving and asking Love. In the West this idea is confined to religious poetry, and even there is repressed and merely hinted at, but in the East it is expressed freely and without restraint. And the Western student of Oriental religions must acquaint himself with this fact, else he will fail utterly in his reading of the Oriental forms of thought and religious expression.

Particularly is the above true of the Persian *Sufi* poets. Even more ardent and unrestrained than the Hindu *Bhaktis*, the Persian *Sufis* express their love for the One in poems in which (following the universal custom of their land and cult) there is always the 'Inner and Hidden Meaning,' so that behind the passionate poem to the 'Beloved Damsel,' there appears the *Sufi* endearment of the One. Just as behind the 'Wine, wine, wine !' of *Omar Khayyam*, appears the *Sufi* doctrines and thought, so in the other Persian poets the 'Love of the One' appears behind the 'Love of the Bright-eyed Damsel,' and the 'Rose Garden,' and the 'Nightingale and Rose' of the erotic Persian love-song. Many Western writers doubt this, and laugh at the attempt to read Divine Ecstasy between the lines of some burning love stanzas of the Persian poets, but all who have studied Persian literature, and Persian *Sufi* philosophy and religion, at the same time, agree upon the facts of the case, as above stated. Misunderstood, the *Sufi* poems must seem indeed like a blasphemous mingling of sensuality and religion, so that one can scarcely blame writers like the Rev. W. R. Inge, who states that "The *Sufis*, or Mahommedan Mystics, use erotic language very freely and appear, like true Asiatics, to have attempted to give a sacramental or symbolic character to the indulgence of their passions." The Rev. Inge also accuses the *Sufis* of being most shocking and blasphemous, but his idea of shocking blasphemy may be understood when it is remembered that he blames Emerson with "playing with pantheistic Mysticism of the Oriental type," and accuses him of resembling the Persian *Sufis* in some respects. He merely lacked the crystal-spectacles of Understanding when he read the Persian poems—that is all.

Let us quote you from some of these "shocking and blasphemous" erotic Persian poets—these God-drunken souls, using the poetical imagery of their land to express that which was the love of the All Good; All-Beautiful, to them. The following lines are from the poems of *Jalal-ud-Din Rumi*, one of the greatest of the *Sufi* poets :

Our journey is to the Rose-Garden of Union.

Come ! Come ! Thou art the Soul, the Soul so dear, revolving !
Come! Come! Thou art the Cedar, the Cear's Spear, revolving;
Oh, come!, The well of Light up-bubbling springs;
And Moning Stars exult, in Gladness sheer, revolving !

I am silent. Speak Thou, O Soul of Soul of Soul,
From desire of whose Face every atom grew articulate.

Give my heart-babe milk, relieve us from its weeping,
O Thou that helpest every moment a hundred helpless like me.
Thy heart's home first to last, is Thy City of Union :

How long wilt Thou keep in exile this heart forlorn?

The Prince of the Fair goes proudly forth to the chase at morning;
May our hearts fall a prey to the arrow of His glance!
From His eye what messages are passing continually to mine!
May my eyes be gladdened and filled with intoxication by His Message!

My body is like the moon which is melting for Love,
My heart like Zuhra's lute—may its strings be broken!
Look not on the moon's waning nor on Zuhra's broken state;
Behold the sweetness of his affection—may it wax a thousand fold !

What a Bride is in the Soul! By the reflection of her face
May the world be freshened and coloured like the faces of the newly married !

Eternal Life, methinks, is the time of Union,
Because Time, for me, hath no place there.
Life is the vessels, Union the clear draught in them;
Without Thee what does the pain of the vessels avail me ?

Show me Thy face, for I desire the orchard and the rose-garden;
Ope thy lips, for I desire sugar in plenty :
O sun, show forth Thy face from the veil of cloud,
For I desire that radiant glowing countenance.

The souls love-moved are circling on,
Like streams to their great Ocean King.
Thou art the Sun of all men's thoughts;
Thy kisses are the flowers of spring.
The dawn is pale from yearning Love;
The moon in tears is sorrowing.
Thou art the Rose, and deep for Thee,
In sighs, the Nightingales still sing.

I, All-in-All becoming, now clear see God in All;
And up from Union yearning, takes flight the cry of Love !

On that his wedding-night in the presence of his bride,
His pure soul attained to kiss her hands.
Love and mistress are both veiled and hidden.
Impute it not a fault if I call him "Bride."

The sect of lovers is distinct from all others,
Lovers have a religion and a faith of their own.
Though the ruby has no stamp, what matters it?
Love is fearless in the midst of the sea of fear.

The love of the Soul is for Life and Living One,
Because its origin is the Soul not bound to place.

Eternal Life is gained by utter abandonment of one's own life,
When God appears to His ardent Lover, the Lover is absorbed in Him,
And not so much as a hair of the Lover remains.
True lovers are as shadows, and when the sun shines in glory

The shadows vanish away.
He is a true lover to God to whom God says :
I am thine, and thou art Mine!'

When one has attained Union with God he has no need of intermediaries.

> Earthly forms are only shadows of the Sun of Truth—a cradle for babes, but too small to hold those who have grown to spiritual manhood.

By Thy grace I keep fixed on Eternity my amorous gaze.

The poet from whose verses we have above made a few quotations, where quite a young man, once advised singing and dancing at the funeral of a friend. When remonstrated with by the horror-stricken and indignant mourners, he replied : "When the human spirit, after years of confinement in the cage and dungeon of the body, is at length set free, and wings its flight to the Source whence it came—is not this an occasion for rejoicing, thanks, and dancing?"

Jami, another *Sufi* poet, bath sung of the Divine Love of the Divine :

Gaze, till Gazing out of Gazing, grew to Being Her I gaze upon,
She and I no more, but in One Undivided Being blended.
All that is not One must ever suffer with the Wound of Absence;
And whoever in Love's City enters, finds but Room for One,
And but in Oneness, Union.

Omar Khayyam, whose 'Rubaiyat' is well known in the West by reason of the popularity of Fitzgerald's translation, had much to say of Love, the Beloved and the Lover, but beyond the few verses quoted by us in the first part of the lesson, Fitzgerald gives us but few touching upon this subject, leaving the balance untranslated and unused, seemingly preferring to give prominence to those using the figurative symbols of 'the Wine.' But still Fitzgerald included many showing that old *Omar* understood the doctrine, and taught the philosophy. The following quotations will show this :

Some for the Glories of this World; and some
Sigh for the Prophet's Paradise to come;
Ah, take the Cash, and let the Credit go,
or heed the rumble of a distant Drum.

(In the above quatrain *Omar* classed alike the Earthly Glory and the Heavenly Glory, both being impermanent—he bids hold fast to the Realization of the Oneness, heeding not the future planes, or states, which are merely another form of impermanence).

Into this Universe, and "Why" not knowing
Nor "Whence," like Water willy-nilly flowing;
And out of it, as Wind along the Waste,
I know not "Whither," willy-nilly blowing.

What, without asking, hither hurried "Whence?"
And, without asking, "Whither" hurried hence !
Oh many a cup of this forbidden Wine
Must drown the memory of that insolence !

Then of the THEE in Me who works behind
The Veil, I lifted up my hands to find
A lamp amid the Darkness; and I heard,
As from without—"The ME within Thee blind."

And then the Tulpi for her morning sup
Of Heavenly Vintage from the soil looks up,
Do you devoutly do the like, till Heav'n
To Earth invert you-like an empty cup.

Perplext no more with Human or Divine,
To-morrow's tangles to the winds resign,
And lose your fingers in the tresses of
The Cypress-slender Minister of wine.

And if the Wine you drink, the Lip you press.
End in what All begins and ends in—Yes;
Think then you are To-day what Yesterday
You were—To-morrow you shall not be less.

So when the Angel of the darker Drink
At last shall find you by the river-brink,
And, offering his Cup, invite your Soul
Forth to your Lips to quaff—you shall not shrink.

And fear not lest Existence closing your
Account, and mine, should know the like no more;
The eternal Saki from that Bowl has poured
Millions of Bubbles like us, and will pour.

Whose secret Presence, through Creation's veins
Running Quicksilver—like eludes your pains;
Taking all shapes from *Mah* tc *Mahi*; and
They change and perish all—but HE remains;

A moment guessed—then back behind the Fold
Immerst of Darkness round the Drama roll'd
Which for the pastime of Eternity,
He Both Himself contrive, enact, behold.

We are no other than a moving row
Of Magic Shadow—shapes that come and go
Round with the Sun—illumined Lantern held
In Midnight by the Master of the Show;

But helpless Pieces of the Game He plays
Upon his Chequer-board of Nights and Days
Hither and Thither moves, and checks, and slays,
And one by one back in the Closet lays.

The Ball no question makes of Ayes and Noes,
But Here or There as strikes the Player goes;
And He that tossed you down into the Field,
He knows about it all—He knows—HE knows !

And this I know : whether the One True Light
Kindle to Love, or Wrath-consume me quite,
One flash of it within the Tavern caught
Better than in the Temple lost outright.

This is a glimpse of old *Omar*, with his Love and Sorrow so closely intermingled—his Trust and his belief in Fate twin-like sharing his soul. His distrust of the speculations of the philosophers causing him to ever seek the Wine of the *Sufi* teachings which lead to God-intoxication. Life to him was but the "Game He plays upon the Chequer-board of Nights and Days"—the Release coming only from "the Grape, the Grape !"

And this, then, is a glimpse into the flower-scented land of Persian *Sufiism*—we trust that the flowers that we have plucked from its Rose-Garden will not have withered by the time they reach you. And we trust that the thorn on the stem may not prevent your seeing the beauty of the flower—nor the distance prevent your hearing the thrill of the Nightingale.

We shall not attempt to point out wherein the *Sufi* Teachings agree with those of the Inner Teachings of the *Yogi* Philosophy—nor wherein they disagree. You who have studied both should be able to make the comparison without trouble—to point out the place at which *Sufiism* emerges from the common Thought-branch, and also the direction in which it grows away from our own stem of Truth. You should be able to analyze the *Sufi* conception, separating its glorious perception of the Ever-Effulgent One, and its expression of Love for Him, from the fatal touch of Pessimism, Fatalism, and Belief in the 'Show World' in which all is but scenery moved by—and puppets on strings pulled by—"The Master of the Show." Instead you should be able to see the Universe as an ever-evolving manifestation of the One Life, under the control of the One Will, and under the direction of the One Mind—and animated by the One Spirit; moving on to greater and greater heights and expression, in accordance with the Divine Plan. What that Purpose of that Plan is neither *Omar* nor ourselves know—and both must content ourselves with the answer: "He Knows—HE KNOWS !"

SPECIAL MESSAGE VIII

By Yogi Ramacharaka

For this month, we invite you to listen to the following strains borne from afar, coming from the harps of Spiritual Truth sounded by the trained fingers of the Hindu Sages :

"The Truth embraces all real consciousness and in embracing all it unites the doer and the deed and the witness of the deed; the actor and the act and the witness of the act; the thinker and the thought and the thing thought of; the living and the life and the witnesses and incidents of the life. As the lamp of the theatre embraces in its rays the audience, the actors, the theatre, and the stage, each and all alike, in one sweep of its light; and as it continues to shed its light when all have departed from the stage and the seats; so is Truth as related to the universe."

"The Seer of thy sight thou shaft not see; the Hearer of thy hearings thou shaft not hear; the Thinker of thy thoughts thou shaft not think; the Knower of thy knowledge thou shaft not know; nay, not until thou hast transcended these mortal things, and risen to a knowledge that Thou art THAT."

"Thou art thy Real Self in Truth, All-pervading, ALL—everything else is mortal, illusion, naught, untruh."

"Truth is the unseen Seer; the unheard Hearer; the unthought Thinker; the unknown Knower. Besides Truth there is no other Seer; no other Hearer; no other Thinker; no other Knower. Truth is THAT, thy Real Self, ever immortal, ever in being, omnipresent, omnipotent, omniscient—all besides is mortal and unreal."

"Know ye one ! Know ye all ! The All is One; the One is All. In the Beginning of Beginninglessness, there was but One. At the end of Endlessness, here is but One. And Beginning and End are One and the Same, and both are Not. Truth is All that is, has ever been, and ever will be."

"Brahma, Indra, Prajapati, and all the lesser gods, the five elements, and all that breathes or moves about, or flies above, or stands steadfast and unmoved, exist through Thougt, depend upon

Thought, are held in Thought—the Thought of the One. Otherwise they are not—but the One depends upon Nothing, not even upon Thought, for All, and Thought emanate from It."

Our Meditation for the coming month is :

"TRUTH IS EVER-ABIDING WITHIN. HE WHO REALIZES THIS TRUTH BECOMES MASTER OF HIS LIFE."

Chapter IX

The Religions of India *(Part I)*

India has ever been the Land of Religions. From her sources have emerged the streams that have travelled to far and distant lands, there to be known by other names, the original source having been lost sight of, or else denied when men have tried to trace the connection and relationship. Modern research along the lines of Comparative Religions has explored the long rivers of Religious Conceptions, and there are but few of the great rivers of the dominant religious conceptions that are not known to have their origin in some conception of a Hindu mind centuries back. Even as in some cases, where the river of thought seems to emerge suddenly from the ground, springing from some unknown depths and apparently furnishing an exception to the rule of original source—even in such cases, careful research will show that still further back some river of Hindu thought has disappeared in an underground cave, thence wending its way onward, silently and unobserved, only to emerge into new activity at some far different point, where it is given a new name, only an analysis of its waters and a careful study of directions and geological formation giving the earnest investigator the clue.

The various philosophies, of which the principal ones compose the Six Great Systems of India, are based upon the Fundamental Philosophy of which we have spoken at length in the Second Lesson and as we have seen in the subsequent lessons. And these six philosophies, with their subdivisions, penetrate every form of religion in India, some favouring one school, and some another, while some are quite eclectic and choosing from each that which appeals to them—and all are regarded as but different interpretations of the Fundamental Philosophy. So, you see, there is an astonishing Oneness about Hindu Philosophy, Religion and Thought, which is understandable only in view of the common origin and root of them all, as well as the fundamental principle of THAT upon which they all unite. The work of the Early Fathers was well done—it has lasted through fifty centuries, and in spite of countless division and subdivision of thought—it is Basic—it is Fundamental—it is Elemental Philosophy.

In India it always has been thought that Truth could never be harmed by adverse criticism and examination, argument, debate or discussion, and consequently the people of that land have always welcomed the teachers of new philosophies and religions among them, provided that the missionaries or reformers were filled with the spirit of toleration and respect for the opinions and beliefs of others. Religious persecution in India has been almost unknown, and even unto this day the average Hindu relishes nothing better than a philosophical, metaphysical or theological discussion with someone opposed to him in doctrine. In the smallest villages, the people will gather around teachers, and listen to discussions of points of belief and doctrine, and will eagerly flock to listen to some new teacher who boldly and vigorously attacks the prevailing views. But there seems to be no desire to crush out or to smother the voice of the new teachers. There is an intuitive sense which has taught this age-old race that these differences are merely different points of view, and but varying interpretations of some great fundamental truths underlying the many doctrines. A favourite aphorism in India is: "The Truth is One—men call it by many names."

And so, side by side, in India, we find representatives of the Six Great Systems of Philosophy, with their subdivisions; also representatives of the countless religious sects and cults, with their hairs-splitting points of doctrinal difference; also the schools of the agnostics, or those who hold that Truth is Unknowable; the Sceptics whose business it is to deny and refute all that the others claim, without offering any theory of interpretation of their own; also the school of *Charvakas* or Materialists, whose teachings are akin to those of the Western Materialistic school; also representatives of the Buddhists, who are dying out in central India, but who have some ten millions of followers in Burmah and adjacent sections, and a number in the Himalayas and Thibet; and all respecting the opinions of the others, and not attempting to interfere with them or to restrain their activities. India has never offered the religious reformer or heretic the stake; the scaffold; the cross; the dungeon; as the reward for his energy. While the Mahommedans proselyted by the sword and spear, and destroyed their enemies as the grass-hoppers destroy the fields of grain before them—while Christianity, contrary to the teachings of the Master who founded it, punished heresy and schism by the most cruel methods and practices, even to-day in Western lands these being boards of Heresy-Hunters in the churches, and punishers of unbelievers and infidels among the people—'heathen' India has maintained perfect freedom of religious conscience and worship throughout all the many centuries of her history, and has always met the new-comer, not with sword, fire or gibbet, but with argument, free discussion, and earnest thought, friendly rivalry, and shriving for success in gaining followers.

Among the Hindus the words 'Hinduism' and 'Brahminism' are never used in connection with their Universal Religion, in its many forms. The word 'Hindu' was applied to the people of India by the Persians and Greeks, the term having its origin in the name of the '*Sindu*' or '*Indus*' River. The natives of India called themselves Aryans, or *Aryas*, the name of their original race. They also resent the term 'Brahminism,' which was given to their religious system by the missionaries, who held that it was the religion of the 'Brahmins' or native priests, while the Hindus claim that it existed long before the days of priests and was divine in its origin, having no founder, no special creed, and no central ecclesiastical authority. Among the Hindus their Universal Religion is known as either the '*Arya Dharma*' or 'Aryan System'; or else the '*Sanatana Dharma*,' or 'Eternal System'—the term '*Sanatana*' being the common term for the system.

The *Sanatana* is most universal and catholic in its views, and allows countless opposing sects to take shelter under its tents, and to participate in the worship of its temples. It is no uncommon thing to see followers of a dozen or more sects engaged in common worship in the temples or holy places. The general feeling among the Hindus is that they are all worshipping the same Infinite Reality under some form or symbol, and consequently there is an absence of that fierce strife and rivalry that is so deplorable in other lands both East and West. So long as the individual accepts the *Vedas* as the Divine Source of Truth, and does not dispute the Fundamental Principles, he is welcomed as a brother-in-religion, and is given the "right hand of fellowship." The Buddhists and *Jains*, however, while not persecuted, are looked upon as outsiders, and the Mahommedan is, of course, a 'stranger to the Faith,' and the Christian is regarded as a well-meaning (if he really happens to be so) follower of an 'unscientific faith' erected on the original pure teachings of Jesus the Christ, for whom all educated Hindus have a profound respect, deeming Him to have been a great Spiritual Master, and an Illumined Soul. They also regard *Buddha* as an *Avatar* or Deity, but deplore Buddhism, which they claim is the degenerated form of *Gautama's* original teachings. The Jews are respected, but are held to have but little in common with the Hindu faiths, by reason of the narrow claim that Jehovah was the Deity of only one race of 'Chosen People'—a Race-God, rather than a Universal Divinity. The *Parsees* are Zoroastrians and Fire Worshippers, and have little in common with the Hindus.

× × ×

It is interesting to trace the rise and progress of the *Sanatana*, or 'Eternal Religion,' from the earliest writings. The early *Vedas* show a peculiar dual-aspect, inasmuch as while there is always an undercurrent of Monism or Pantheism—that is, the belief that there is but One ALL in All, still there was always the outer teaching of a something like Nature Worship, with its countless personifications and polytheism. While there was ever the influence of an over-shadowing ONE brooding over All, still there was at the same time the mythology of the nature gods and entities that always mark a certain stage in the religious development of a race. The careful student deduces from this that while the knowledge of the Inner Teachings was with the race, having been inherited from the former civilization from which the Aryan Race sprung, still that Inner Teaching was in the hands of the Few, and that the Many were not as yet ready to receive the teachings in their purity. And so the masses were indulged in their Nature Worship, and their minor deities and mythology, the Few endeavouring to get a knowledge of the Truth into the minds of the people through kindergarten methods, symbols—by reflection, as it were. But still there was always noticeable a gradual and. steady inclination toward the Teachings regarding the ONE.

Even in the early hymns of the *Rig-Veda*, there are to be found numerous references to a Something that is above even the gods—a God of gods, as it were, without any attempt at explanation or speculation but merely the beginning of a suggestion to the people that there was something beyond their mythology—some Universal Something from which all things, even their gods, proceeded.

The ancient Aryans were a joyful, happy, playful lot of Pagans in their everyday life, resembling the early Greeks.

They revelled in the joy of living, "eating, drinking, and making merry," and endeavouring to extract the greatest joy from each passing moment—not as the result of Hedonistic reasoning, but out of the sheer animal joy of living. Their gods were like the mythological deities of the early Greeks, very much like themselves, and not requiring very much thought on the part of their worshippers, nor a special code of conduct or ethical, hair-splittings—a little matter of sacrifices settling the matter and fulfilling the requirements. This, coupled with the usual requirements of the rulers, and the observance of primitive social duties, was about all there was to it.

But gradually there appears an awakening sense of responsibility regarding a future state depending upon the present, in place of the return to Life by Metempsychosis that had been the original future life. The idea of an Inexorable Law of *Karma* crept into the field of religious thought, coming doubtless from the teachers who dealt out the old truths in tiny bits, easily assimilated by the people. Then came the talk of *Samsara*, or the Cycle of Existences, that was not a thing of joy, but an evil thing occurring to the race, placed upon it in some mysterious way. Life began to be regarded as "a barren vale between the peaks of two eternities" filled with pain, and grief, and woe, and from which escape was most desirable. Thus entered that sad, pessimistic minor note that has ever stayed with the Hindus, in their philosophical and religious thought, and which was so different from their former Paganism, which resembled the Greek conception of life and existence—death and rebirth. Some strong teacher had directed the Hindu face toward the Pessimistic side of the shield, and it was so fascinated and horrified by the sight that it was unable to withdraw its eyes, and failed to perceive the reverse side of Truth, which showed the aspect of Optimism. Students have suspected that some foreign influence caused this sudden change of the race-thought, but others have attributed it to some great teacher unloosing some hitherto concealed fragment of the Secret Doctrine of the Fathers, to a race not yet quite ready to receive it, nor to understand it in its true relations.

It was not the idea of Metempsychosis that so changed the race-nature of these early people, who had always believed in Rebirth, but the undue emphasis laid upon the Law of *Karma*, that oppressed them. *Samsara* was pictured to them as a terrible cosmic mechanism, resulting from Ignorance or Mistake of some kind on the part of The Powers-That-Be, and into the wheels of which the race was caught and entangled almost beyond the possibility of escape. Particularly was this the case with the idea of the accused bad *Karma*, which was not possible of exhaustion in the present life, but which would remain over as "unused *Karma*—as an unpaid debt—and which would entail effects which would serve as a nucleus for new *Karma*, and so on, and on, binding the soul to the Wheel of Causation, or *Samsara*, for ever and ever, with only the shred of a chance to escape.

This doctrine in all of its unrelieved severity was poured out to this primitive people, as yet unprepared to consider it philosophically or to weed out the "half-truths" which appeared among its blossoms. To them it was the grim Law, as terrible as was the Law of Causation as stated many centuries afterward by *Gautama Buddha*, which again held the race to this side of the shield of Truth. There was no escape from the Law—"As among a thousand cows a calf finds its mother, so does the previously done deed follow after the doer thereof," says the writings. The root of the teachings regarding Desire, which afterward was retaught by *Gautama*, is found in these early teachings; Desire was the Root of Evil. And Desire was held to have sprung from *Avidya*, or Ignorance, which was the Seed of Evil. And so *Samsara*, or the Cycle of Existences, was thought to have arisen from *Avidya*, or Ignorance, which had crept upon the

ALL, and overshadowed its Wisdom. This was the beginning of the Hindu conception of *Maya*, or the Illusory Cause of the Phenomenal Universe. And then came the other teaching that by *Vidya*, or Wisdom, the chains of *Samsara* could be destroyed. And so the race began to take life very seriously, and to endeavour to attain Wisdom, in order to escape *Samsara*.

Van Deussen thus concisely states these fundamental conceptions regarding *Samsara*, and the escape therefrom : "Life is held to be precisely meted, in quality and quantity, as an expiation (absolutely just and adequate) for the deeds, thoughts and actions of the previous existence. This expiation is accomplished by deeds of action and enjoyment, which in turn is converted into fresh works and therefore cause of *Karma*, which must be expiated afresh in a subsequent existence, so that Atonement or Expiation is like a clock-work that in running-down always rewinds itself afresh, to be then again run-down, and again rewound, until all eternity. All this unto all eternity—unless there appears the Wisdom and Knowledge, which does not depend upon merit, but which breaks into consciousness with connection with it. This Wisdom or Knowledge dissolves *Samsara* or Life into its innermost elements, and burns up the seeds of works; and thus makes impossible for all future time a recurrence of the rebirth in *Samsara*."

× × ×

It is no wonder that this one-sided statement of Truth affected the Hindu race and coloured its religious conceptions for centuries to come, until the higher philosophical reasoning was able to separate the grain from the chaff of the teachings. Never has the race had a doctrine so compelling of Fear and Despair as this crude idea of *Samsara*, unrelieved by, philosophical explanation. To the minds of these primitive people, it must have indeed appeared that a Devil, stronger than all their gods, had appeared from the clear sky. For even their gods were held to come under the

Law, and to act as its administrators and instruments. And from that period, which shows its distinctive marks in the *Vedas*, the nature of the religious conceptions of the Hindus changed—Paganism vanished and the Life under *Samsara* succeeded it.

× × ×

But other influences were at work. Among the scattered mythological teachings of India there began to be manifested an insistence upon the fundamental truth of the ONE, over All, and in All, and which was ALL. No longer a shadowy, indefinite idea, the teaching of the *Brahman* began to assert its supremacy among the people. It did not do away with the gods, for they continued to be worshipped, and new ones still appeared—but *Brahman* was the Source of gods and people alike—the Universe coming from his Being. *Brahman* was regarded as the World-Soul, or Universal Spirit. *Brahman* had returned to the Aryans, who had lost sight of It during their years of wandering from the land of the Former Civilization—and nevermore has its Conception of the ONE-ALL, INFINITE, ETERNAL, ABSOLUTE EXISTENCE-INTELLIGENCE-POWER departed from the Aryan Consciousness in India. The race did not rise at once to the full Realization of this Truth—it has not fully risen to it, as a race, even to-day. But there set in an evolution of the understanding and realization of this great Truth, which is the basis of All Truth—this ONENESS—this Essence of Monism—to which all human thought and speculation invariably and inevitably leads its followers.

And now we shall proceed to trace this evolution of this dawning realization of the Absolute Truth among the minds of the Hindu races, as evidenced by their religious forms and schools, as we have already shown in connection with the philosophical schools. India's philosophies and religions mingle, blend and coalesce—there is no distinct and absolute division between them—but they may be considered as two phases of human thought.

× × ×

As we have said, the earliest conceptions of "gods" and supernatural beings, among the ancient Hindu peoples, were those of beings akin to Nature-Spirits, that is personified, deified Natural Forces. Thus in the early *Vedas* we find records of *Dyaus-Pita*, or 'father-Heaven,' accompanied by *Prithivi*, or 'Mother-Earth'; also *Ushas*, or the 'Dawn-Goddess'; *Surya*, or the 'Sun-God'; *Vayu*, or the 'Wind-God'; and *Agni*, the 'Fire-God.' There was also *Indra*, who was originally conceived of as the 'Lightning-and-Thunder-God,' similar to Jupiter and Zeus, of the Roman and Grecian mythology, but whose character was elaborated as time passed, and the *Indra* myths developed, until he was given a high place in the Pantheon of the early Hindus, and was often regarded as the 'King of the gods.' We also find frequent reference to *Varuna*, the 'Sky-God' whose eye was the blazing sun, and who gradually developed into the great god having charge of natural laws, and who also supervised the morality of the people. There was also *Soma*, the god of the fermented liquor, similar to Bacchus or Dionysus, minus their excesses—the Hindus using the fermented juice of the *soma*-plant in the sacrifices and religious ceremonies. *Soma* juice was also the nectar or sacred drink of these primitive Hindu gods, *Indra* in particular being addicted to its use, thereby increasing his ardent, fiery, warlike character, which made him so popular among the earlier warlike Hindu people.

There were thirty-three popular and celebrated gods in the early Hindu Pantheon, with innumerable demi-gods, minor gods, and demons, and lesser nature-spirits, many of which resembled the godlings of the ancient Greeks, having arisen from the same source, *i.e.*, the personification of natural principles, etc. Among these was the well known *Yama*, the "God-of-Death," who was held to be the first man who died, and who thus assumed godhood. There began to be noticed a peculiar tendency to blend the conceptions of two or more gods into one, and to exchange properties or characters between separate gods. This tendency increased and developed, until finally the distinctions between the several gods began to grow misty, and the people began to regard them all as appearances or personifications of some one Deity, and the fundamental ideas and conceptions of Hindu Pantheism began to assume more definite and much clearer shape and form.

× × ×

As time rolled on, the minor deities were lost sight of, and many survived only in name. The Brahmins, or priestly caste, assumed a still greater control, and impressed its teachings upon the people, shaping the popular belief more into a set system, and unifying its conceptions. As the Pantheistic idea developed, the nature and duties of the gods changed. *Indra* lost much of his terrifying power, and became the King of the After-World—the realm of the gods. *Varuna* became the Lord of the Ocean, and so on, many of the minor-gods being merged into the greater ones, as the race-conception moved toward Pantheism.

Gradually the idea of *Brahman*, the Supreme Self of the Universe, began to gain immense headway in India, among the masses, as it had long before been held as truth by the philosophers and priests. And accordingly the god *Brahma*, a personification of the *Brahman*, began to attain great popularity. *Brahma* was regarded as the Creative Deity, akin to the Greek Demiurge or divine agent of the Supreme Being employed to create the material universe and man; the terms *Prajapati*, and *Hiranyagarbha*, also being applied to *Brahma*. But *Brahma* did not altogether displace the older gods, some of which were retained, but which were considered as subordinate to *Brahma*—*Indra* and *Varuna* thus holding their places.

× × ×

Then began to develop the clearer idea of the Hindu

Trinity, composed of *Brahma, Vishnu,* and *Shiva*—the three being held to be aspects of one Supreme Being. *Brahma* was regarded as the Creative Principle of the Trinity; *Vishnu* as the Preserving Principle; and *Shiva* as the Destructive Principle; the manifestations of three principles causing the universal manifestation and life. This idea of the Trinity has never lost its hold on the Hindu mind, although it changed with the rise of *Vishnu* and *Shiva* worship, each sect holding that *Vishnu* or *Shiva*, as the case might be, was the Supreme Being, from which the other two sprung. But the basic Trinitarian idea remains as a part of the Hindu religious conception, and has persisted from the time of its birth. It dates very far back, and many of the ancient sculptures show traces of it; for instance, the well-known rock carving at Elephant which shows the Trinity as having one body with three heads emerging from it.

The rise of the popularity of *Vishnu* and *Shiva*, the two principles of the Hindu Trinity, may be traced in the *Vedas*. Among the early *Vedas* we find traces of *Vishnu* and *Rudra*, the latter being identical with *Shiva*, *Vishnu*, from the first, was pictured as gracious deity, filled with goodness, righteousness, and love, as well as a desire for order and peace—his symbol was the moving sun. *Rudra* (*Shiva*), on the other hand, represented the principle of destruction and strife, having a malevolent and revengeful nature, but being capable of propitiation and flattery for which he rewarded his worshippers with favours, prosperity, health, etc.—he had the storm for his symbol. This conception of *Vishnu*, and *Shiva*, corresponded with the world-wide and world-old conception of the Good Spirit and the Bad Spirit—God and Devil—which all races and religions seem to have had at some time in their history.

The conception of *Vishnu*, as the Lord of Righteousness and Goodness, had a wonderful growth among the people, and although originally opposed by many of the priests, it grew until the latter were compelled to accord it recognition and sanction. Not only was *Vishnu* regarded by many as the Supreme Principle in the Trinity, but gradually the conception grew until he was identified with the Supreme Being, or *Brahman*, itself, and the idea of *Brahman* lost its original philosophical significance among the people, and was regarded as the "nature of *Vishnu*"—*Vishnu* being regarded as the One God. But this idea of the One God was more than monotheism—it was Pantheism, for *Vishnu* was given the quality and nature of *Brahman*, and was held to be the Real Self, from whom all the universe, with its individual souls, flowed or was emanated. In other words, *Vishnu* became a personified THAT.

But growing up at the same time was another cult or school of religion—both within the enclosure of the orthodox Hinduism, and both receiving full sanction and tolerance. This second school was that of *Shiva*, whose former name of *Rudra* was dropped. *Shiva* was the direct contrast of *Vishnu*, the preserver and loving righteous guardian of his people. *Shiva* was the destroyer—the god of change and dissolution. As Lyal says : "*Shiva* represents the earliest and universal impression of Nature upon men—the impression of endless and pitiless change. He is the destroyer and rebuilder of various forms of life; he has charge of the whole circle of animated creation, the incessant round of birth and death in which all nature eternally revolves. His attributes are indicated by symbols emblematic of death and of man's desire; he presides over the ebb and flow of sentient existence. In *Shiva* we have the condensation of the two primordial agencies, the striving to live and the forces that kill. He exhibits by images, emblems, and allegorical carvings the whole course and revolution of Nature, the inexorable law of the alternate triumph of life and death—the unending circle of indestructible animation."

Shiva, under his ancient title of *Rudra*, was a fierce and terrible devil-god of the mountains. Dwelling surrounded by his bands of demons, goblins, and destroying spirits, and accompanied by his bride *Parvati*, in the depths and inner recesses of the Himalaya he held high revel and court, and was accordingly feared and flattered by his followers among the people, who sought to conciliate him by sacrifices and worship. As a symbol of the reproductive principle of nature, he wore the token of the *lingum* or male organ of generation; and as a symbol of subtle and malignant power, he wore a garland of twined serpents—a horrible creature, calculated to inspire fear, horror, and to induce propitiatory offerings. He was wont to haunt the tombs and graveyards at night, accompanied by his band of demons. Many of the cruel self-tortures of the Hindu ascetics arise from the desire to propitiate *Shiva*. But this horrible and fearsome creature, or god, with all of his malignant qualities, drew many followers to him, who manifested the greatest love and affection for him, equalling the love and devotion manifested by other cults and sects toward his opposite, the beneficent *Vishnu*. It is a strange psychological study in religion to witness the love, affection and devotion bestowed by some of the lower cults of *Shiva* toward this god, whose image is that of a naked, fierce being, with blue throat and red skin, or else of a livid white colour, with three eyes, besmeared with cow-dung ashes. Surely in its lower forms, *Shiva* worship is a refined form of devil worship. But there is a higher side of *Shiva* worship, as we shall see when we come to a consideration of the various sects.

Akin to *Shiva* worship, and springing up by its side, is the worship known as *Shakta* worship. *Shakti* is the term given to the principle of Cosmic Energy, or the Principle of Life Activities in the Universe, as contrasted with the Principle of Being. Personifying these two principles as follows : *Shiva* representing Being; and *Shiva's* consort or bride, known as *Parvati* (or *Uma*; *Gauri*; *Tara*; *Kali*; *Durga*, as the case may be) representing *Shakti* or the Creative Energy—the *Shaktas* have built up a cult or sect, devoted to the worship of *Shakti*. *Shiva* is the male-god, and *Shakti* the female-god.

And the worship is entirely that of the Female Principle of the Universe. The *Shaktas* are divided into two schools, *viz.* (1) the *Dakshinachari*, or 'Right Way Walkers,' who worship both *Shiva* and *Shakti*—that is the male and female principles of the deity, and who resemble the ordinary worshippers of *Shiva*, except that they manifest a preference for the destructive and terrible aspects of their god; and (2) the *Vamachari*, who concentrate their worship exclusively upon the feminine and maternal aspects of the deity, and who have been accused of a tendency toward Phallic worship. The ancient *Thugs*, and other terrible cults of India, were degenerated sects of *Shakta* worship. But, so strange is the division of Hindu thought, among the *Shaktas* are to be found many holding high ideals of the female deity as the Universal Mother, or Nature, as such worshipping her with beautiful ceremonies and ritual, and with the highest idealistic expressions, as we shall see presently.

The influence of Buddhism for a number of centuries after the death of *Gautama Buddha*, its founder, was quite marked, and the new religion left its impress upon many of the other forms of religion and philosophy in India. Following directly after the influence of the *Vishnu* and *Shiva* cults upon the orthodox priesthood, and which compelled them to revise and modify the original conceptions and authorized teachings, the teachings and doctrine of the *Buddha* did still more to shake the foundations of the priestly authority, and to render more catholic and universal the Universal Hindu Religion. Buddhism brought about an extreme adherence to the old respect for animal life, and led to the abolition of animal sacrifice. The Buddhist idea of Universal Brotherhood also had its effect in softening the hitherto rigid lines of caste, and led to the extending of religious knowledge to the lower castes who before that time were debarred from this instruction, and had to content themselves with the crumbs that fell from the tables of the higher castes. But in the end the Brahmins reasserted their ascendancy, and although their ideas had been modified by Buddhism, still they managed to crowd out the Buddhistic religious teachers and cults, peaceably but irresistibly, until now there is but a shadow of Buddhism left in India; in fact, in the central part of India proper it is not known at all among the people. Akin to this influence was that of the Jains, whose cult was a part of the general Buddhistic movement, although independent. The *Jains* affected the Brahmins more or less, but were finally compelled to modify their original position, until to-day they are looked upon more in the light of moderate dissenters than as heterodox outsiders.

And so, gradually there came to exist but two great schools of the Hindu Religion—(1) the *Vishnuites*, or *Vaishnavas*, who are the worshippers of *Vishnu*; and (2) the *Shivaites*, or *Shaivas*, or the worshippers of *Shiva*, including the cult of the *Shaktas*, or worshippers of the feminine principle of *Shiva*. Although there are a number of scattering cults and sects outside of these two great divisions of the Hindu Religion, still the majority of the cults and sects, high and low, advanced or degraded, may be classed under the head of one or the other of these two great schools or cults. And in the next lesson we shall proceed to a consideration of these two great cults as they exist to-day, with their many sub-divisions and characteristics of each. But before so doing let us consider the development of the two schools from their ancient condition to the present state, particularly as concerns the influence of the philosophical thought of the land, and the teachings of the several leaders who arose to influence the trend of the religious and philosophical thought in India.

While the cults of *Vishnu* and *Shiva* were developing, and the school of Buddhism and *Jainism* were churning up public opinion and beliefs, the purely philosophical minds of India were not idle. There were many such minds in India, and they held close to the fundamental principles of *Brahman*, the One Supreme Being, and to the Inner Teachings concerning THAT. The *Upanishads* were being studied as never before and additions to their number were being made by the great teachers. The philosophers were advancing the teachings of pantheistic monism along the lines of the *Vedanta* System, and the *Sankhya* System had gained many followers. Especially important was the work and influence of *Sankaracharya*, the great systematizer of the *Vedanta* System, who lived about the eighth century A.D.—he re-established the System which had lapsed in energy, and really founded the *Advaitist*, or non-dualistic, school of the *Vedanta*. This school held strictly to the conception of *Brahman*, or THAT, as Absolute Reality, all else being held to be *Maya*, or the illusory phenomenal universe. *Brahman* was held to be the only Truth, and the individual *Atman*, or Spirit, was held to be identical with *Brahman*. The *Vishnuites* (or *Vaishnavas*) claim *Sankaracharya* as having been one of their school, and his writing seems to bear out this fact, but nevertheless, he seems to have made common cause with the *Shaivas* in the common fight against Buddhism and *Jainism*, and, indeed, both of the schools of the *Vaishnavas* and the *Shaivas*, respectively, might accept the *Vedanta* teachings without any trouble, by the simple process of identifying their respective deity with *Brahman*, or THAT.

In the twelfth century A.D. appeared *Ramanuja*, the other great *Vedanta* teacher, who attacked *Sankaracharya's* position of absolute monism, or non-dualism, and advanced a system of "qualified-dualism," or *Vishishtadvaita*, which held that there exist Individual Souls or Atma, which, though proceeding from *Brahman*, are not essentially one with THAT, but instead bear a high degree of relation to It, as "elements" of Its Being; and which also differed from the *Advaitist* system by holding that *Brahman* was not merely a purely abstract being, but that It possessed real qualities of goodness, love, etc., raised to an infinite degree. Consequently, there at once arose a close degree of sympathy and relationship between the regular *Vaishnava*, or *Vishnuite* school, and this new *Vishishtadvaita* system of philosophy. *Ramanuja* made frequent respectful and worshipful mention of *Vishnu*, and his school were ardent *Vishnu* worshippers and recognized as a branch of the *Vaishnavas* on the religious side, while considered a branch of the *Vedanta* on the philosophical side—thus does philosophy and religion blend in India.

In the fifteenth century there arose another teacher destined to exert a marked influence upon the *Vaishnava* school, one *Vallabhacharya*, a Brahmin. His teachings were very much along the lines of those of *Ramanuja*, but in addition he laid great stress upon the human side of *Krishna*, an *avatar* or incarnation of *Vishnu*, who was represented as of a most attractive human personality. *Vallabhacharya* taught among other things that the best way of worshipping *Krishna* was by sanctifying all human joys and pleasures to his service—the laying of the offering of the sacrifice of human pleasure upon the lap of the deity. This teaching, which was called *Pushti Marga* or "The Way of Pleasure," had its idealistic and refined aspect, but unfortunately it afterward degenerated into sensualism among some of the more ignorant followers. In the early part of the nineteenth century, one *Svami Narayana* did much to reform this cult, and to bring it back to its original purity. He was a man of high morality and exalted religious nature, and he left a devoted band of followers whose successors exist to this day in some parts of India.

The fifteenth century gave birth to another great teacher whose influence in Hindu religion was quite marked. This man, a *Brahman*, was named *Visvambhara* and *Nimai*, but afterward took the name of *Chaitanya* upon the occasion of the taking of vows. He began to show signs of religious fervour in his youth, but at first hesitated to identify himself with the *Vaishnavas*, who were strongly opposed by the *Shakta* cults in his part of the country. However, before long he became overcome with the emotional and ecstatic phases of the *Bhakti*, or love-worship of *Krishna*, and soon was regarded as the chief earthly apostle of the latter. He announced no new doctrine, but devoted himself toward stirring up a strong *Bhakti* movement in favour of *Krishna*, and before long was at the head of a tremendous following of the most ardent, ecstatic, rapturous *Bhaktis*, who filled the air with shouts of "*Krishna! Krishna! Krishna!*" It was one of the greatest "revivals" that India has ever witnessed. Under *Chaitanya*, the worship of *Krishna* (the incarnation or *avatar* of *Vishnu*) received a strong impetus, which persists until the present time. This teacher held that the individual soul emanated from the Supreme Being, but was not identical therewith, his teachings resembling those of *Ramanuja*, with an admixture of the higher parts of those of *Vallabhacharya*.

In our next lesson we shall explain the various *avatars* or incarnations of *Vishnu*, of which *Krishna* was one, and which has much to do with the later development of the *Vaishnava* cults, as above indicated.

The *Shivaite* cults, while numerous, have not had so many divisions created by great teachers; their difference having arisen by reason of the preferences of the people in various sections for certain features of the worship, the choice often depending upon some prior form of worship which influenced the newer conception. These various *Vaishnava* and *Shaiva* sects and cults, together with the several minor divisions of the Hindu Religion, will be considered in our next lesson.

There is another sect which has attained prominence in India, and which is affiliated with the *Vaishnava* sects, and which is by some considered as a 'dualistic' form of the *Vedanta*, and which is known as the *Madhva* sect. It was established by *Madhvacharya* in the thirteenth century A.D. It is sometimes known as the *Dvaita*, or 'dualistic' philosophy, as contrasted with the *Advaita* or 'non-dualistic' philosophy of the branch of the *Vedanta* by that name. Departing from the *Advaita* non-dualistic, and the *Vishishtadvaita* 'qualified-dualistic' conceptions, this *Dvaita* system postulates an eternal distinction between *Brahman* and the individual souls, the latter being held to be akin to the individual spirits, or *Purushas*, of the *Sankhya* System, which resemblance is heightened by the fact that Matter is postulated as existing eternally, separate and distinct from both *Brahman* and the individual souls or *Purushas*. In fact the basic conceptions of this sect seem to have been taken bodily from the *Sankhya*, and then attached to the conception of *Brahman*. This *Madhva* sect teaches the efficacy of the adoration of *Vayu*, the son of *Krishna*, whom they hold to have been incarnated as *Madhvacharya*, the founder of the sect. *Madhva* departs radically from the prevalent Hindu conception of the universality of Emancipation of Salvation from *Samsara*—theory that all souls alike may gain Freedom. On the contrary he assumes a Calvinistic position, and separates the individual souls into three classes, *viz.* (1) the souls destined to pass to the realms of eternal bliss when they have escaped from *Samsara*; (2) the souls who are destined to eternal *Samsara*, without possibility of escape; and (3) the souls who are destined to everlasting hell by reason of the vileness of nature.

There are a number of minor sects and cults each having followers scattered throughout India, among whom are the following :

The *Nimbarka*, founded by *Nimbarka* in the twelfth century, who are held to be a branch of the *Vishnuites*, and who worship *Krishna*, and his consort *Radha*. They have no distinctive tenets, and are regarded more as a religious 'denomination' than as a 'school' or 'system.'

The *Ramananda*, founded by *Ramananda*, the pupil of *Ramanuja* the *Vishishtadvaitist*, and which adheres somewhat to the *Vishishtadvaitist* teachings, with additions and changes. Its adherents are among the poorer classes in the northern part of India.

The *Kabirpantha*, which was founded by *Kabir*, a disciple

of the founder of the last mentioned school, *Ramananda*. His teachings were largely those of his own teacher, with a strong tincture of Mahommedism. He taught a monistic Pantheism, warmed by a fervid *Bhakti* tendency, inclining toward ecstasy and emotion. The *Sufi* influence is apparent in his teachings. He held to a Supreme Being, which was the essence of all spiritual being, and soul-manifestation, the material universe being the 'body' of the Supreme Being. The latter is held to have evolved *Maya*, which in turn brought forth the Hindu Trinity of *Brahma, Shiva,* and *Vishnu,* who brought forth other gods, who begot the universe. This sect is still popular in the north of India, and has a following in Bombay.

The *Nanakpantha*, which is somewhat akin to the last mentioned sect, has its origin in *Vishnuite Vedanta*, coloured strongly by Mahommedism. It was founded by *Nanak*, in the sixteenth century A.D. Its essence is the worship of a formless Supreme Being (akin to the Mahommedan *'Allah'*) by godliness, meditation, tolerance, etc. The Sikhs take their teaching from Nanak, and this teacher has influenced many minor cults and sects in India, some of which have developed an advanced religious conception, and considerable philosophical merit.

In our next lesson we will consider the religions of Modern India.

SPECIAL MESSAGE IX

By Yogi Ramacharaka

For this month, we invite you to inhale the perfume arising from the flowers of the Spiritual Gardens of India, planted, reared and watered by the hands of the Sages :

"When one becomes freed from the bondage of the senses, he transcends all material relations, and realizing the inward light, regains his knowledge of Himself. This is indeed a realization of the Truth. It dwells beyond Mortality and Fear. Truth, Wisdom, Self, Spirit Absolute, are all but names for the same thing."

"There is no room for separateness in that intransmutable, formless, characterless Truth, which is beyond the relations of subject, object, time and space, cause and effect, beginning and end, absoute and relative, all and part. It is in every way full to the utmost, like the waters surging above all things at the great cyclic deluge. In it merges the cause of illusion, like darkness merges into light. Verily, there can be nothing like separateness in It, the highest essence of Truth—the One without a second."

"Truth is the highest and only real plane of Being. In it there is no world of subject and object. It is as a void, and yet is full. Though void, still does it contain innumerable worlds upon worlds, upon worlds. And yet it is void in Truth."

"As all light belongs to the sun; and all coldness to cold; and all warmth to heat; so do existence, consciousness, bliss, eternity, inteligence, belong to Truth."

"Truth is all bliss of every kind. Attaining this realization, one realizes his nature to be all-bliss. Truth, therefore, is the ultimate measure and standard of all bliss."

"Truth is unborn; ever-awake; free from dream; having no form and no name. It is one continuous thought, all- knowing. There is no metaphor, whatever, in this saying."

Our Meditation for the coming month is :

"REJOICE AND BE GLAD, FOR WITHIN YOU IS THE LIGHT OF THE WORLD."

Chapter X

The Religions of India (*Part II*)

From the sources mentioned in the preceding lesson, the Religions of India of to-day have arisen, subject to the mellowing influence of time, and the inevitable blending and mutual modification and influence of each upon the others. The old lines are maintained, but the doctrines have modified each other, and the lines are softened and blended until often it is difficult to point out the exact distinctions between some of the many cults of the several schools, the shading being so gradual. At the present time the three hundred millions (300,000,000) and over, of the Hindu people, are divided into several great divisions, with the numerical strength approximately stated as follows :

Orthodox Hindu Faiths	225,000,000
Mahommedans	63,000,000
Buddhists (in Burmah, etc.)	10,000,000
Animistic Religions	10,000,000
Christians	3,000,000
Sikhs	2,500,000
Jains	1,500,000
Jews	25,000
Parses	100,000

In the above list we have included the Jews, who are found principally in the large cities like Bombay, Calcutta, etc.; and the Christians, who are found in certain sections where the missionary work has been vigorous for several centuries. About one-half of the native Christians in India belong to the Roman Catholic Church, the other half being divided among a number of Christian denominations. The Parsees are found principally in the Bombay Presidency, and are the descendants of Persian Fire-Worshippers who settled in India over one thousand years ago, and who have never been interfered with in their faith by the orthodox Hindus, so tolerant is the Hindu race. Another instance of this tolerance is found in the case of the million of aboriginal people in India, the descendants of the dark-skinned natives of India who were found there by the Aryans when they came into the land many thousands of years ago; and these natives have never been disturbed in the original worship, nor have they been exterminated as were the native American Indian tribes who were the aborigines in the land now called America. They have been allowed to maintain their original nature worship, ancestor worship, or spirit worship of their forefathers, without opposition or hindrance, and without being subjected to 'missionary work' on the part of the Hindus. These people are included in the list of 'Animistic Religion,' the remaining nine million of this class being composed of scattering tribes, peoples, and sects who adhere to the ancient nature worship, or worship of the early personifications of natural forces, under the name and form of numerous 'gods,' and demi-gods, as mentioned in the preceding lesson. In the above list we have included the sixty-three million Mahommedans in the British Indian Empire and Provinces, who are the descendants of those who were converted to Mahommedism during the period when the adherents of that religion overran India (where they maintained a foothold for several centuries), together with the descendants of the original invaders. The Buddhists, numbering ten million in all India, are principally located in Burmah, and the Indo-Chinese Peninsula, Ceylon, Nepal, etc., at least nine million of the whole number being in Burmah alone; Buddhism being extinct in many parts of India, and existing only as a dead religion there.

Under the head of 'Orthodox Hindu Faiths' are included

followers of the several sects and schools of religion and philosophy, or religious-philosophy, which are generally grouped under the term and class of 'Brahminism,' the various sects and schools differing very materially from each other, but all having a common root, origin, and relation to that Original Religion of the Hindus, which they themselves call the *Sanatana* or Eternal Religion, and which has as its basis the belief in a One Infinite Reality, Being, or Existence, from which the phenomenal universe and the individual souls proceed. The different Hindu sects, while practically appearing as different religions, in reality regard themselves as but different sects and divisions of the One Eternal Religion of India, of which each, of course, considers itself the best and most favoured channel of expression and interpretation. None of the cults, or sects, or schools are regarded as 'outlanders,' heretics, or unbelievers—all are included in the great fold—all are regarded as seekers after the great Truth—all are looked upon as travellers upon many roads, each choosing his own path, of which the number is countless. As a respected Hindu has said: "The prevailing religion of India may be compared to a great mosaic, inlaid with every kind of religious idea, and every form of worship which the human mind can possibly conceive." And, as Max Müller says: "No phase of religion, from the coarsest superstition to the most sublime enlightenment, is unrepresented in that country."

The various sects and schools of the Hindu Religion, which is generally regarded under the head of "Brahminism" or 'Hinduism,' by Western authorities, but which is spoken of as the *Sanatana* or 'Eternal Religion,' or the 'Religion of India' by the Hindus themselves, and which comprises two hundred and twenty-five millions (225,000,000) of people in India, may be grouped into three general classes, namely: (1) *Vishnuites*, or *Vaishnavas;* (2) *Shivaites*, or *Shaivas*; and (3) Abstract Monists. The origin of the first two classes has been given in the preceding lesson, where the rise of the worship of *Vishnu* and *Shiva* has been described and the various influences operating in the development having been noticed. The third class, or Abstract Monists, are comparatively few in number, and are those people who refuse to acknowledge the need of names of personification of *Brahman*, and who maintain a philosophical religion based upon Pure Reason, with *Brahman*, THAT, or The Absolute as their object of veneration, love, and meditation.

The worship of *Brahman*, the personification of the Creative Principle in the Hindu Trinity, has almost disappeared as a separate form of religion. *Brahma*, as the Creative Principle in the Trinity, or as the Personification of *Brahman*, is considered too much of an abstraction to be the object of love and worship, and is generally passed by in favour of either *Vishnu* or *Shiva*, often being held to be really in the nature of a Demiurge, or Creative Agent of either of these two great Deities, particularly in the case of those *Vishnuites* who attribute to *Krishna*, in his highest conception, the nature of *Brahman*, or THAT. It is true that, nominally, the Hindu Treaty is spoken of as existing and ruling the religious conception of India, but in reality it is not so, and the two great classes of the modern Hindu Religion have practically discarded the Trinity, and have substituted the worship of *Vishnu* or *Shiva*, as the case may be. *Brahma* is still seen in the temples, in the shape of his images with their red bodies and several heads, all of which is merely symbolic, of course—but as an object of worship he has faded from view, being outclassed by the other two conceptions of Deity. And, accordingly, let us now pass on to a consideration of the two great classes or divisions of the Hindu Religions of to-day: (1) the *Vishnu* worshippers, or *Vaishnavas*; and (2) the *Shiva* worshippers, or *Shaivas*, including the *Shaktas*.

The Vaishnavas

The *Vaishnavas* are those Hindus who worship the Supreme Being under the name of *Vishnu*, the second person of the Hindu Trinity, or-the Preserving Principle of Deity. We have spoken in our last lesson of the rise of the conception of *Vishnu* from that of a separate god of goodness, and kindness—the beneficent god—to the second person in the Trinity of the Hindus, as *Vishnu* the Preserver; and of his subsequent rise to the position of the Supreme Being Absolute, in the eyes of his followers, the *Vaishnavas*. And this latter position he now occupies in India to-day, at least among his own followers, who compose one of the great two classes of the Hindu religions; the opposing faction, or Shaivas, refusing this exalted position to *Vishnu*, relegating him to a secondary place, and claiming the first place for their own god, *Shiva*. It is the custom of many Hindu writers to say that the worship of *Vishnu* and *Shiva* is practically the same, and that the followers of the one class cheerfully join in the worship of the opposing conception—both being but different ideals of the One Reality. This statement is true, when understood correctly, but the fact remains that when a *Vaishnava* worships *Shiva* he qualifies his worship with the belief that he is really worshipping *Vishnu through Shiva*, the secondary aspect; and the *Shaiva* pursues the same policy when he is worshipping *Vishnu* in company with his *Vaishnava* friends. It is true that both agree that they are worshipping *One*, but the fact remains that each believes *that One* to be *his own One*; that is, he believes his own Deity to absorb the other, *the other being but an aspect of his own Deity*. So that while it may be claimed that there is a "Unity in the Diversity," it likewise may be stated that there is a decided difference of opinion as to the nature of that Unity. There are two classes of worship, in spite of the kindly attempts to make it appear as one.

The *Vaishnavas* hold that *Vishnu* may be considered in both the impersonal and the personal aspect. As the impersonal *Vishnu*, he is the Supreme Being, omnipresent, omnipotent, and omniscient—exciting everywhere, and being the Reality or Spirit in all manifestations—having all power—and possessing infinite knowledge. In fact, the impersonal *Vishnu* is considered as *Brahman*, THAT, or the Absolute. But the *Vaishnavas* consider him in this impersonal aspect only in their philosophical minds, and when it comes down to worship the personal aspect is ever in evidence. The personal *Vishnu* is held to dwell in the highest heavens, which he rules. His image in this aspect appears in the temples, blue or black in colour. But there is another and far more important personal aspect of *Vishnu*, and one that causes him to be so popular among the Hindu people—his aspect as the various *avatars* or incarnations in human form.

While the term *Vaishnava* is strictly applied to all worshippers of *Vishnu*, still it is generally restricted to those sects which worship him in the form of either of his two chief incarnations, *viz.*, *Rama* or *Krishna*, more particularly the latter, and which comprise the great majority of the *Vishnu* worshippers, those who worship him either in his general personal aspect, or his general personal aspect as the Lord of the Heavens, being few as compared with those who worship him in his *avatars*. These *avatars* or human incarnations were for the purpose of regenerating the race, and lifting it up from the mud of materiality. There are promised other avatars, from time to time, as they are needed. The *Bhagavad-Gita* promise, which is held sacred by the *Vaishnavas*, says: "Although I am above birth and rebirth, or Law, being the Lord of all there is, for all emanateth from me—still do I will to appear in my own universe, and am therefore born so by my Power and Thought, and Will .... Whenever the world declineth in virtue and righteousness ; and vice and injustice mount the throne—then come I, the Lord, and revisit my world in visible form, and mingle with men, and by my influence and teachings do I destroy the evil and injustice, and re-establish virtue and righteousness. Many are the times that I have thus appeared—many are the times hereafter when I shall come again." (*Bhagavad-Gita*, part IV).

The Rama Avatar

The first great *avatar* which is dear to the *Vaishnavas* is the seventh, in which *Vishnu* incarnated as *Rama-Chandra,* or *Rama,* the hero of the Hindu epic, the *Ramayana. Rama* was the son of King *Dasaratha* of *Ayodhya,* and whose youth wad marked with wondrous performances. He married the beautiful princess *Sita* (whose memory is revered by all Hindu women, to whom she is held up as an eternal example of purity and goodness), but afterwards either voluntarily relinquished the throne, or else was exiled by his father for his religious austerities, and then lived in the jungle for fourteen years. *Sita,* his wife, was stolen by the demon-king *Ravana. Rama,* flying to her rescue, defeated and destroyed the hosts of *Ravana,* and saved his wife; whereupon he returned to his own country and was crowned as king. Influenced by the idle gossip and envious talk of the people, *Rama* sent his wife *Sita* away from him, to the hermitage or convent, where she bore him two sons, *Kusa* and *Lava,* and was afterward reunited to him in the heaven-world. The story of *Rama* is forever preserved in the great Hindu epic, the *Ramayana,* one of the masterpieces of Hindu literature, which is highly regarded and venerated by the Hindu people, and which forms a Bible to many who worship *Rama* as the *avatar* or human incarnation of *Vishnu,* and the Saviour of Mankind. These worshippers of *Rama* are known as *Ramat-Vaishnavas,* and number many millions of people. They are noted for their high degree of morality and ethics, and for their complete theological system. They hold not only that *Vishnu* has qualities of positive goodness, instead of being merely an abstract Being, but that moreover there is a heaven of pure bliss in which the righteous emancipated soul will spend eternity instead of being absorbed into the divine Being, as held by the *Advaitist Vedantists.*

The Krishna Avatar

The large body of the *Vaishnavas,* known as the

Krishna-Vaishsnavas, worship *Vishnu* in his eighth *avatar* or human incarnation, in which he appeared as *Krishna*, and whose history and teachings appear in the Hindu epics known as the *Mahabharata*, with its supplementary writings known as the *Harivamsa*, the *Pancharata*, and the *Bhagavad-Gita*, which compose a gigantic Hindu epic, in the first part of which *Krishna* is represented as a demi-god and powerful prince, the latter part (particularly in the *Bhagavad-Gita*) showing him in his aspect of the *avatar* or full incarnation of *Vishnu*, the Supreme Being. The Hindu records hold that *Krishna* appeared about 1400 B.C., and he is claimed as the greatest of the *avatars* of *Vishnu*. He is represented as having been born in a cave, during a time when a Hindu king named *Kamsa* had ordered all young infants to be killed. He was named *Krishna*, by reason of his blue-colour. His father, *Vasudeva*, in order to save him from the hands of the murderous king of *Mathura*, gave him into the keeping of Nanda, a herdsman. *Krishna* spent his youth as a shepherd in *Vraja*, and many myths and legends are related regarding this part of his life, some of which concern his relations with the Gopis, or shepherdesses, but which his followers claim to have a symbolic significance instead of the literal one which the casual reader might be inclined to place upon them. The spread of the *Krishna-Vaishnava* cult has been remarkable, and it has hundreds of thousands of adherents in India to-day, numbering among its ranks some of the most prominent people in the land. There are several divisions of this cult, the principal of which are known as the *Bhagavatas* and the *Pancharatras* respectively. The *Bhagavad-Gita* is the principal sacred writing esteemed by these schools, and its general doctrine is that of the cult. It identifies *Krishna* with the Supreme Being, and accordingly the term '*Krishna*' is heard a thousand times to one of *Vishnu—Krishna* being regarded not only as the term for the *avatar* of *Vishnu*, but also as the favourite term for the Supreme Being itself. Another favourite term applied to *Krishna* is '*Hari*.'

There are many minor divisions among the *Krishna-Vaishnavas,* which arose from the preference for the details of the teachings of several great teachers which arose from time to time. Among these schools, founded by the teachers, are the followers of the following great leaders, respectively; *Sankaracharya,* the founder of the *Advaitist* school of *Vedanta; Ramanuja,* the founder of the *Vishishtadvaita* school of *Vedanta; Vallabhacharya,* a follower of *Ramanuja,* who established the *Pushti-Marga* teachings ; *Ramananda; Nimbarka; Madhva,* the founder of the dualistic or *Dvaita* school of *Vedanta;* and *Chaitanya,* the great *Krishna-Vaishnava* teacher—these several schools and their founders have been described in the preceding lesson. We do not consider it necessary to repeat the descriptions here, and must content ourselves with the bare mention in connection with what we have said in the preceding lesson regarding them.

We make an exception of the school of *Chaitanya,* however, for his influence was most marked on the *Krishna-Vaishnava* cult, and, in fact, there are schools of the cult that hold that he, himself, was a subsequent incarnation of *Vishnu,* or *Krishna.* The teachings of *Chaitanya* have exerted a great influence over the entire cult of the *Krishna-Vaishnavas,* inasmuch as he laid such great stress upon the *Bhakti* or 'Love' doctrine. The result has been that the entire body has been noted for its extreme manifestation of the 'Love-of-God' conception, rather than for its philosophical teachings. The followers of *Chaitanya* exalt *Rahdi,* the consort of *Krishna,* to a high position, regarding her as the Love-Principle which emanated from *Krishna.*

There have been a number of 'reform movements' in the various schools of the *Krishna-Vaishnavas* and some of the reformers have carried their followers far beyond the original bounds of the cult, some tending toward an extreme liberal eclecticism, while others tend toward a very narrow form of deism scarcely resembling the broader pantheistic idea. Some of the schools are marked by a very high degree of morality and form of worship, while others have wandered off into low forms of ceremonial and worship, in a few cases degenerating to a degree but little removed from the old Phallic worship, and in which the 'Love' element is prostituted into low and ignoble forms. This, however, should not be urged as a reproach against the general cult, as these degenerating tendencies have been evidenced in nearly every religion the world has ever known at some time in their history; and are really departures from the pure religion, rather than a development of it.

Some of the several *Krishna-Vaishnava* schools are noted for their insistence upon the worship of the 'infant *Krishna*,' with a related Madonna worship, which was a departure from the older schools, and which bears interesting resemblance to certain forms of ceremony and worship in the Roman Catholic Church. It seems that India is destined to manifest every possible form of religious ceremony and worship, and to exhibit a correspondence to the religions of all countries—always antedating them, however.

As an instance of the degree of 'hair-splitting' theology manifested by some of these schools and cults, let us call your attention to a matter of theological dispute that has raged for centuries between two schools of the *Ramat-Vaishnava* cult. The school of the north of India, known as the *Vadagalis*, are found opposing the school of the south, known as the *Tengalais*. The Southern school holds that the Lord saves the sinning soul as does the mother cat, picking up the young and carrying it away to a place of refuge; while the Northern school insists that the Lord saves the sinning soul as does the mother monkey, urging her young to embrace her so that they may be carried off. The former school holds that the work of salvation must be done altogether by the Lord, who, mother-cat-like, picks up the sinner and saves him ; while the latter holds that the saving is done by the Lord in the manner of the monkey-mother who bids her young reach out for salvation, and thus saves them by reason of their love, faith, and individual effort. This point, of course, is applicable to other religions besides those of the Hindus, and shows the degree of theological reasoning employed in these schools, as well as the tendency to illustrate the doctrines by parables, in which the common animals are brought in in a manner startling to the Western mind.

Krishna is usually represented in the images as playing the flute, and often with his consort *Rahdi* standing behind him, encircling him with her arms. The *Vaishnavas* often mark their foreheads with two perpendicular marks, as a cult sign. They hold in high esteem the symbols of the *Tulsi* plant, and the *Salagrama* stone, which latter is a clear white pebble.

As a rule, the Hindus with *Vedantic* affiliations are inclined toward the *Vaishnava* cult, in some of its many branches, and many of the great *Vedanta* teachers have been teachers and founders of *Vaishnava* schools, as we have noticed in passing.

The Shaivas

In our preceding lesson we called your attention to the rise of *Shiva* from the earlier conceptions of him as *Rudra*, the Destroying God; on to the higher conception of him as the third principle of the Hindu Trinity with the added quality of the god of change and reproduction as well as his original quality of the destroying principle; and then on to the still higher conception of him as the Absolute Supreme Being, the latter claim, however, being made only by his special following, the *Shaivas*—the claim being contested by the *Vaishnavas*, who claim that distinction for their own deity, *Vishnu*. To the *Shaivas, Brahma* and *Vishnu* are merely emanations from, or else high agents or demiurges springing from *Shiva* and performing parts of his universal work.

There is one great difference between the respective *Vishnu* and *Shiva* cults, and that is that the *Vishnu* worshippers have their god appearing in human form in his *avatars*, of which we have spoken, and they claim that he is thus brought nearer to them in the matter of worship—that instead of being an abstract being he is a real, human entity, partaking of the nature of man, and thus understanding other men the better. To the *Ramat-Vaishnavas*, the incarnation of *Rama* is a great and dignified leader, teacher and guide, of the highest morality and offering a splendid example of right living—ever the 'great Example,' as he is called. And to the *Krishna-Vaishnavas, Krishna* is regarded as the Saviour of mankind, inspiring love and fervid devotion to a degree impossible in the case of an abstract deity—a touch of the intimate personal relation akin to the love for the Master among the Christians, which is nearer than the love for Jehovah, the Father of the Trinity, who is regarded rather more with awe, reverence, and fear, than with the human love bestowed upon the second aspect of The Son. In fact, as strange as may appear to the Western mind, many of the simpler-minded Hindus beseech *Krishna*, the *avatar*, to intercede for them with *Krishna*, the Supreme Absolute Being —and when remonstrated with by the missionaries for the absurdity and inconsistency of the proceeding, often reply that it is no more absurd than the missionaries teaching that prayer to God should be made through the Mediator, or Christ—"through our Lord, Jesus Christ," or "for Christ's sake," when Christ is equal to, and identical with the Father.

But the *Shiva* worshippers have no such intimate approach to their deity—for *Shiva* is not held to have had any incarnations or *avatars*. *Shiva* must be approached directly by his worshippers. But, nevertheless, among some of the *Shaivas* there is manifested a wonderful fervour of worship and devotion, scarcely second to that of many of the *Vaishnavas*.

There is a paradox in the conception of *Shiva* that is most difficult of comprehension by the Western mind, even when a study of the subject is made. There are two distinct aspects of *Shiva*—two totally opposing conceptions of him—one or the other of which is favoured by the various sects in the general cult. And this gives rise to the paradox of the character of the *Shaivas* noticed by all Western writers and students of *Shiva* worship. The highest and the lowest are represented in this form of worship, and the followers of the sects represent some of the brightest philosophical minds in India, and also some of the most degraded and brutal and uneducated among the Hindu races or tribes-people. The tendency of the *Shaivas* to ignore the caste distinctions has attracted many of the low-caste people to some of the lower *Shaiva* sects.

In fact, there are really *two Shivas*—that is, while there is merely one *Shiva* in name, there are really two aspects of him as conceived by his followers. The one aspect or conception is derived from the legendary *Shiva* of the ancient Hindus, in which he is pictured as a fierce, revengeful, warlike, angry god, of a destructive tendency—the *Rudra* of the ancient peoples. And this aspect attracts to him the rude, uncultured minds of the uneducated people and tribes, and also those whose minds turn toward selftorture, asceticism, etc., as a means of worship. And some of the lower sects are composed of people having these debased ideals. The *fakirs* of India—those false *Yogis*—the mendicant class, ignorant, superstitious, and given to self-torture and displays of low forms of magic and conjuring—all of these are numbered among certain lower sects of the *Shaivas*. And the descendants of some of the lower tribes of India—the semi-barbarous people who represented the negative-pole of the ancient Hindu race—have naturally evolved into *Shaivas* of certain lower sects. The fanatical and almost savage people of the more remote districts also incline toward certain forms of *Shiva* worship, and many of their ceremonies and rites show an unpleasant resemblance and origin from the rites and ceremonies of their barbaric forefathers. Many of these tribes, you must remember, were of Non-Aryan extraction, and are quite different from the Aryan races in culture and attainment. And, even when we consider certain degenerate tribes and peoples of Aryan extraction, we have only to compare them with some of the semi-barbarous and brutal classes and sub-races of certain European countries, who, while claiming the name of Christians, certainly are sunk in the deepest mire of gross superstition and ignorance, and are incapable of even faintly understanding the true principles of the religion whose name they bear. Comparison, like these will give us a fairer perspective and point-of view, as well as a clearer understanding of the degenerate forms of certain sects of *Shiva* worship.

Among these sects worshipping this aspect of *Shiva*, some of the representations of their deity are revolting and shocking. His images are hideously ugly, disfigured by lines showing rage, anger, and the attributes of the devil-gods of other peoples. Snakes are intertwined around his head, and he is daubed with the ashes of cow-dung. Skulls form a part of his adornment. His atmosphere is one of dread and terror. Demons and evil spirits attend upon him, and the pallor of death is upon his countenance—the fetid odour of the graveyards is his delight. The stage fittings and general atmosphere surrounding *Shiva*, among such sects, are appropriate to the conception or aspect of the god which attracts this class of his followers. The sects favouring this aspect or conception of *Shiva* are of three classes, *viz.* (1) Those who have descended from the semi-barbarous tribes and people of the past, and whose crude and savage conceptions of deity have been absorbed naturally as an inheritance from the past—these people generally dwelling in remote districts, far from the educating influences of the cultured centres of Hindu life and teachings; (2) Those whose sects have degenerated and become debased, from numerous influences, and who have sunk to a low degree of civilization and life, and whose religious ideals have become degenerated—these people also, as a rule, live in remote districts, although some of them are among the various lowest classes of the more thickly populated sections and cities and belong to the 'submerged millions' which exist in India and the West alike; and (3) Those who are attracted to this low form of *Shiva* worship by reason of their attraction for low forms of magic art, sorcery, witchcraft, and general conjuration, known to the Western occultist as 'Black Magic.' The reason for this is that *Shiva* is ever regarded as the god of Magical Art, of Psychism, and while for that reason he attracts some of the followers of higher forms of Hindu Magic, Supernatural Science, etc., the same fact draws to the lower sects the followers of the dark side of the subject. To these people *Shiva* is little more than a sorcerer-god of a sublimated Satan, or Beelzebub—and their worship of him but little more than a devil worship. To understand some of the lowest forms of this worship, and the worshippers, one has but to remember the degraded Voodoo worship of some of the Afro-American negroes, with their charms, fetishes, and black-magic practices and devilish rites. As a writer says : "These abortions of religion are *in strange contrast to the higher schools of Shaivaism.*"

Now let us turn to the lighter and brighter side of the picture of *Shaivaism,* such as alluded to in the closing words of the above quotation. The second aspect or conception of *Shiva,* and which is held by many influential sects of the cult, represents the extreme opposite pole of religious thought, and is held by the extreme opposite pole of human society. Western travellers who have witnessed only the degraded forms of *Shaivaism* and who have returned home and written of what they saw, while honest in their intentions, nevertheless have done a great injustice to the cult of the *Shaivas,* inasmuch as they have told merely a half-truth, leaving the brighter half untold, because unwitnessed. The higher *Shaiva* sects are composed of the persons of high social position and education, many being drawn to them by reason of the interest in the more subtle features of philosophy as taught by their teachers. The sects of the *Dandis*; the *Dasnamis*; and the *Lingayats*, respectively, represent the higher phases of *Shaiva* philosophical and religious thought. The *Dandis* and the *Dasnamis*, while ascetic to a degree, avoid the excesses of the lower devotees, and a high form and degree of religious life and morals is manifested among them. Their philosophy very much resembles that of certain of their *Vaishnava* countrymen, inasmuch as it is based on the *Advaita Vedanta* teachings of *Sankarachayya*, the great *Advaitist* teacher. They devote themselves to the study of, and contemplation of *Brahman*, or the Supreme Being, or THAT, with which they hold the impersonal *Shiva* to be identical—in other words, they worship *Brahman* under the name and form of *Shiva*, just as some of the *Vaishnavas* worship *Brahman* under the name and form of *Vishnu*, or *Krishna* in the Absolute aspect. The *Lingayats*, while wearing the phallus or symbol of the male generative power, are almost puritanical in their views, regarding sex as a most sacred thing, and severely condemning impure views or actions relating to it.

Other of these higher sects have attracted many highly educated Brahmins and high-caste Hindus, and those of philosophical or, more particularly, metaphysical tendencies, and such dwell upon the metaphysical features of the doctrine. Other high sects are composed of the better class of *Yogis* and followers of *Patanjali*. The *Spanda* sect in the north inclines to a mystic philosophy of a high order, somewhat resembling certain of the *Sufi* doctrines. There, are also, in the south, other mystic sects within the cult of the *Shaivas*, whose poems are in the same fervid strain as the Persian *Sufi* poetry (see lesson on *Sufiism*).

In strange contrast to the hideous images of *Shiva* favoured by the lower sects are those used by some of the higher sects, more particularly those having *Yoga* tendencies. Instead of the horrible skulls and instruments of vengeance and death, *Shiva* is represented as a venerable *Yogi* Ascetic, wrapped in profound meditation and in the *Samadhi* ecstatic stage, representing the highest *Yogi* ideal—Transcendental

Consciousness through Meditation and Concentration. To these sects *Shiva* represents renunciation and unworldliness, and a complete manifestation of the *Yoga* Stages as recommended by *Patanjali*. And this is why *Shaiva* is the "god of the *Yogis*," when they seek an outward or personified form for the Supreme Being with whom they desire Union. And to such, *Shaiva* is the "god of the *Yoga* Powers," that is, of the super human powers and qualities claimed by the *Yoga* school for their advanced teachers and students—the Deity of High Magic and Psychic Power.

So, you see, there are two entirely distinct and opposite conceptions and aspects of *Shaivaism*—the extremely high, and the extremely low. And back of all is the *Shiva* of the transcendental philosopher, or metaphysician, who, divesting *Shiva* of all human attributes or qualities, thinks of him as identical with *Brahman*, The Absolute, or THAT—the One, without attributes or qualities—the Abstraction of Reality. Such is the variety and quality of the Hindu religious and philosophical mind. And, after all, the West offers a correspondence in the varying conceptions of Deity, as witness the difference between the conception which pictures Deity as a 'tribal-god,' or 'war-god,' accompanying the armies of a favoured nation, helping them to victory, and destroying their enemies (and this is common to many modern nations in time of war, nearly all of whom claim that "God is on our side"); and the other conception of Him as the God of Love and Peace, abhorring strife and bloodshed; and the third conception of Him as an abstract, impersonal Being, beyond human thought and imagination—all of these conceptions exist side by side among the Western people of the same faith. Let us remember this when we wonder at the 'paradoxes'" of Hindu religious conception and worship. We have but to compare the conception of Deity held by the earlier writers of the Old Testament (which many moderns still favour) with those of the highest form of Modern Christianity, to understand that the same Deity can mean totally different things to different people. After all, there is great truth in the well-known sayings that "A man's God is himself at his highest," and that "A man's idea of God is but the man himself magnified to infinity." In spite of the symbol and name, men insist upon giving to their gods their own attributes, qualities and feelings—and if one knows a man's idea of God, he may form a very fair idea of the man himself; and if he knows the man himself, he may form a very fair idea of his God.

The Shaktas

In our preceding lesson, we pointed out to you the relation of *Shakta* worship with that of *Shiva* worship. *Shakta* worship is the worship of *Shakti* or the Creative Principle of the Universe, conceived of as being of the female nature or quality—the Universal Mother. It is believed by some authorities that *Shakta* worship is the survival of an elementary worship of the Female Principle in Creation, or the Female Side of Nature or Divinity, possibly acquired by the Aryans from the native tribes of India with whom they came in contact. However this may be, the conception has taken a strong hold on the *Shaivas* in its high and low forms, corresponding to the high and low forms of the *Shiva* worship itself, and generally accompanying it.

In its higher form, *Shakta* worship consists of the worship and adoration of the Mother Aspect of Nature, or the Divine Motherhood. It attracts many *Sankhyas* who see in *Shakti* the principle of *Prakriti*, or the Creative Energy of Nature, or Nature itself, as contrasted with *Purusha* or Spirit, which latter they held to be represented by *Shiva*. Others are attracted to *Shakta* worship in a manner similar to the attraction that Nature Worship has for certain of the early Greeks and other peoples, and which has led many of our Western poets to rhapsodies over Nature, personified as a Being. Admirers of Walt Whitman and other Nature lovers among the poets could understand some of the more refined and subtle of the conceptions of the *Shaktas*. Some of the higher *Shakta* cults have a beautiful ritual and interesting ceremonies, inspired by poetic idealism.

But, as is the case in the *Shiva* worship which it accompanies, *Shakta* worship has its unpleasant side. In contrast with the beautiful images and ideas of *Shakti*, favoured by the higher sects which dwell upon the beauty and beneficence of Nature or *Shakti*—the lower sects picture *Shakti* in hideous forms, representing death, disease, plague, horror and other undesirable aspects of Nature and Nature's Laws. And just as the higher sects picture the Divine Feminine in *Shakti*, endowing her with the attributes of maternal love, and feminine influence and affection of the highest kind, in all of its gentleness and attractiveness—so do the lower sects picture *Shakti* as representing the gross side of the female nature, partaking of licentiousness, and lust, and fierce animal passion. Just as Woman herself may rise to the highest heights, or sink to the lowest depths, so have the conceptions of the *Shaktas* risen high, or fallen low, according to their natures. And just as the higher sects consider the 'Magic of Nature' as shown in her wonderful transformations and phenomena; and endeavour to obtain control or mastery of these processes and forces by studying the underlying laws, according to their theories of physics and psychology—so do the lower sects prostitute this study into witchcraft, or sorcery, or degraded and debasing forms of psychic phenomena, resembling the practices of the lowest Voodooism and Conjuration, thus giving a fit companionship to the lowest *Shaiva* practices. And so in the case of the *Shaktas*, as with the *Shaivas*, there is the paradox of the Very High and the Very Low.

The Sikhs

The *Sikhs*, dwelling for the greater part in the Punjab, or north-western province of India, comprising 2,500,000 people, follow the teachings of *Nanak*, who lived in the sixteenth century B.C., as stated in our preceding lesson. The *Sikhs* regard *Nanak* as a minor incarnation of Divinity, and highly revere his writings and teachings. They are intensely opposed to images or symbols, resembling the Puritans in that respect, and forming a contrast to the majority of the other Hindu sects or cults who revel in imagery and symbols. The *Sikhs*, however, are inclined to make a Sacred Thing of the Holy Writings of *Nanak*, which are their Scriptures, and which they regard as 'The Word of God,' placing it upon their altars, and paying it sacred honours. Their teaching shows the influence of both the *Vedanta* and Mahommedism—they holding to the existence of One Supreme Being or God, which they hold to be formless, and in many ways akin to the *Allah* of Mahommedism. Their Scripture inculcates a high order of religious and moral doctrine, and a broad tolerance and kindliness, and a high ideal of purity and godliness. The followers of this religion rank very favourably among the other Hindus of the better sects, and with the better class of the Mahommedans.

The Jains

There are also about 1,500,000 followers of the religion of the *Jains* in India, principally in Marwar, Bombay Presidency, and Mysore, drawing its numbers from the respectable middle-classes and small merchants, etc. It stands well among students of Oriental religions, although a minor religion, and its literature is generally of a high order, and its people orderly, and manifesting a morality and ethics which compare favourably with the other sects and cults. The *Jain* teaching is similar to that of the Buddhists, but the orthodox Hindus consider them agnostic rather than atheistic. The *Jain* doctrine is dualistic, consisting of a belief in Soul and Non-Soul or Matter. Their conception of God is that He is but little more than the Totality of Cosmic Energy. They have a number of revered prophets, or teachers, called *Tirthankaras*, who have passed on to higher planes, and to whom, and *Mahavira*, the founder of their cult, they pay homage and intense devotion and reverence, akin to Saint Worship. The *Jains* are great respecters of life, even outdoing the Buddhist in that respect, and go to absurd lengths to avoid the destruction of life, even in seeds, etc. At the same time they look forward to Death with pleasure and delight, as a release, and some fanatics among them have starved themselves to death as a religious act, but at present this practice is almost unknown.

The Theistic Sect

During the nineteenth century there arose a number of modern Theistic Sects in India, closely resembling the Unitarian Movement in America. The principal sect of this kind is the *Brahma-Samaj*, which is called a 'natural religion,' denying the infallibility of the *Vedas*, and adhering to the worship of One God, or Supreme Ruler of the Universe, rejecting all images or symbols. *Kesab Chandra* was the prime mover in establishing this sect, about 1870. Another similar sect was founded in Bombay, about the same time, called the *Prarthana-Samaj*, which holds to the general Unitarian doctrine, but discourages Christian influence or affiliation; preferring strictly Hindu control and membership. The *Arya-Samaj* is another sect of this kind, which was founded by *Dayananda Sarasvati* about the same time as the other two similar schools. This sect discards caste, images, mythology, and tradition, but respects the *Vedas*, which embrace its doctrine of a strict Monotheism. The teachers of this school interpret the *Vedas* in the light of modern religious thought, including the teachings of modern science.

Ramakrishna

A marked influence on modern Hindu religious thought was exerted by *Bhagavan Shri Ramakrishna*, who lived and taught in India during the last part of the nineteenth century, and who founded a school which now includes many Hindus of the better classes of the community. His teachings were based on the Fundamental Doctrines, as interpreted by the *Advaitists*, but his views were extremely broad and catholic. He claimed all men as his brothers and co-religionists; all countries as his home; and all religions as his very own. By many of his followers he is regarded as an Incarnation of Divinity. His teachings created a great revival of religious interest in India, the effects of which are still very apparent. A branch of his movement was established in America by the late and respected *Swami Vivekananda*, who was one of his disciples and ardent admirers, and who brought forth his teachings in America at the occasion of the World's Parliament of Religions in 1893. *Ramakrishna* was a *Bhakti Yogi*, as well as a teacher of philosophical religion, and his theme was ever 'Love, love, love!' By many 'Western people he is regarded as the Modern Hindu Saint, equalling the teachers, sages and founders of cults of early days.

Hindu Religious Images

We wish to add a word here regarding the Western misconception of the use of Images in the Hindu religious worship. According to the Western travellers, particularly the missionaries, the Hindus are a race of Idolaters. This is an erroneous idea. While it is true that many of the ignorant and uneducated Hindus worship images without a high conception of the symbology, still there is always "the god above the image" in the mind of the worshipper, and the image is used in order to fix the mind of the worshipper upon the object of his adoration. And the higher and educated use the images merely as a symbol and "outward appearance of an inward reality." The Hindu mind is poetical, and tends toward imagery in expressing thought and worship—just as does the Latin mind of the West, as evidenced by the Italians, Spaniards, and French, and the Spanish-American peoples. Consequently the Hindus naturally turn toward imagery in their worship, in a manner incomprehensible to the average Anglo-Saxon mind. And this imagery has its low as well as its high aspects. The key to the whole matter is the thought and idea that the Image is always the Symbol of an Underlying and Overshadowing Being. A stone, a stick, a bit of earth—or the sun itself—it matters not. It is always the God back of, underneath, yes, IN the object to which the worship and adoration goes out. This is the key to the Mystery—the Indwelling, Underlying and Overshadowing God—symbolized by the material form, name or object. It is Symbology carried to its extreme.

SPECIAL MESSAGE X

By Yogi Ramacharaka

For this month, we invite you to taste of the spiritual confections compounded by the skilled hands of the Hindu maker of Spiritual Confections, which bring delight to the soul of the spiritually minded :

"As the eagle of the mountains, having soared high in the air above the earth, wings its way back to is resting-place, being fatigued by its long flight—so does the soul, having experienced the life of the phenomenal, relative, and mortal, return finally unto Itself, where it can sleep beyond all desires, and beyond all dreams."

"As the lump of salt melted in the water cannot be experienced by the eye, but may readily be detected by the tongue, so indeed the ever-existent and ever effulgent Truth, shining in the depths of the heart, cannot be realized by the external senses, but only by the light of that sympathetic awakening which comes from the word of the teacher of the Truth. In the vessel of water, which thou tallest thyself, there is ever present that flavour of the salt of Truth which, while undetected by the eye, may yet ever be tasted by the spiritual sense."

"Truth is not realizable by study alone, nay, not even by intelligence or by much learning, alone. Truth unfolds its full essence to him alone who applies his whole soul to Truth. He who has not given up the ways of sense; he who has not acquired self-control; he who hath not gained inward peace; he whose mind is not at rest; can never realize the Truth, even though he be filled with the learning of the world."

"Talk learnedly of the philosophies; worship devoutly at the altars of the gods; carefully observe the minute details of the ceremonies and rituals; sing loudly the favourite hymns of the deities; do all these things, if you will, yet shall you not gain merit, or wisdom, or freedom, even at the end of a thousand kalpas, unless you realize the Oneness of Truth."

"He who hath grasped the Secret of Oneness of the Truth passes beyond the gates of Death, and enters into the realms of Immortality."

Our Meditation for the coming month is :

"IN THE PERCEPTION OF THE EVER-EFFULGENT ONE ALONE IS THERE FREEDOM, WISDOM AND BLISS."

Chapter XI

Hindu Wonder-Working

The majority of Western readers are more or less familiar with the accounts of the Wonder-Working feats of the Hindu fakirs, or so-called '*yogis,*' whose feats have been witnessed by Western travellers in India, who have related wonderful accounts of what they have witnessed upon their return home. Of course, many of these accounts are exaggerated and distorted, but there is a basis of agreement upon the fundamental facts which should satisfy the fair-minded Western student that there are "many things in heaven and earth not dreamed of in our philosophy"—that is, in the philosophies of the West. All educated Hindus, however, know that while these feats are performed, that they are not *supernatural* in any sense of the word, but are in strict accordance with natural laws, although some of these laws may not be known to the general public, and some of the applications of ordinary natural forces are strange to the Western world. Moreover, the educated Hindu knows that these exhibitions and manifestations of strange forces are not necessarily proofs of a high degree of spiritual attainment on the part of the performer, for these men are often quite low in the ranks of spiritual attainment—but are rather the result of the control of certain of nature's forces by means of the development of certain psychological powers, chiefly by the control and application of the Will. It is true that the great spiritual Masters of India—the Sages, Adepts, or Masters, are possessed of high spiritual powers which are far above those manifested by the fakirs, but these people never stoop to exhibit 'feats' for the amusement or entertainment of the populace—the very fact that a man will give an entertainment of this kind stamping him as one of the class of fakirs who work on a lower plane and who does not possess the higher powers.

The secret of the fakir's power generally consists in his ability to produce a mental illusion, or *Maya,* whereby the senses of the bystanders are deluded and the people made to appear to witness things that have no basis in fact, as we shall see as we proceed. Another class of effects are produced by the control of *prana* (or Vital Force) by the concentrated Will of the performer, so that heavy objects are moved around in defiance of the law of gravitation, and even the human body at times being floated about in the air, which feat is called Levitation, and is not unknown to the Western world. Then the marvellous degree of development along the lines of Telepathy among these people, and many of the Hindus for that matter, renders possible feats that would be practically impossible in the West. Many of these feats could be produced in no other land but India, owing to the psychological conditions maintaining there, the material mental atmosphere of Western lands tending to counteract the effects. Let us examine a few typical cases of this phenomena of Wonder-Working in India, that we may arrive at an understanding of the methods employed.

In the first place the Hindu mind, by reason of the training of centuries and the mental attitude of the majority of the people, is peculiarly receptive to strongly concentrated thought-waves—telepathy among these people is so common a thing as to merit but scant notice. English people in India always have been aware of the fact that news and information have been and are flashed from one end of India to another in a few hours. Let some peculiar occurrence happen in one corner in India, perhaps quite remote, and away from railroads and telegraphs—some uprising or revolt, for instance, or the appearance of some religious teacher preaching new truths—and before the day is passed the news will be known in every corner of the land, much to the surprise of the English residents, who see that something strange is occurring, but who will not learn the true cause for several days afterward. At the time of the native uprisings and revolt, some fifty years ago, the news of each move was known all over India a few hours after the occurrence, a fact which baffled the efforts of the English authorities to fathom or explain.

The same is true in India of to-day. As all careful readers of the journals know, there is in India to-day a strong spirit of revolt against English rule, and there are many manifestations of unrest. Many careful observers claim that sooner or later there will be a national uprising among the Hindus, the result being that the English rule will be over—the yoke cast off. As some of the Hindus say, "India is a huge elephant lying asleep, beside her being her keeper—a red-coated boy with a goad in his hand. Some night the elephant will roll over on the boy and then there will be no keeper, and the goad will be useless." Well, however this may be, the fact remains that in this year 1908 there is a perfect system of *telepathic* news service kept up among the different parts of India, whereby the various local readers of the 'underground movement' are kept fully posted on the progress of the movement elsewhere. In the morning, in some large town, everything will be moving along as usual, while in the afternoon the English residents will notice strange glances being cast at them, and sneering smiles and meaning glances passing between the natives in the bazaars. Some news has been gained—some word of some point of advantage secured by the plotters. And the only way that the news travels so quickly is by the *telepathic* route.

This power of telepathy, and the receptivity to its influence on the part of the populace generally, renders a Hindu crowd susceptible of being impressed quite easily by the psychological power of the fakirs, who have reduced mental concentration to a fine art and who created a condition of mental illusion as a foundation for their more difficult feats. And not only are the natives affected by this influence, but Western people who happen to be in the crowd catch the contagion of the thought and fall victims to 'the psychology of the crowd,' as it is known in the West. All this is a kind of hypnotism or mesmeric influence, of a certain form known to the fakirs, and to those who have made a study of the subject. The crowd is placed in a 'suggestible condition,' and filled with the 'expectant attention' which is so important a condition for the successful carrying off of these feats. In addition to this method, the fakirs also possess the power of 'mental materialization' in which they produce illusion by sending forth strong 'thoughtforms' of that which they wish the crowd to see, and which are then apparently 'seen' by the people witnessing the performance, although a photograph snapped at the time will fail to disclose any of the remarkable scenes being witnessed, thus proving that the effect is purely psychological. Let us describe a typical performance of this kind, by one of the best and most successful travelling fakirs of India, in which the various classes of phenomena are manifested.

At the beginning of the performance, which is given in the open air, in a large vacant space, the fakir seats himself on the ground in the typical Hindu fashion, his legs being folded in front of him, and his hands arranged in the style familiar to those who have seen the image of a Hindu deity in the temples, and with his eyes closed. The crowd has gathered around him, at a respectful distance, and prepares for the usual long wait. Then the assistants of the fakir, usually youths of a tender age, begin to beat cymbals and drums, not loudly but with a muffled peculiar monotonous sound. Then the fakir begins to chant slowly and drowsily, choosing words that end in "*um-m-m*" sounds (not a difficult thing in India), until after a bit a rhythmic vibration is set up and the air seems to quiver with its tremulous movement. Then, perhaps, the assistants will release several cobra snakes from jars, or boxes, and the serpents will writhe around in harmony with the music, and lo ! they are seen swelling and stretching and increasing in size, until at last they become as immense boa-constrictors swaying before the affrighted audience; then at a wave of the fakir's hand the music changes a little and the snakes begin to decrease in size until they vanish from sight entirely. This snake feat is often dispensed with by some of the leading fakirs, who consider it too crude, and worthy only of the lower order of performers or snake charmers.

Then the fakir rises, and taking a slender long rope from his assistants, he casts the knotted end high into the air. The rope spins out its length for several minutes, rising higher and higher until the knotted end is lost to sight. Finally it stops, and the lower end is left dangling a few feet above the ground, as if suspended by some invisible hook or beam far above the ground. Then the fakir bids his smallest assistant climb up the rope, which he does, nimbly passing up and up, until he too fades from sight. Then the fakir claps his hands, and lo ! the rope itself vanishes. After a wait of a few minutes the boy who has disappeared comes rushing into the circle of the crowd as if coming from a great distance, and all out of breath. Sometimes this feat is varied, and terminated by the boy appearing high up in the air, as a tiny speck, and then gradually descending to the ground by means of the rope. This feat has several variations, but the general outlines are the same.

Then the fakir proceeds to perform the celebrated Mango Feat, so often witnessed by English travellers in India. He begins by building up a little hillock of earth, into which he places a mango seed. Then he begins his chant, accompanied by the drums and cymbals, and a waving of his hands over the little pile of earth. In a few moments a little sprout of green manifests itself from the top of the pile, and, growing rapidly, soon reaches the height and appearance of a young mango bush, which still keeps on growing until it has reached the size and maturity of a full grown mango tree, with leaves and blossoms. Then the blossoms change into young fruit, which ripens before the eyes of the crowd, until finally it is picked and passed around the crowd to be eaten. Then the fakir reverses the process, and the tree begins to shrink and retire into itself until finally it has again resolved itself into the original seed which was planted in the hillock. In some cases the fakir varies the feat by bidding the people hold carefully in their hands the mangoes which he distributes, the result being that when the tree disappears the fruit disappears also.

Another favourite feat of these fakirs is the Spinning Boy, in which he takes his young assistant and whirls him around like a top, the motion growing more and more rapid until the boy spins around rapidly by himself, without assistance. Finally the spinning boy begins to ascend in the air, higher and higher, until he vanishes from sight. The feat is terminated either by the boy coming running back to the crowd from a distance, or else by a reversal of the disappearing act, and a return from the heights as a human spinning-top, growing more and more distinct until the earth is again reached, when he gradually slows down until he comes to a perfect rest, when he squats unconcernedly by the side of his master.

The Rope-Snake Feat is another favourite manifestation of these fakirs. They will take plain bits of rope, often cutting the bits from a long thick rope with a knife, and then knotting an end on each bit. Then begins the chant, and waving of hands, and the drum and cymbals. Soon the bits of rope begin to tremble, and a moment later are seen to be slowly transforming themselves into cobra snakes. Finally the knotted end turns into the hooded head of the deadly cobra and the serpents are seen moving hissingly and threateningly toward the crowd, which retreats in terror. A word from the fakir and the snakes begin to resolve themselves back into the original bits of rope, and in the end are as they were at the beginning—bits of severed rope with a knotted end—much to the relief of the spectators. Then the fakir will stand up, and leaning backwards will lift his feet from the ground, until at length is seen to be floating in the air as a good swimmer floats in the water. Often he passes over the heads of the crowd, circling around until he finally returns to his original place and position.

Sometimes this 'Floating Feat' is varied by the fakir snatching a child or young boy from the side of its parents, and causing it to float around in the air, often rising up out of sight in the manner before mentioned. There is no end to the variety of changes that these people work in performing this feat. ' They will also toss into the air various objects that may be lying around, and make them float easily in the air, rising and lowering themselves at the command of the fakir.

The well-known Cocoa-nut Feat is another favourite illusion of the travelling fakirs. It is performed by producing an empty cocoa-nut shell, which is passed around for examination. Then from the nut is seen to bubble up great streams of water, which is poured into a bucket; then into another vessel or jar; and so on until many gallons of water have been produced from the shell, and many jars filled. Then he reverses the process and slowly pours vessel after vessel of water back into the shell, where it disappears, until finally the vessels have been emptied and the shell is again passed around, perfectly empty and as dry as in the first place.

There are many variations and combinations of this class of feats as performed by these travelling fakirs and others, the variety and interesting features depending materially upon the ingenuity and power of invention on the part of the fakir. As a rule, however, these people merely repeat the feats which have been taught them by their parents or masters, with little or no variation, change, or improvement, their inventive faculties not being highly developed seemingly. The majority of the fakirs have served long apprenticeships with either the fathers or else with some old master fakir to whom they were apprenticed in early youth. And it is the tendency of a certain type of Hindu mind to follow an example as closely as may be, without any attempt at improvement. But here and there are to be found rather enterprising fakirs who are not satisfied with the mechanical repetition of the feats as taught them, but who wish to achieve special renown by performing some new feat, or new variation on some old one. And when this desire possesses a fakir there are no limits to the variety of feats that he produces, which, however, are mainly variations upon and combinations of the principal feats, such as are mentioned above.

Some of these variations take the form of materializing objects from the air; producing the forms and shapes of men, women, children and animals—in short, that which is similar to what in the Western world are called 'materializations' in spiritualistic seances, although there is really no connec-tion between the two classes of phenomena, as we shall see as we proceed. There is practically no limit to the variety possible to the person possessing the ability to produce or rather to induce the illusive mental state which lies at the bottom of this class of manifestations. An enterprising Western magician, were he possessed of the power of producing this illusion, would startle the world by sensational exhibitions of his wondrous power. But the Hindu fakir does not seem to wish to 'spread himself out' in this way—such would be contrary to the traditions of his class and race, and he prefers to move along in the same old ways that have been followed by the many generations of teachers and pupils before him—for his trade is an old one, and each fakir descends in a direct line from hundreds who have preceded him, and from whom he has acquired the little 'knack' of producing the illusion, as well as the methods whereby he has acquired the power of concentration.

For, let the truth be known, while the basis of these feats is the strong, concentrated will and mind of the fakir, trained by methods handed down from the centuries, still the details of the performance are practically those of the magician of the West, and are arranged with an eye to effect and 'stage business.' This must be so necessarily, for the fakir is a public performer and his business must be managed so as to produce the best effects. He is not filled with the scientific spirit, nor is he possessed of high spiritual ideals. He simply has come into the possession of certain methods of mental training, whereby he is able to 'psychologize' his audience, and to project 'thought-forms,' which will seem as realities to his spectators, and he uses the power to entertain, amuse, and bewilder the crowds that flock around him in his travels. Many Hindus and many Western men have endeavoured to extract the secret of the process from these itinerant wonder-workers, but without avail—large sums of money have been offered them, but they have spurned it. The truth is that they have taken sacred oaths to the instructors to preserve the secrets of their craft, and besides they are afraid of the vengeance sure to be meted upon them by their brethren of the craft should they divulge their methods. A fakir will die rather than tell his secrets. But nevertheless the secrets are known to the advanced occultists among the Hindu sages and adepts, who are acquainted with the laws and methods of development concerning the production of the feats. But these advanced souls would not think of exhibiting these powers, as does the fakir, nor would they make the methods public, for fear that they might be used for improper purposes.

But there is no doubt in the minds of the Hindu investigators that the feats are mere illusions, in fact the process and general methods are known to some who have investigated closely along these lines. The fact that photographs snapped during the performance of these feats have failed to reveal anything but the fakir sitting still in the centre, with his eyes fixed in a concentrated glare, and an entire absence of the many illusory features, shows conclusively that the "feats" exist merely in the minds of the audience upon which they have been superimposed by the mind of the fakir. Many experiments in photography have been made along these lines, but the result is always the same—the plate shows nothing unusual—in the boy and rope feat there is seen no rope, no boy, no climbing, nothing but the fakir sitting still and *concentrating*, CONCENTRATING, CONCENTRATING. Moreover, other experiments have been made along these lines. It has been discovered, accidentally, that if the spectators move in too close upon the fakir the illusion vanishes from the minds of those approaching him, although remaining as fresh and strong as ever in the minds of those remaining in the 'charmed circle.' And the same is true in the case of those who retreat beyond a certain distance of the circle. People have tried this experiment in numerous cases, and with the same result. Moreover, some have witnessed the performance from the roofs of buildings higher than the average, and have seen nothing unusual, while their friends on the ground have witnessed all the strange and wonderful features above narrated. There can be no doubt that herein lies the secret of the phenomena.

But even though these feats be merely illusion, and not a reversal of nature's laws, is it not wonderful that such psychological power can have been cultivated and developed? It shows the possibilities of practice and concentration of the mental powers, of which the Western world is just beginning to understand. The West is merely in the kindergarten stage of the Power of the Mind, but we venture the assertion that the American spirit of investigation will bring many new things to light along these lines within the next twenty years—the investigators are on the right track already, and wonderful possibilities are before the race.

And now let us pass on to a consideration of the higher class of phenomena of the Hindu Wonder-Workers, of which the Western world is not so well informed as of the above mentioned class exhibited by the fakirs. For there is a higher phase, possessing real scientific interest, and manifesting a wonderful control and management of the powers of nature, along the lines of vital forces, etc., and which is devoid of the illusory nature of the fakir's feats. The Western world may doubt some of these higher feats, but many Hindus, and a few Western travellers, know them to be facts.

Among the instances of the exercise of a high degree of control over some of nature's forces, along scientific lines, and devoid of the illusory features of the phenomena previously mentioned, is that of the celebrated Boiling Water Feat which has been witnessed and reported by several Western writers and travellers, but which is not nearly so common as the class of phenomena due to mental illusion. The feat is performed as follows : The fakir takes between the palms of his hands a glass, or other vessel or receptacle, filled with clear water—both the water and the receptacle having been examined by the witnesses of the performance. Then showing signs of mental concentration, and at the same time practising the *Yogi* Rhythmic Breathing, the fakir seems to be sending to the water a current of power or force of some sort. In a few moments the water seems to be filled with tiny bubbles similar to those showing in boiling water, and gradually the entire glass is bubbling away as if a great heat were being applied to it. Investigators have then insisted that the glass be placed on a table away from the hands of the fakir, the result being that the ebullition gradually subsided, and the glass of water resumed its normal appearance, with the exception that tiny bubbles of air gathered and remained on the sides of the glass, just as they do in ordinary instances when a glass of water is allowed to remain for a length of time.

It is said by those who have experimented with this phenomenon, that the water does not grow hot, nor does it really 'boil' in the sense of being agitated by heat, the appearance being that of 'effervescence' rather than that of 'boiling' by heat. It should be noted here that the investigators took steps to prevent the insertion of any effervescent chemical into the water, in some cases the precautions taken being so great that the investigators brought their own glasses, which they filled themselves, and then covered carefully, in one case a covered 'Mason jar' being used to obviate any change or the insertion of any chemical substance into the water. In one instance, we understand, the water was connected with a registering instrument similar to a galvanometer, and no signs of an electric current were observed—and in the same test the water was subjected to a chemical analysis, but no traces of foreign chemical substances were found. Some have remarked that the water seemed to be slightly warmer than that of the water before the manifestation upon it, but this may have been caused by the natural heat of the hands of the fakir—we have heard of no cases in which the heat has been recorded by the use of a thermometer. Some have thought that after the manifestation the water tasted 'flat,' as does water that has been subjected to boiling, in fact this seems to be the general verdict, but there is a chance of the effect of auto-suggestion or imagination in this case, in absence of any scientific test. As to the genuineness of the phenomenon of the effervescing or boiling, however, there seems to be no doubt.

Some of the fakirs performing the above feat, when closely questioned, insisted that they were unable to explain what force was used, as they merely 'concentrated their minds on the water,' according to methods taught by their instructors and masters, and the result followed naturally. Some attempted to give some fantastic explanation, or to account for the phenomena by the theory of 'spirits,' but these people were suspected of endeavouring to surround the phenomenon with supernatural 'fringes,' and a close cross-examination generally resulted in their admitting that they did not understand the real cause underlying their work—they knew that "it worked," and that was all. Others, however, who were better informed, held that it was caused by the manifestation of *'Prana'* under the control of their concentrated will, and assisted by their Rhythmic Breathing, and such is the opinion of Hindu occultists who are familiar with the phenomenon and who claim that it is merely a simple manifestation of the operation of *Prana* generated by the Rhythmic Breath, and directed by the focused Will. In short, it is merely a more marked manifestation of the same natural force which is employed in the production of the 'magnetized water' so frequently employed by the 'magnetic healers' of the Western world.

We have heard of experiments performed privately by advanced occultists who were investigating the force-producing effects of water subjected to concentrated *Prana*, in which the vessel containing the water was connected by a pipe attached to a miniature toy steam-engine boiler, the result being that when the effervescence began to manifest in a high degree the tiny boiler was filled with the 'steam' (?) or other ethereal form of matter arising from the water, and the little engine began to work. We never have witnessed this experiment, personally, but have heard of several cases of its having been performed in India. In these cases, however, the persons capable of exerting the force decline to exhibit the feat in public, having no desire for notoriety or 'fame,' the Hindu mind working along lines of its own in this respect, and which are foreign to the Western point of view, which sees the advantage and virtue of publicity. The Orientals hold firmly to the idea that the Truth is for the favoured few who can appreciate it; the Westerner holds that Truth should be spread widely among all, irrespective of the capacity to understand and correctly apply it to the best advantage—each view has its own arguments and merits, and the real wisdom probably lies in the middle of the road between the two.

Another feat which has caused much interest among educated Westerners in India is that of the germination of seeds under the influence of *Prana* directed by Rhythmic

Breathing and Concentrated Will. This feat is entirely different from the Mango Feat and similar exhibitions along the lines of illusory mental influence as mentioned in the first part of this chapter, and in which there is no real sprouting or growth, but only an appearance or illusion of the same. In the present case the germination is real, as evidenced by photographs and the preservation of the germinated sprout attached to the seed after the termination of the performance. It is unnecessary to say that in a feat of this kind the chances of sleight-of-hand are great, and that the investigators have taken means to obviate the chances of the same by employing the methods familiar to the investigators of psychic phenomena. In this feat the fakir takes seeds of certain quick-growing plants of India, which are brought by the investigators and which subsequent analysis shows to be free from foreign chemicals, and enclosing them with a handful of earth, likewise examined and afterward tested, holds the mass of earth in his hand for a space of about half-an-hour to an hour, at the same time concentrating the *Prana* upon it by means of Rhythmic Breathing and Concentrated Will. After a time there appears a tiny sprout of green working out of the earth, which is allowed to grow until it attains a height of several inches. Examination shows the remnants of the seed clinging to the sprout, as is the case in natural and normal germination, and the presence of a tiny root which has been sent in the opposite direction to the sprout. The reports are that this feat has been performed frequently under the strictest test conditions, the elements of deception having been eliminated. The explanation given is that the energy of the *Prana* operates precisely as do the rays of the sun in a tropical country, only in a more concentrated degree, and that the energy employed and that contained in the sun's rays is identical. No heat is noticeable, but then the higher, rays of sunlight are not heat rays, as all scientists know. Another point of resemblance to the Actinic Rays of the sun is shown in another feat in which the fakir places his hand on the fair skin of a newly arrived European or American, and after holding it there for about fifteen minutes or a half hour, leaves a 'sun-burnt' impression of his hand on the flesh of the fair-skinned visitor. We would like to hear of the experiment being tried of placing a covered sensitive photographic plate under the hand of the fakir so that it might be ascertained whether the imprint of his hand would appear thereon, as is the case when the X-Ray is so applied—but so far we have not heard of this last mentioned experiment having been attempted. In the Germination Feat it should be noticed that the seeds employed are always those of some native quickgrowing plants of India, many of which will sprout naturally in twenty-four hours under the rays of the Indian sun.

Another feat performed by the same methods is that mentioned by a few people who have witnessed it, it being a rare one and one which is seldom manifested or exhibited, and which is known as the Fish Feat. It is performed by the fakir holding in his hand a glass or tiny bowl of water in which have been placed a few of the *ova* or eggs of small native fish (fertilized, of course), and upon which he concentrates the *Prana* for about half-an-hour, along the lines of the methods stated above, the result being that the *ova* or eggs would hatch and produce tiny young fish swimming freely about in the glass or small bowl, just as if they had been hatched naturally, and in the usual time. The Hindu occultists held that this result is produced purely by the application of the power of concentrated *Prana*, by means of Rhythmic Breathing and Will-Power, as was the germination of the seed, the phenomena being identical. We have heard of a few isolated cases in which certain Hindu fakirs have been able to cause the hatching of the egg of small birds, quite a time, however, being necessary in such cases, in one instance the entire day (twelve hours) being necessary to produce the result. The principle in all of these cases is the same, the application of *Prana*, which hastens the vital processes inherent in the germ of the seed or egg itself, the work being performed along purely natural lines; merely being hastened or stimulated to a marked degree by the action of and increased and concentrated supply of *Prana.*

Another interesting manifestation of the same force is that which has been related by the travellers in certain parts of India, whereby the temperature of water is lowered to the extent of a number of degrees, not in the way of an actual subtraction of the heat by the direct action of *Prana,* but in a manner similar to that of artificial refrigeration by evaporation. The method is as follows : The fakir takes into his hands, and at the same time rests upon his lap, one of the large water jars common to all tropical countries, which is wrapped with cloths moistened with waters and which are usually placed in the sun that the heat may cause the water on the cloths to evaporate, the evaporation drawing the heat from the water within the jar and thereby cooling it—the process being according to well-known physical laws. The fakir, by directing a supply of *Prana,* upon the moistened cloths (which are re-moistened from time to time) manages to set up a process of evaporation similar to that mentioned in the Boiling Water Feat, and this constant evaporation drawing the heat from the water within the jar gradually reduces it to a degree of coolness quite perceptible and agreeable to the taste. This manifestation shows quite plainly that *Prana is* the force used, and gives us an additional proof of the nature of this class of phenomena.

There are other cases, however, in which *Prana is* used in an entirely different way, and in accordance to different laws of nature. We allude to 'the action at a distance,' in which bells are rung and objects moved as if by an unseen hand. Laying aside for a moment the cases in which this class of phenomena is produced by the projection of the Astral Body charged with *Prana* let us consider the cases in which the *Prana is* directed along the lines of Thought form projection, or 'Vitalized Thought.' There are a number of feats produced in this way by the Hindu fakirs, some of which resemble some of the manifestations of the Western spiritualistic mediums. Bells are rung, small objects are shifted in position, and the strings of musical instruments are sounded, etc., although the fakir is bound and surrounded by watchers. These manifestations are performed in a dim light, darkness not being deemed necessary as in the cases in which the Astral manifestations are performed. In the latter cases there are conditions manifested which resemble the 'materializations' of the Western spiritualists, and in which in the dimly lighted room the form of the fakir is seen floating about, and in which the other physical manifestations are shown. In many cases the fakirs attribute the phenomena to 'spirits' or disembodied entities, but in many cases they frankly admit that they "go out of themselves" in some way unknown to them, but which they produce by means of trance-states, etc., and in which they find themselves able to move objects, etc., while their physical body is tied in a chair, or while it reclines on the ground, held by some of the spectators. These séances resemble in many ways the spiritualistics séances of the West, and we shall not dwell upon them as they are not distinctively Hindu. As a matter of interest, we would note that many Western investigators now claim that much of the so-called 'spirit phenomena' of the West is really caused by the unconscious astral projection of the medium, instead of by disembodied entities dwelling on other planes of being. If such be the case the West has stumbled on one of the methods of the Hindu fakirs, a fact which is most interesting and instructive.

There is another class of phenomena manifested by these fakirs which is of a very different type, and which perplexes the majority of investigators, but which is thought to arise from the employment of *Prana* in some peculiar way. We allude to the phenomenon of Levitation, whereby the body is caused to 'levitate' or become so buoyant that it floats in the air as the body of the swimmer floats in the water. This phenomenon is not identical with a similar one caused by 'mental illusion,' in which the spectators are made to imagine that they see the feat, but is an actual physical phenomenon duly attested to by numerous Western people in India, and which has also been manifested in other countries. It is generally attributed to a suppositious quality called 'Levity,' which is held to be the opposite of Gravity, and which counteracts the effect of the latter. But other authorities hold that Gravity is not neutralized but rather is overcome by the effect of *Prana* directed in a manner similar to the other feats. The fakir generally leans backward gradually, and when he begins to feel buoyant he calls upon the attendants to lift his heels from the ground and to support him in the air for a few moments, after which they withdraw, leaving him suspended in the air. After a few minutes the fakir is generally able to move himself about—to "float" in fact—until the power gradually decreases and he sinks slowly to the ground. It must be remembered that he passes into a state of intense concentration, becoming oblivious to the outside surroundings, and at the same time *he breathes rhythmically* in slow measured time.

In the above connection it is interesting to compare the above-mentioned complete levitation with the partial levitation so often resulting from the familiar Western experiment whereby a heavy person is lifted into the air by the finger-tips of his companions who have been breathing rhythmically and in unison. While the process does not appear to come under the classification of the other feats performed by the use of *Prana*, there seems to be very good ground for believing that in some way *Prana is* employed to counteract the effects of Gravity.

The fakirs themselves seem to be at a loss to account for the phenomena, saying merely that they merely "let themselves go," holding at the same time a strong mental image of suspension in the air, and then "hold themselves up" by a concentrated effort of the Will directed into the Mental Image, or Thought Picture. They claim that it tires them out in a short time, and that they can feel themselves "giving out," just as under a physical strain. They acquire the means of producing the feat by frequent practice under the instruction of their masters in youth, but they also declare that some of the pupils never acquire the method at all, in spite of the instructions and practice, and that the teachers are unable to induce the power where it does not exist naturally. They refuse, as they always do in any case, to describe the methods of practice, except to their own apprentices, and they refuse large sums of money for the 'secret' which they have sworn to preserve. Under no circumstances would they betray the secret to an outsider, for they fear the vengeance of their particular deity or god, Shiva, for they belong to the credulous and superstitious portion of the race, and are far from being advanced spiritually or intellectually. All of which goes to prove the contention of the developed and advanced occultists that these fakirs possess powers of a low degree, and which have no connection with true "soul-power," which is possessed only by advanced individuals, and which depend upon a high degree of knowledge concerning the nature and powers of the Soul.

We will not take up space and time in endeavouring to explain the nature of *Prana* and Mental Influence in this lesson. In the first series of our lessons, known as "The Fourteen Lessons in Yogi Philosophy and Oriental Occultism," we have gone into the subject of these two forces, showing what *Prana* is and how it is employed in connection with Psychic Influence. We would refer students to the lessons in the said book touching upon the forces named. But in order that this lesson, and the above references to *Prana* and Mental Influence, may be intelligible to the general reader, we feel that we should state briefly the nature of *Prana*, and to describe the underlying principles of Mental Influence.

"Prana" is the Sanskrit term used to designate that great natural force or energy which is universal in its manifestations, and which appears in the human being as Vital Force, or Nerve-Force, in other words as the power which makes Life-Action possible. This *Prana,* although manifesting as Vital Force, is more than this—it is the great power or energy or force which manifests in all things throughout the universe, showing now as electricity, now as light and heat, now as magnetism, now as gravitation, etc.—in short, the Energy Principle of the Universe. *Prana* may be, and is directed by the human will, to the different parts of the body—as when the will commands the muscles to contract by means of a current of *Prana* sent there—and it may be projected beyond the limits of the body in certain forms of occult phenomenon.

There are various forms of Mental Influence, as all students of the subject well know, but the form or phase which is manifested by the fakirs in the feats of illusion mentioned in the first part of this lesson is in the form of Vibration, and *Prana*-charged Thought Forms projected toward the spectators. The fakir has cultivated the power of Mental Imaging to a high degree, and then forming a Thought Form along the mould of his Mental Image, the same being charged with *Prana* to give it vitality and force, by means of his concentrated Will he projects it towards the circle of spectators, thus producing similar Vibrations in their *Chitta* or Mind-Stuff which causes them to think they see in actual manifestation the scenes that the fakir has seen by Mental Imaging. It is as if the fakir was using a Mental Magic-Lantern containing a slide with the desired picture painted on it—when the lantern-ray strikes the surface of the brains of the other persons the scene is reproduced there, and they think that they are actually witnessing the scene of the lantern-slide. This illustration is somewhat crude, but it gives an idea of the process employed. References to our other series of lessons, as aforesaid, will give detailed explanation of the nature and laws of the phenomena of Mental Influence.

In the Wonder-Working of the fakirs of India we have to deal with a great variety of feats and manifestations, which would require a large book to describe or even mention in detail. We have selected certain typical cases in order to illustrate the subject, and have given you an explanation of the laws and principles underlying each, so that you may be able to distinguish between the various phases of the phenomena. We think that with our explanation you will be able to classify, distinguish and understand any particular feats of which you may hear henceforth.

We wish to be distinctly understood, however, in stating that the explanations given do not apply to the higher class of phenomena manifested by the Advanced Masters and Higher Occultists of India, who have mastered the secret of many of nature's finer forces, and who employ the same from time to time for the good of humanity and the advancement of the race. These developed souls, however, *never* exhibit these powers for the purpose of satisfying the curiosity of travellers or others, or even for the purposes of scientific investigation—they hold themselves above these things and would scorn to 'give exhibitions' for any such purpose. Some of their favoured students have been able to witness some of these remarkable manifestations of power, during the course of their occult instruction in which the principles were applied in order to illustrate certain points of teaching. This class of phenomena belongs to another plane of life and activity, and may be considered as 'Spiritual' in nature rather than Mental or Physical. And the acquirement of such power is possible only to those who have trodden the Path of Attainment and who have won the battle of Self Mastery, which must precede the Mastery of the Finer Forces. Many people make the mistake of confounding this Higher Phenomena with the manifestations just mentioned, or else the Psychic Phenomena of the Astral Plane, both of which are immeasurably below it in the scale. As we have said, many of these lower powers are acquired by persons of but a low grade of spiritual attainment or development, and their success depends principally upon those commonly known but little used faculties—Concentration, Perseverance, and Work, to a degree uncommon to the average person who wishes to be shown a Royal Road to Power, while no such road exists.

SPECIAL MESSAGE XI

By Yogi Ramacharaka

For this month, we invite you to taste of the spiritual wine of Wisdom, from the grapes of Understanding, pressed forth by the Hindu Sages of old :

"Truth cannot be realized by want of spiritual strength; nor by indifference; nor by austerities unaccompanied by renunciation. The self of that knower who applies himself to Truth, enters the great Self. Sages have found it, and do thou stand ever content in Spiritual Consciousness; remain thou ever centred in Truth, being free from all attachment, and always at peace within and without. Find the unconditioned and all-pervading, and realizing the Truth within you, become one with All. With faith firmly fixed on the Truth; with the mind purified through renunciation; with the soul illumined with Spiritual Consciousness—become One with the Immortal—one with the One."

"When thy mind reaches the stage of intuitive knowledge, follow thou it—be led by the Truth within thee. Until then, be thou guided by the best books, and the best teachers, and the logical instruments of knowledge—though these be but as crutches, yet wisdom dictates that they be not thrown away until outgrown. When latent desire is burnt out by the fire of the Spirit, and the One is realized, then wilt thou have no concern with outward instruments of knowledge, however good these may be, these teachers, and books and logical reasonings."

"The rivers flowing to and gaining the ocean, lose themselves in it, yea, lose even their name and form, and become one with the Ocean, and even bear its name. So do all the myriads of individual selves flow into and gaining the One, become lost in it, losing name and form and being known by its name. This One, in which all is lost—and by which losing all is found—is the immortal, transcendent Truth. In Truth are all forms, like the centring of the spokes of the chariot-wheel in its hub."

"Knowing Truth, the great all-pervading One, through whom

is experienced dream and waking, the wise rise above pain, and sorrow, for Wisdom neutralizes these illusions."

Our Meditation for the coming month is :

"THE WISE EVER SEEK THAT WHICH ONCE KNOWN ALL IS KNWON."

Chapter XII

The Vedas

Students of the Hindu Philosophies and Religious Systems meet with frequent and constant allusions to the '*Vedas*' and '*Upanishads*,' the Sacred Books of India, but as a rule find little or no description or explanation of what the *Vedas* or *Upanishads* are; of what they consist, or of their history. We have thought it advisable to give our students a brief description and account of the *Vedas* and *Upanishads* in this lesson.

The Vedas

The *Vedas*, generally speaking, may be defined as :

The Hindu Sacred Books comprising the Hindu Scriptures, *viz.*, *Rig-Veda;* the *Yajur-Veda;* the *Sama-Veda;* the *Atharva-Veda;* and also the *Brahmanas* and the *Upanishads;* and also comprising the poems, hymns, sacred literature, rituals, and general religious philosophy of the Hindu religious systems.

But strictly speaking, the term 'The*Vedas*' is used to designate merely the Sacred Scriptures of the Hindus, which we shall now consider.

The *Vedas* have a most ancient origin, their early history fading into "the days before history." There are accounts of the Sacred Writings extending back for several thousand years, but before this time there were evidently still older manuscripts; and before the constant verbal transmission of the Sacred Teachings from mouth to ear—from father to son—from teacher to student—which has always been the custom in Oriental countries. There are over one hundred of these Sacred Books, but their base is found in the "Four *Vedas*," known as the *RigVeda;* the *Yajur-Veda;* the *Sama-Veda;* and the *Atharva-Veda.*

The *Rig-Veda is* considered the oldest of the Four *Vedas,* and is probably the most important. It consists of over one thousand great hymns, of extraordinary length, and chiefly concerning ceremonial worship and ritualistic rites of devotion. These hymns are arranged into ten books, called *Mandala,* six of which are Family Books, that is, are written by some sage or poet in the first place, and then added to by his descendants. The subjects treated in the *Rig-Veda* are numerous, mythology being strongly in evidence, the successive stages of the work showing the growth of the mythology of the Hindus, and also showing how some of the more elementary and simple conceptions of the earlier Hindus developed in systems of gods and demi-gods.

The *Yajur-Veda* is devoted principally to ritualism or sacerdotalism. Its form is metrical, as a rule, although certain forms of prose appear at times. The influence of the *Rig-Veda* is noticeable in it, and the latter is regarded in it as authoritative. The *Yajur-Veda* concerns itself with sacrifice, priestly functions, ceremonial of worship—the machinery of 'the Church' in fact, very little of philosophy, metaphysics, or spiritual teaching being found therein—formalism, ritual and ceremony being the themes.

The *Sama-Veda* has been called 'the *Veda* of Hymns,' which indeed it is. It comprises many verses, melodies, librettos, and naming of pious exclamatory words which were interjected into the singing, in the manner of the exhortations and pious exclamations manifested by some of the Christian sects during the prayers or sermons of others, such as "Amen! Glory to God ! Praise the Lord !" etc., which practice was common among the early Hindus, and even to this day is found among some of their sects in which ardent enthusiasm is encouraged.

The *Atharva-Veda* has been called 'the *Veda* of Psychic Powers,' for the reason that it devotes much attention to the various methods regarded as conducive to the development of supernormal faculties, senses, and powers. There is mention of both the low as well as the high use of the powers, the discussion ranging from highest forms of psychic power to the lowest forms of witchcraft, sorcery and black magic, the habit of the Hindu mind being toward thoroughness, the logical conclusion being sought after without fear or hesitation. The books composing the *Atharva-Veda,* some twenty in number, contain countless 'recipes' and formula for blessings, curses, charms, incantations, magical ceremonies, invocations, evocations, etc., etc., far exceeding in variety and detail any of the similar writings of the Hebrews, Greeks, etc., and showing to what extent the human mind may travel along these lines. But strange to say, among this mass of 'methods,' etc., there appear certain portions of the work touching upon high ideas, thoughts and speculations, having evidently been written about the same time, and included with the other work by reason of the period of their writing, rather than by any relationship or connection of thought. The modern Hindu, and in fact the Hindus for many centuries past, have recognized a decided division between the parts of the *Atharva-Veda,* separating them into divisions corresponding to the Western terms of 'White Magic' and 'Black Magic' respectively.

The Brahmanas

There are many schools of interpretations of the *Vedas,* each of which have many commentaries arising from the interpretations. Proceeding from these differences appeared the several *Brahmanas,* which are in the nature of theological commentaries concerning the *Vedas,* more particularly in the matter of forms, ceremonies, creeds, etc., accompanied by a copious reference to the original books, and a quoting of 'texts' in a manner familiar to those familiar with the customs of the Western sects and denominations. From these original *Brahmanas* developed a later form of commentaries which are known as the *Aranyakas*, or 'Forest Treatises,' named after the teachers who wrote them and who dwelt in the forests. These works are of a higher character than the earlier *Brahmanas*, and are . of a mystical character and touch upon the higher phases of the Hindu religious thought. These works may be considered as a connecting-link between the *Brahmanas* and the *Upanishads*. The two important *Aranyakas* are known as the *Aitareya*, and the *Taittiriya*, respectively.

The Upanishads

The term '*Upanishad*' means, literally, "a sitting down beside," or what in the West would be called a 'heart-to-heart' instruction. The word is also used as meaning 'the esoteric doctrine' The general use of the word, however, is as the designation for the "End of the *Vedas*," that is, for the philosophical writings which conclude the general *Vedas*, or Sacred Books of India. The *Upanishads* are devoted to theological, philosophical and metaphysical speculation, argument, discussion, teaching and consideration, whereas the *Vedas* proper; the *Brahmanas*; and the *Ayanyakas* (see previous reference in this lesson) are devoted rather to mythological, ritualistic, ceremonial subjects than to those treated in the *Upanishads*. The earlier Sacred Books devote themselves to explaining the religious, ethical, and ecclesiastical duties, together with a reference to. super-normal powers in one case—but the *Upanishads* devote themselves chiefly to a consideration of the nature of man and the universe, and their relation to the Infinite Being. The *Upanishads* reach much higher planes of human thought and reasoning than do the earlier books, and are decidedly the writings preferred by the Hindu philosophers and metaphysicians, although priests naturally prefer the earlier works which are nearer to their profession and calling, and consequently nearer to their hearts.

The *Upanishads* are closely related to the *Aranyakas,* and are often found either 'imbedded' in their substance or else forming their conclusion, showing their common origin among the 'Forest Sages.' And both the *Aranyakas* and the *Upanishads* are frequently found at the end of some of the *Brahmanas.* So from the early *Vedas* to the latest *Upanishads* there is an unbroken line of continuity and relationship. And, accordingly, the general term 'The *Vedas' is* applied to all of these Sacred Books or Writings. The date of the earlier *Upanishads* is unknown, but it is certain that the oldest ones antedate the Christian Era by over one thousand years—probably by many more centuries than even that time. The older *Upanishads* belong to the original *Veda* school, while some of the later have schools founded upon themselves.

Perhaps the two most important of the *Upanishads* are the *Brihadaranyaka,* and the *Chandogya,* respectively, both of which belong to the *Vedic* school. Other important *Upanishads* are the following : The *Aitareya;* the *Kausitaki;* the *Taittiriya;* the *Kathaka;* the *Maitrayaniya,* or *Manava;* the *Kena;* the *Talavakara;* the *Isa;* the *Svestasvetara;* the *Mahanara;* the *Prasna;* the *Mandukeya;* and many others of more or less importance and popularity and authority. In fact, there are about 235 *Upanishads* considered to carry authority with them and known to the Hindus to-day, besides which there are many shorter and secret writings respected and treasured by some of the sects and schools of India, and which never have been allowed to be translated, and many of which are never committed to print, but are passed along verbally, or else in private copies written by hand. The Hindus hold that the canon of the *Upanishads* is not closed, and that the future may add to the number of the admitted books.

In the *Upanishads* will be found the entire system of the Hindu philosophical and religious thought, in its many forms and varieties of interpretation. It is the largest collection of philosophical writings in the world, ancient or modern. And, moreover, the subject is considered with such wonderful subtlety of analysis and detail, that it is thought to include every possible variation of metaphysical thought of man up to the present time—that is, no other nation has ever been able to form a metaphysical conception that is without its counterpart in some of the *Upanishads.* The *Upanishads* stand as a monumental memorial to the energy, persistency and keenness of the Hindu metaphysical mind. But this fact has its weakness as well as its strength, for just as it is often said in the West that "one may prove anything, or disprove anything, by texts from the Bible"—so in India every sect, school, or division of thought is able to fortify itself with authoritative 'texts' from the *Vedas* or *Upanishads,* proving each position and disproving the others. But nevertheless, there is a fundamental agreement upon basic principle—and between the lines of all may be read the words of The Inner Teachings. And those Teachings all have as their essence the Truth :

"THERE IS BUT ONE AND ONE ONLY."

Explanation of Hindu Terms

One of the difficulties of the Western student of Hindu philosophies and religious systems has been the lack of understanding of the technical Sanskrit terms used in the works on these subjects. Accordingly we have thought it desirable to issue a plain, simple Glossary or Partial Dictionary, containing a definition of, and short explanation of, the technical Sanskrit terms used in our lessons, and in other works on the subject. This Glossary does not claim to give an 'authoritative,' academical definition of the terms, but rather a plain explanation of each term, stated as clearly and as simply as possible. There has been no attempt toward academical preciseness or technical exactness in this Glossary—the sole desire and intent hating been to enable the student to know "what the term means in English." The definitions given are 'free,' rather than in the 'exact,' precise style and form of the scholastic teachers of Sanskrit.

Pronunciation

It is almost impossible to give in English an exact Key to Pronunciation of the Sanskrit. The Sanskrit, you know, is the ancient language of the Hindus—a most classical and polished language—now employed only in the literary work, and sacred writings of India, and not in common use in that country, the popular, common dialects having superseded it. Sanskrit is highly technical and difficult, and even its correct pronunciation is possible only to the advanced scholar, even in India. Its finer shades and distinctions are beyond the ordinary student, particularly of the West, and we have made no attempt to give them here. We have thought it better to confine ourselves, and our students, to the general rules of pronunciation, which are all that are necessary for the casual reader and student. The following are the General Rules of Pronunciation of Sanskrit words :

A has the sound of *a* in *a*rm, far, or f*a*ther. It has also a secondary sound of *u* in b*u*tter, *u*p, b*u*d, etc. The general English pronunciation used is that of the first sound (as in *a*rm) slightly sliding in the direction of the second sound (as in b*u*t)—the result being the sound of the last *a* in Philadelphi*a*, or the *a* in mut*a*ble, vill*a*, sal*a*ry, etc.

E has the sound of *a* in f*a*te, n*a*me, g*a*y, etc.

I has the sound of *i* in *i*ll, p*i*t, adm*i*t, etc., sliding into the sound of *i* in mach*i*ne, p*i*que, intr*i*gue, etc. (derived from the French), which is akin to the *e* in s*ee*.

U has the sound of *u* in p*u*t, b*u*ll, p*u*sh, etc., rather than that of the *oo* in t*oo*.

S generally has the sound of *s* in *s*at, *s*un, *s*ister, etc., although there is another use of it giving the sound of *sh* in *sh*ip; for instance, *Siva* is pronounced *Sheeva*, not *Seeva*, but generally *sh* is used in the words having this *sh* sound—for instance, *Shiva*, instead of *Siva*.

Ch has the sound of *ch* in ri*ch*, and not the *k* sound.

C (without the *h*) is generally sounded as *k*, not as s.

Ai is generally sounded as *i* in l*i*ght, f*i*ne, br*i*ght, etc.

The other letters generally are sounded as in English.

SPECIAL MESSAGE XII

By Yogi Ramacharaka

For this month we invite you to partake of the fragments of the Bread of Truth, baked from the flour of Wisdom, by the Hindu Sages of old :

"I know the One to be the All. The Great Self, the Truth, all effulgence, transcending all darkness. Knowing this, one can transcend even death."

"As oil is found in sesamum-seeds; as ghee is found in curds; as water is found in the streams; as fire is found in the flame; so is the One Self seen in the self by him who tries to realize it through universal love and perfect control over mind and body."

"Three are the supports of religion: Renunciation; Knowledge; and Compassion."

"Beyond desire; without parts; above egoism; being and non-being—whatever thou art, still thou coast not escape being the One. Thou protectest, destroyest, givest, shinest, speakest, though ever free from egoism—wonderful is the power of Illusion which concealeth thee, and yet revealeth thee—but more wonderful still art thou beyond the Illusion"

"Then, when Truth was still unmanifest, It, of Itself, became manifest through name and form, endowing everything with this or that name, and this or that form. All things even until now are defined by some name and some form. This is the import of Its entering into the objective formed and evolved from Itself."

"In dreams there are in reality no chariots; no horses; not even the course on which the chariot may run; and yet all these are mentally created in a moment. There are in reality no joys; no pleasures; no delights; and yet all are mentally seen and felt at the instant. There are in reality no ponds, no lakes, no rivers, and yet all are there at the merest thought. The power of evolving any number of forms from Itself is the creative power of the One."

"This, therefore, is the Truth, that as from fire well-lighted, fiery sparks flow off in every direction by the thousands, so do all beings of every variety come out, O Great One ! from the ever Immutable, and are resolved also into the same. It is the self-illumined, formless Spirit of Truth, all within and all without; unborn; without breath; without mortal mind; above all conditions; beyond the eternal cause of the phenomenal and relative objective."

Our Meditation for the coming month is :

"THERE IS BUT ONE TRUTH—MEN CALL IT BY MANY NAMES. ABOVE TIME AND BEYOND SPACE, AND FREE FROM CAUSATION, EVER DWELLETH THE ONE THAT IS ALL."

Chapter XIII

Glossary

ABHEDA Sameness; not-distinct; non-separateness.

ABHAVA. The Principle of Non-existence; Without Qualities.

ABHIDHYA. Non-covetousness; non-revengeful; non-vainglorious.

ACHARYA. A *Guru;* spiritual teacher, etc., of high rank.

ADARSA. A mental mirror; psychic vision.

ADHIDAIVIKA. Supernatural; above ordinary experience.

ADHIKARI. A worthy student of Truth.

ADITI. Infinity.

ADITYA. the Sun.

ADITYAS. The twelve Planetary Spirits.

ADHARMA, Unrighteous; lacking virtue.

ADVAITA. Non-dualistic; monistic; the designation of the Monistic sect of the *Vedanta.*

ADHYASA. Reflection of an outside object; the chameleon duality of taking on appearances, hence the illusory aspect of things.

AHAM. The Ego; the "I"

AHAMKARA, Egoism; Self-consciousness; the *Sattva* or Principle of Self-consciousness.

AHARA. The drawing in of nourishment for body or mind.

AJNA. The Sixth Lotus of the *Yoga* Teachings of *Patanjali,* situated in the centre of the brain, just back of the eyebrows; also used in the sense of 'divine perception.'

AJNATA. One possessing divine wisdom, or superhuman psychic perception.

AKASHA. The Universal Ether, which pervades all space.

AKHANDA. Whole; undivided.

AKHANDA-SATCHITANANDA. "The Undivided Existence—Knowledge—Bliss Absolute"; the knowledge of which is perceived in *Samadhi.*

ALAMBANA. Contemplation on outward things.

AMRITATVAM. Immortality.

ANAHATA. The Fourth Lotus of the *Yoga* of *Patanjali,* situated in *Shusumna,* directly in line with the heart.

ANANDA. Absolute Bliss.

ANTAHKARANA. The Internal Organ of the Mind, including the deliberative faculty, the determinative faculty, and the Self-conscious Principle.

ANUBHAVA. Realization.

ANUMANA. Inference.

APANA. The nerve-currents governing the excretory organs one of the five manifestations of *Prana.*

APARAPRATYAKSHA. Psychic sensing, beyond the realm of sensuousness.

APARAVIDYA. Knowledge of externals, as contrasted with knowledge of internals; superficial knowledge.

APAS. The element of Water.

APTA. One who has attained Illumination.

APURA. Merit.

ARJAVAM. Directness in intention; straightforwardness.

ARUPA. Formless.

ASAMPRAJNATA. The extreme and highest state of superconsciousness.

ASANA. Posture; bodily attitude assumed during meditation; the Third Step in *Patanjali's Yoga* System.

ASAT. Non-being; non-existence.

ASVADA. Psychic taste; or faculty of taste.

ASTI. To exist; to be.

ATIKRANTA-CHAVANIYA. Meditation leading up to and culminating in the state of *Samadhi,* or Transcendental Consciousness, or Ecstasy.

ATMAN. The Spirit; the Real Self.

AUM (or OM). A symbolic "Holy Word" signifying The Absolute Idea.

AVARANA. The outward sheaths of the mind.

AVATARA OR AVATAR. A divine incarnation; an incarnation of Deity in human form.

AVIDYA. Ignorance.

AVYAKTAM. Undifferentiated state or condition of *Prakriti,* or Nature, before there is a manifestation.

BHAGAVAD-GITA. A sacred book of India, or *Upanishad.*

BHAGAVAN. A high title denoting all-powerful; allwise; all-inclusive; generally applied only to the highest teachers.

BHAKTA. An ardent lover of God; a *Bhakti Yogi.*

BHAKTI. Ardent love of God. *BHAKTI YOGA.* The Yoga, or Doctrine of the Love of God. *BHAKTI YOGI.* A disciple of *Bhakti Yoga.*

BHAVANA. Meditation; thoughtful reverie.

BHEDA. Separateness; lack of unity.

BHIKSHU. A Buddhist mendicant monk.

BHOGA. Sensuousness; sensual pleasure.

BHUTAS. The gross elements of nature.

BRAHMA. The personified conception of *Brahman;* the conception of Deity as the Creating God; the Creative Deity of the orthodox Hindu Trinity.

BRAHMAN. The Absolute; THAT; the One Existence; the Primal Being; God, in the highest sense of the term.

BRAHMAVIDYA. The knowledge of the Absolute; Supreme Wisdom; the Highest Knowledge.

BRAHMIN. A member of the highest caste of India; a 'twice-born,' according to the Hindu term.

BUDDHA. The great founder of the Buddhist philosophy, and held to be an incarnation of *Brahman* by some; *Gautama Buddha,* who lived about B.C. 600.

BUDDHI. The determinative faculty of the mind; the Determinative Principle arising from *Prakriti* by reason of the involvement of *Purush.*

CHAITANYA. Pure Intelligence; also the name of a high Hindu teacher, who lived about 1500 A.D., and who is regarded by some as an incarnation or *avatar* of *Krishna.*

CHARVAKA. A materialist; the Hindu term for one who rejects the spiritual philosophies.

CHIDAKASA. The mental space, in which the advanced soul perceives knowledge of the universe.

CHITTA. Mind-Stuff, or the subtle elements from which Mind is evolved or manifested.

CHITTAKASHA. The area or space of the mind.

DAMA. Control of the organs of the senses and the body.

DEHA. Gross matter.

DEVAS. The angelic beings, who were originally human beings, but who have advanced in the spiritual sole into a state of semi-divinity; 'the shining ones,' according to the Hindu popular term.

DEVACHAN. The heaven-world. DEVALOKA. The higher regions or planes.

DHARANA. Concentration. One-mindedness. The *Yoga* Sixth Step.

DHARMA. Duty; virtue; the Path of Right Action.

DHYANA. Meditation on the Divine; the *Yoga* Seventh Step. DHYANAMARGA. The Path of Knowledge through Meditation.

DRAVA. The Ultimate Substance of *Kanada's* Philosophy.

DVAITA. The Dualistic School of Philosophy, opposed to *Advaita.*

DVANDAS. The 'pairs of opposites,' or dual-aspects of nature, such as heat and cold; pleasure and pain; high and low; sharp and dull, etc. ; the 'polarities' of natural objects.

DVESHA. Hatred; dislike; aversion; repulsion.

EKAGRA. A state of Concentration.

EKAM. One; hence, EKA-NISTHA, or devotion to one ideal; EKANTA-BHAKTI, or single-love for God; EKATMA-VADAM, or Monism in philosophy; EKAYANA, or the one-support of the universe, *i.e.,* God.

GAUTAMA. The founder of Buddhism; the *Buddha.*

GNANA. Wisdom. GNANA YOGA. The *Yoga* of Wisdom.

GOTAMA. The founder of the *Nyaya* Philosophy.

GRAHANA. Sense-perception.

GUNAS. The Three Qualities of *Prakriti,* or Nature. (See lesson on the *Sankhya* System.)

GURU. A spiritual teacher; a term of great respect.

HATHA YOGA. The *Yoga* of Physical Well-Being, or Physical Control, the aim of which is physical perfection, or the preparing of a worthy temple of the Spirit; but which, when perverted, is, applied to the degrading and abnormal practices, austerities, and self-torture of the fakirs and false-*Yogis* of India. HATHA YOGI. A follower or practitioner of *Hatha Yoga.*

HUM. A mystic word used in mediation, as in the sacred verse, *"Om, Mani, Padme, Hum."*

IDA. The left-side nerve-current ; the left nostril.

INDRA. The "King of the gods," in the ancient Hindu mythology.

INDRIYAS. The Internal Organs of the Mind.

ISHTA-NISHTA. Devotion to one's highest ideals.

ISHWARA. The Personal God; the Logos; the Demi-urge; the Universal *Purusha;* sometimes used as the highest personification of the Absolute possible to the mind of man, the Absolute in itself being incapable of conception or thought.

JAIMINI. The founder of the *Purva Mimansa* Philosophy.

JIVA. The individual life, or individual soul. JIVA-ATMAN. The *Atman* in its manifestation of Divas.

KAIVALYA. Isolation from the Material World. Oneness with the Absolute.

KALA. Time.

KALPA. A cycle of time.

KAMA. Desire; passion; sense-longing.

KANADA. The founder of the *Vaisheshika* Philosophy.

KAPILA. The founder of the *Sankhya* System of Philosophy; the great teacher of Evolution in India.

KARMA. Action; also the effects resulting from action; also the Law of Spiritual Cause and Effect, which underlies the Hindu Philosophies and Religions.

KARMA YOGA. The *Yoga* of Work, or Action, or Duty-Well-Performed Without Hope of Reward. KARMA YOGI. A disciple of *Karma Yoga.*

KHANDA. Differentiated; divided; separated; or the action which separates, divides, or differentiates.

KRISHNA. An incarnation of *Vishnu;* an *avatar* of Deity; a Great Teacher who lived about 1400 B.C., and whose general teachings are stated in the *Bhagavad-Gita;* the term is also used by the *Vaishnavas,* or worshippers of *Krishna,* as the name of the Absolute or THAT, as well as in the sense of the personified Deity.

KUMBHAKA. The retention of the breath in the practice of *Pranayama.*

KUNDALINI. The subtle nerve-energy, or concentrated psychic force, located in the lotus at the base of the spinal column, and which, when aroused, develops the psychic and spiritual powers of the *Yogin.*

LINGA SHARIRA. Subtle Body. Etheric Body.

MAHA. Great.

MAHAKASHA. Great space.

MAHAPURUSHA. A great soul; generally applied to an incarnation, or *avatar*, or sometimes to a great sage or teacher.

MAHAT. Universal Consciousness; the term literally meaning 'the great one.'

MAHATATTVA. The great principle of Consciousness first evolved and proceeding from *Prakriti,* according to the *Sankhya* philosophy.

MANAS. The deliberative or reasoning faculty of the mind.

MANTRAM. An affirmation; prayer; holy word; verse thought; idea, etc., expressed in words, or meditated upon in the form of words, during worship, meditation, or concentration.

MANIPURA. The Third Lotus of the *Yoga* of *Patanjali,* which is situated directly opposite to the navel, on the *Shusumna,* along the spinal column.

MAYA. Illusion; the Unreal Appearance of Nature; the phenomenal cloak or covering of the Absolute, which is not real but exists merely as an appearance; phantasmagoria.

MIMANSA. The name of two schools of the Hindu Philosophy, *viz.* : the *Purva Mimansa;* and the *Uttara Mimansa,* generally known as the *Vedanta.*

MOKSHA. The state of Liberation; Emancipation; Freedom; Divine Absorption, etc., often used in the same sense as *Nirvana.*

MUKTI. Deliverance, or Emancipation from *Samsara,* or Rebirth.

MULADHARA. The Basic or First Lotus of the *Yoga* of *Patanjali,* situated at the base of the spinal column; the termination of the spinal cord; in which the *Kundalini* is stored or 'coiled-up.'

NADA-BRAHMA. The sacred word *Aum* (or *Om*), which was the first vibration of the newly-created universe.

NAMA-RUPA. Name and form.

"NETI-NETI." "Not-this—Not-this"; the term used by the teachers in describing THAT, which is considered as "Not-This" to everything—that is, as a Something that is No-Thing.

NIRALAMBANA. 'Without Support'; an extremely high state of meditation in the *Yoga* practice.

NIRBIJA. 'Without-Seed'; the highest possible form of *Samadhi,* or *Yoga* superconsciousness, in which the seed of *Karma* is killed, and the soul is no longer bound to *Samsara.*

NIRGUNA. 'Without-*Gunas*'; that is, without qualities or attributes.

NISHKAMAKARMA. Actions performed unselfishly, from duty, and without desire or hope of reward; according to the teachings of *Karma Yoga.*

NITYA. Eternal; without end; permanent; indestructible.

NIRVANA. The state of Emancipation, or Freedom from *Samsara,* or Rebirth; the state of Absorption by the Divine; generally used by the Buddhists, but sometimes by the Hindus.

NIRVICHARA. Without discrimination, or preference.

NIRVIKALPA. Without change in time; changeless duration; a 'lesser eternity.'

NISHTHA. Oneness of attachment; singleness of attraction.

NIYALI. Fate; Necessity; Determinism.

NIYAMA. Religious Duty; consisting of inward and outward purity; right-thought; right-action; contentment; avoidance of luxury, vanity, and sensuousness; performance of religious duty, etc.; the Second Step of the *Yoga* of *Patanjali.*

NYAYA. The Philosophical System of *Gotama.* (See the lesson on the Three Minor Systems.)

OJAS. The subtle energy of the system, conserved by continence and purity.

OM, or OMKARA. See *Aum.*

"OM TAT SAT." A sacred expression of the Hindus, applied to THAT, and meaning "Thou art the Supreme and Absolute Being, Wisdom, and Bliss"; *tat* meaning 'that,' and *sat* meaning 'being'; and *Om* meaning the term for THAT, including his Absolute Aspects.

PADARTHA. A Category, or Ultimate Classification.

PARA. Supreme; greatest; highest (superlative term used as a prefix).

PARA-ATMAN. The Supreme Spirit.

PARA-BHAKTI. Supreme Love of God.

PARA-BRAHM. *Brahman* considered in its Absolute Aspect, devoid of manifestation or emanation—*Brahman*-in-Itself.

PARA-NIRVANA. The Supreme *Nirvana,* which by many is held to mean Absolute Extinction or Nothingness, but which the Inner Teachings hold to be Absolute Absorption in THAT and Infinite Consciousness.

PARAMAHAMSA. Supreme soul, or being.

PARAVIDYA. Supreme Wisdom, or knowledge.

PARVATI. The wife of *Shiva,* in the ancient mythologies

PATANJALI. The founder of the *Yoga* System of the Hindu Philosophy, who lived about 200 B.C.

PINGALA. The right-side nerve current; the right nostril.

PITRIS. The forefathers, or ancestors, highly venerated by the Hindus and all Orientals, and generally held to exercise a watchful interest over their descendants.

PRADHANA. Nature, or primordial element.

PRAJNA. Divine Wisdom, leading to the Realization of the One.

PRAJNAJYOTI. An Illumined One; one who has attained divine knowledge.

PRAKRITI. Nature; or the Primal Substance of Nature ; one of the two fundamental bases of the conception of the Universe advanced by the *Sankhya* philosophy of *Kapila;* the source of the material and mental phases of the universe, as distinguished from the Spiritual Basis, or *Purusha.*

PRANA. The Universal Principle of Energy; also used to designate the Vital Force of the body, which is a manifestation of the Universal *Prana.*

PRANAYAMA. The Science of Control of the *Prana,* principally by means of the Breath; the Fourth Step of *Patanjali's Yoga* System.

PRASANKHYANA. Contemplation of the Abstract.

PRATIBHA. Illumination by Divine Wisdom.

PRATIKA. A symbol, or image, of *Brahman,* the Infinite Being.

PRATIMA. The use of images of the gods as symbols for the Supreme Being. The worship before these symbols is intended as the worship of the Supreme Being, in some of its phases, and is not idolatry as the term is generally understood.

PRATIVISHAYA. The sense-organs.

PRATYAHARA. Control of the Senses ; a part of the *Yoga* discipline and practice; the Fifth Step of the *Yoga* of *Patanjali,* which consists in making the Mind introspective—that is, turning it back on itself, and releasing it from the power of outward impressions.

PRATYAGATMAN. The state of internal self-illumination, or spiritual knowing.

PRATYAKSHAM. Perception by means of the illuminated consciousness, and without the necessity of sense-organs.

PRITHIVI. Solid matter; earth; cohesive mass.

PURAKA. Inhalation of the Breath.

PURUSHA. The Spiritual Principle; the Spirit. (See lesson on the *Sankhya* System.)

PURVA MIMANSA. 'Prior Investigation'; one of the Three Minor Systems of Hindu Philosophy.

RAGA. Attachment of the Senses.

RAJA. Royal; Chief; Superior; Superlative.

RAJA YOGA. The 'Royal *Yoga*'; 'Superlative *Yoga*'; a form of *Yoga* advocated by the *Yoga* School of *Patanjali* and others, which has for its object the development of the psychic and spiritual faculties, and the control of the Mind. (See lesson on the *Yoga* System.)

RAJAS. Activity; Energy; Lively; One of the Three *Gunas*. (See lesson on the *Sankhya* System.)

RAMA. A celebrated ancient Hindu sage and teacher, regarded as an incarnation or *avatar* of *Krishna*.

RECHAKA. Exhalation of the Breath.

RIG VEDA. The oldest part of the *Vedas*, and which is composed principally of hymns, etc.

RISHI. A great sage or teacher who has attained the stage of Super-Man, and who is possessed of the power of supersense perception.

RUDRA. The name formerly given to *Shiva* in the ancient mythology.

SAGUNA. Possessing qualities.

SAHASRARA. The final lotus, situated in the brain, described in *Patanjali's Yoga* System; sometimes regarded as the brain itself; "the thousand petalled lotus."

SAKTI. Power; Authority.

SAMA. The form of mental control which consists in directing the mind inward, and preventing it from externalizing.

SAMADHI. Transcendental Contemplation, or Ecstasy; Cosmic Consciousness; a supernormal state produced by meditation, concentration, etc.; the Eighth Step of *Patanjali's Yoga* System.

SAMANYA. The Principle of Generality, or Genus.

SAMAPATTI. The figurative term, meaning 'the casket of treasures,' used by the *Yogins* to describe the stages of meditation.

SAMAVAYA. The Principle of Coherence.

SAMPRAJNATA. The preliminary stage of *Samadhi*, or superconsciousness resulting from *Yoga* meditation etc.

SAMSARA. The World of Phenomenal Existence; the Chain of Rebirth ; the Cycle of Existences; used particularly to distinguish the universe of manifestation and phenomena from the Real Existence which lies behind and under it.

SAMSKARAS. The impression in the mind-stuff that results in fixing habits.

SAMYANA. A term used to designate the Three Higher Steps in *Patanjali's Yoga*, known as *Dharana Dhyana*, and *Samadhi;* or, in other words, the steps of Control of the Mind, Meditation, and Transcendental Contemplation, collectively; the word means Restraint or Control.

SANANDAM. The third stage of *Samadhi*, or superconsciousness.

SANATANA. The 'External Religion' of India.

SANKARACHARYA. A great Hindu teacher who lived about A.D. 800, and who was the leading expounder and commentor of the *Vedanta.*

SANKHYA. The great system of Hindu Philosophy founded by *Kapila* about 700 B.C., the leading features of which are the conception of the dual-principles of *Purusha,* or Spirit, and *Prakriti,* or Nature, or Universal Creative Energy. (See lesson on the *Sankhya* System.)

SANNYASA. Renunciation; non-worldliness; the forsaking of position, name, possessions, family, and all connected with the world of sense-attraction. SANNYASIN. A follower of *Sannyasa;* an ascetic; one who forsakes all and follows the Spirit.

SAT. Absolute Existence; one of the terms applied to The Absolute, *Brahman* or THAT.

SAT-CHIT-ANANDA. A term applied to The Absolute, *Brahman* or THAT, consisting of three terms, and meaning "Absolute Existence or Being—Absolute Wisdom and Knowledge—Absolute Bliss or Happiness."

SATTVAS. One of the Three *Gunas;* the *Guna* of Brightness, Goodness, and Light. (See the lesson on the *Sankhya* System.)

SHAKTAS. Worshippers of *Shakti.*

SHAKTI. The Principle of Life Energy or Cosmic Energy, or Nature.

SHAIVAS. The cult of *Shiva* worshippers.

SHIVA, or SIVA. The Third Principle of the Hindu Trinity, representing the Destroying or Changing Principle ; also the conception of the Supreme Being of the *Shaivas.* (See lessons on the Religions of India.)

SHUSUMNA. The canal running through the centre of the spinal cord, and through which the *Kundalini* ascends in the *Yogi* practices. (See the lesson on the *Yoga* System.)

SIDDHANTA. The Knowledge of Decision; positive knowledge.

SIDDHAS. *Yogis* who have attained semi-divine powers, through superconscious knowledge, etc. SIDDHIS. The supernormal powers of the *Siddhas.*

SHISHYA. A student, neophyte, or disciple of a Guru; a *Chela.*

SHLOKA. A verse of a poem or sacred writing.

SMRITI. Memory; also a term sometimes applied to the sacred books outside of the *Vedas,* which have been transmitted in the past by Memory.

SOHAM. A term meaning "I Am He," used by the enthusiastic *Bhakti Yogis,* and others, and implying the perception of their relation to *Brahman* or THAT; equivalent to the radical *Sufi* statement of "I am God Himself."

SOMA. The nectar of the ancient gods; an Indian plant.

SHRAVANA. The supersensuous hearing claimed to be developed by the *Yoga* practices; Clairaudience.

SRI, or SHRI. A term meaning 'blessed one,' or 'holy one,' applied to the great sages and teachers of India by their followers.

STHULA SHARIRA. The gross physical body, as distinguished from the LINGA SHARIRA, or subtle body, or etheric double.

SHUNYA VADA. The doctrine that behind the phenomenal world there is an Infinite Void, or Nothing; a form of philosophical Nihilism.

SUSHUPTI. The state of profound, dreamless sleep.

SVADHISHTHANA. The second lotus of the *Yoga* System of *Patanjali,* and which is situated back of the navel.

SWAMI. A spiritual teacher.

TADIYATA. A state of exaltation common to certain of the advanced *Bhakti Yogis,* in which the man loses his sense of personality and feels that he is merged with the Lord's "radiation or light" by reason of his Love-of-God.

TAMAS. Darkness; one of the *Gunas;* the *Guna* of Sloth, Ignorance, and Slowness. (See lesson on the *Sankhya* System.)

TANAMATRAS. Subtle or fine elements of Nature, from which the gross elements proceed.

TAPAS. Ascetic practices for controlling. the body by fasting, austerities, self-torture, etc.

"TAT TVAM ASI." A term meaning "That thou art," used by Hindu teachers to their students, and which informs them of their relationship with *Brahman,* through the Indwelling Spirit.

TATTVAS. Principles; Categories; Ultimate Classes; Truths.

TEJAS. The element of Fire.

TRISHNA. Desire; thirst; longing; craving.

TURIYA. The highest state of consciousness.

TYAGA. Renunciation of the lower for the higher.

UDANA. Nerve-current controlling the speech organs.

UDGATHA. The awakening of the *Kundalini.*

UPADANA.

UPANISHADS. The later Sacred Books of India.

UPAYAPRATYAYA. The state of intense abstraction, or meditation upon abstract things; abstract meditation, or meditation upon nothing.

UTTARA MIMANSA. A term applied to the *Vedanta* System of Hindu Philosophy, and meaning 'subsequent investigation,' or 'investigation of the subsequent part,' the "investigation" applying to the *Vedas.*

VADA. Knowledge by Argument, or Discussion.

VAIRAGYAM. Renunciation of, and non-attachment to, the objects or allurement of the senses.

VAISHESHIKA. The school or system of Hindu Philosophy founded by *Kanada*, one of the distinguishing features of which is the 'Atomic Theory.' (See lesson on the Three Minor Systems.)

VAISHNAVAS. The disciples and worshippers of *Vishnu*, or *Krishna;* one of the leading religious sects of India. (See lessons on the Religions of India.)

VARUNA. A god in the ancient Hindu mythology.

VASUDEVA. A manifestation of the Infinite Being.

VAYU. The Principle of Air.

VEDANA. The supersensuous faculty of Feeling developed by the *Yogis.*

VEDAS. The Sacred Books of India. (See latter part of this lesson.)

VEDANTA. The great system of Hindu Philosophy, the distinguishing feature of which is Idealism. (See lesson on the *Vedanta* System.)

VIDYA. Wisdom; Knowledge; Science.

VIMOKSHA. Absolute freedom from Desire; Emancipation.

VIRYA. Strength; vitality; energy; virility.

VISHNU. The First Principle of the Hindu Trinity; the Preservative Principle of Deity; of whom *Krishna* was an *avatar;* the conception of *Vishnu* and *Krishna* is often identical. (See the lessons on the Religions of India.)

VISHESHA. Atomic Individuality.

VISHISHTADVAITA. The branch of the *Vedanta* which holds to the conception of 'qualified nondualism,' and which teaches that the individual soul is a part of God. (See lesson on the *Vedanta* System.) VISHISHTADVAITIN. A disciple or follower of *Vishishtadvaita.*

VISHUDDHA. The fifth lotus of the *Yoga,* of *Patanjali,* and which is situated in the *Shusumna,* back of the throat.

VIVEKANANDA. A term meaning "Bliss-in-

Discrimination"; the name adopted by a celebrated Hindu *Advaitist* teacher who visited America in 1893.

VIVEKA. Discrimination between the true and the false.

VRITTI. A whirlpool, vortex, or wave-action in the *Chitta* or Mind-Stuff; a mental activity or thought-action.

VYANA. The nerve-currents of the physical body.

VYASA. An ancient Hindu teacher who is held to be the author of the *Mahabharata,* and of the Aphorisms of the *Uttara Mimansa* or *Vedanta.* VYASA SUTRAS. The Aphorisms of VYASA.

VYUTTHANA. Arousing or awakening from meditation, or concentration.

YAMA. Self-Control; the First Step in *Patanjali's Yoga* System.

YOGA. A term meaning "yoking; joining, etc."; also meaning "mental control and advancement" resulting therefrom; the name of the *Yoga* System of Hindu Philosophy established by *Patanjali.* (See lesson on the *Yoga* System.)

YOGI, or YOGIN. A follower of *Yoga;* a practitioner of the *Yoga* methods; or in a more general sense, "one who seeks Union, Realization, and Attainment by means of Wisdom, Divine Love, Action, or Control—or by all."

Index

B

C